SOUTHAMPTON'S
LUCKY JIM

A County Borough Copper in the 50's and 60's

SOUTHAMPTON'S LUCKY JIM

A County Borough Copper in the 50's and 60's

JIM BROWN

This edition published in Great Britain in 2013 by DB Publishing, an imprint of JMD Media.

ISBN 9781780913308

Printed and bound in Great Britain by Marston Book Services Ltd, Oxfordshire

Contents

ACKNOWLEDGEMENTS

I am deeply indebted to the following; without their assistance this book would not have been possible:

The ever helpful staff of the Local Studies, Southampton Reference Library and the Southampton Record Office; Sue Woolgar, City Archivist; David Thomas, Paul Stickler, Derek Stevens, Peter Stoddard and Dr Clifford Williams, Hampshire Constabulary History Society. (I am especially indebted to Derek Stevens, HCHS Curator, who supplied archive photographs and bound copies of the Southampton Police Standing Orders from 1952 to 1967).

In addition to photographs held in my personal collection, I am appreciative of being given permission to use photographs from their collection by Ian Abrahams, Bitterne Local History Society; Ian Murray, Editor Southern Daily Echo; Dave Goddard; Janet Holloway; Bill Moore; Jeff Pain; Bert Moody; and the late Eric Gadd.

I am also extremely grateful to my wife, Marion, who carried out an initial proof read to reveal ambiguity and typing errors; ex-DS Ken Holmes, who checked my account for accuracy, but most especially my daughter Amanda. She not only patiently checked my account in detail for grammatical errors, but gave me sound advice on its construction.

This book is dedicated to all those committed police officers who served in the Southampton County Borough and City Police prior to its amalgamation with Hampshire Constabulary in 1967. We were a close-knit family, supporting each other at all times, and I hope that those who have survived to read the book will have nostalgic memories of what is now a bygone age.

J.W.M. Brown, July 2013.

INTRODUCTION

I have endeavoured to give an accurate and factual account, warts and all, of how the County Borough of Southampton, later to become a City, was policed by me and my colleagues in the 1950/60s. It cannot be overemphasised that the attitudes and behaviour of officers at this period, both supervising and subordinate, reflected the age; it was a different post-war world with vastly differing standards. Modern officers do not behave in the same way today; they are governed by different criteria.

Such issues as Human Rights, Women's Liberation, Racial Discrimination, Gay Rights, Health & Safety, Rehabilitation of Offenders, and European Directives, these were all matters that just did not come into the equation; they were for the far distant future. If anybody had seriously suggested that a woman could be a Superintendent, let alone a Chief Constable, that would have been as ridiculous an idea as having a woman Prime Minister; it could just never happen. Women were believed not to have the physical or mental capacity to undertake such demanding positions. Policing certainly was very much a man's world and fully accepted as such.

The reader will perhaps appreciate the strong points of the now old fashioned policing methods, as well as the weaknesses, and may be surprised at the vast differences. Serving officers will be possibly staggered by the absence of modern technology and amazed at the working conditions meekly accepted by their earlier colleagues.

To this end supervising officers, especially section sergeants and inspectors, were obsessed with ensuring that patrolling constables did not remain in the station for a moment more than necessary. The emphasis throughout was that officers should be on the street, seen by and available to the public. Beat officers taking temporary refuge in a 'tea hole' on their beat – usually the rear of a shop or café, where a cup of tea was readily provided – had to take care to avoid being caught by the section sergeant or inspector.

No doubt the Victorian attitudes towards discipline had persisted throughout generations of supervising officers, because of the drink problems of patrolling officers that were widespread in the very early days of policing.

Readers need only look at the unacceptable behaviour of early 19th century police officers, as seen in the excellent book *"111 Years Policing Winchester"* by Clifford

Williams, to realise why beat officers had to be closely supervised. The high incidence in that book of early patrolling officers disciplined or dismissed for drunkenness and/or found away from their beat was striking.

Zero tolerance was the norm and the protection of the law abiding public was the overriding concern of every officer, but their behaviour when carrying this out would often be completely unacceptable today. Obscene language in a public place, for example, was an arrestable offence, under section 28 of the Town Police Clauses Act, 1847, and this was always immediately exercised; not so today it seems, according to some TV police documentary programmes.

Although I have named officers wherever possible, I have not identified those individuals whose actions warrant criticism from a modern perspective, although former Southampton officers of my generation will frequently know who I refer to. I have also only used the second Christian name of offenders, or omitted it altogether, to protect the guilty, as well as to conform to the Rehabilitation of Offenders Act.

By initially including the minutia of daily police work I hope I have painted the real picture of a good deal of boring, routine and monotonous work for the uniformed officer, not the glamorous and exciting life as portrayed in films and TV. That is not to say that there were no incidents that were exciting and interesting to deal with, but each one was followed by the laborious completion of essential paperwork, although nowhere as much as today. Detective work did have its moments, but even that involved getting the paperwork exactly right to avoid a case collapsing.

The reader will hopefully fully appreciate what police work was really like for me by the time they have completed my story of policing Southampton in earlier times. What only takes up a paragraph or two in the book usually meant many hours, if not days, of enquiries. Even for petty criminal offences, or traffic accidents, witnesses had to be traced and interviewed, offenders identified and questioned, and the paperwork completed in accordance with strict legal guidelines.

One major difference, I believe, in policing today, is that in my time the many routine duties brought us into close contact with so many members of the public. Policing is essentially dealing with people, not abstract ideas or theories or number crunching on a computer; it rests in having direct contact with individuals from all walks of life and having a good relationship with them. The financial rewards for an officer today are considerable compared with the many hours of unpaid duty carried out by their predecessors; it was most certainly a different age during my police service.

Before joining the Force the only homes I had ever entered were those of friends and family. During my service I entered many thousands of homes, discovering that although the majority of individuals were decent and law abiding, and their homes and behaviour showed it, a far too large minority lived in a fashion that I at first found unbelievable. Encountering filthy conditions and extreme unsocial behaviour gave me a somewhat jaundiced view of a large section of the great unwashed general public.

Council estates, in particular, reflected these two sides of the public. Council officials seemed to have the ability to segregate prospective tenants into two groups, those who were genuine working class and those who were not, allocating them into different areas. Thus certain sections of some estates had a concentration of the worst elements of society, and these were treated as such from the outset. A suspected person being checked giving an address within those worst sections would therefore be questioned more thoroughly than others. Possibly unfair, but it only too often proved to have been the correct action as offences were then frequently revealed.

Details of the Force structure and aspects of some procedures are given in Appendix 'A' and some idea of how different the earlier procedures were can be gleaned from the 1949 "Notes for the Guidance of Police" booklet issued to every officer. A synopsis of this is given in Appendix 'B'.

The 'Judges' Rules', governing the questioning of suspects and taking voluntary statements, as issued to me in 1952, is reproduced as Appendix 'C'. It was not only an insert in my pocket book leather holder, it was also reproduced on the inside cover of the uniformed officer's notebook, but not, paradoxically, in the CID officer's notebook. (Detectives were expected to have an in-depth knowledge of the legal rules governing evidence.)

Throughout the book I have used the following abbreviations: PC – Police Constable; PS – Police Sergeant; Insp – Inspector; C/Insp – Chief Inspector; Supt – Superintendent; C/Supt – Chief Superintendent; DC – Detective Constable; DS = Detective Sergeant; DI – Detective Inspector; DCI –Detective Chief Inspector; D/Supt – Detective Superintendent

I trust that by reading my account of life as a Southampton police officer in the 1950s and 60s you will not only understand how the TV 'Dixon of Dock Green' image was a reality at this period in Southampton, but also just how much a police officer's dedication was exploited by his senior officers.

Finally, I very much hope that this account of my life as a Southampton police officer in the 1950/60s will be considered not just as an account of part of my personal life but as a piece of social history that will be of some interest to future historians.

J.W.M. Brown, July 2013.

1. EARLY DAYS

It was my very first court appearance, at the Southampton Juvenile Court housed in the Marlands Hall, directly opposite the Civic Centre Law Courts.

(Bitterne Local History Society)
The Marlands Hall, with its long flat roof and small car park in front, is in the centre right of the photo, with the Juvenile Court located at the right hand side of the building, directly opposite the police headquarters and law courts entrance. The site has since been completely replaced by the BBC local television and radio station.

Following a guilty plea from the 11 year old defendant, the police inspector prosecuting the case explained the circumstances. He stated that the boy's father was away at sea, serving in the Merchant Navy, and in his absence the roof of the outside toilet at their home in Graham Road was found to be leaking.

Directly opposite the rear garden of their house, in Brinton's Terrace, was the store of William Dibben & Sons, Builders' Merchants, and the defendant had been seen by a neighbour climbing over the perimeter fence and returning with a sheet of corrugated iron. This had been used by the boy to repair the roof and when interviewed he had readily admitted the theft.

The presiding magistrate looked at me (because I was that 11 year old defendant.) with a grim face and I fully anticipated being told that I would be sent to an Approved School. That was what my mother had warned would be the likely decision. However, to my immense relief, he gave me a Conditional Discharge for12 months, warning that any future offence would result in a more serious outcome. I left the Court resolving that never again would I run the risk of being sent to an Approved School.

Prior to this court appearance I had been involved with other boys in my neighbourhood in the common wartime practice of entering newly bombed and abandoned houses, armed with a small iron bar, which we used to break open the lock on the gas and electric meters. The proceeds, substantial to us, were always shared, and we considered the practice to be quite normal. It was also a regular custom to enter empty bombed properties in order to rip up the floorboards, used for firewood at home. Again, we saw nothing wrong in that, it was considered the spoils of war; most of the houses were to be demolished anyway.

Empty shops were also targeted and I recall finding a large jar of lemonade powder, together with a supply of small paper bags. Selling bags at school for tuppence (roughly 1p) each, ideal for sticking in fingers and licking the powder, proved a profitable enterprise.

However, the Magistrate's warning certainly worked as I was too scared to continue joining my friends in entering properties. The fear of the consequences if caught over-rode the peer pressure of taking part again, and my new outlook on life was reinforced when I later passed the 11 plus and gained entry to Taunton's Grammar School.

Up to that time, with my mother too fond of Guinness in my father's wartime absence at sea, leaving me completely uncontrolled, I had little or no sense of self pride and suffered from low self esteem. Taunton's transformed my life, building on the Court appearance, giving me self confidence and a pride in my school and its uniform. The dedication of the staff gave me a strong sense of belonging to something worthwhile, with the potential of a good career ahead of me. It was their outstanding teaching qualities that enabled me to obtain a University of London matriculation when I eventually reached the Sixth Form. Their example ensured I remain a staunch member of the Old Tauntonian's Association to this day.

An equally strong factor that determined my future was meeting, at the age of 13, the girl who has been my wife for the past 60 years. Her staunch Methodist mother helped to guide me on the right lines and this continued in 1950 when I joined the army for my two years National Service.

I became more mature during my army service, helped by being an 18 year old sergeant in the Royal Army Educational Corps stationed in BAOR, Germany, with the 1st Battalion the King's Royal Rifle Corps. As the youngest sergeant in the mess I initially took a good deal of stick from the veterans, who had seen active service during the war. But their attitude changed when I acted as a section sergeant during manoeuvres, in charge of a platoon with Bren guns and a half-track. It was the proudest moment of my army service when I was later called into the mess and the regimental sergeant major presented me with the regimental black belt and lanyard as an honorary member of the KRRC.

I then had to decided my future when demobilised in 1952. By this time my future wife and I, with her parents, enjoyed old-time dancing, and one of the "Gay Nineties Club" members was Archie Davies *(left)*, a detective with Southampton Police. (The club name had a very different connotation in 1952) Archie, who was a former War Reserve officer, managed the local Criminal Record Office and thus was only too aware of my juvenile conviction. However, I approached him for help in applying to join the police, and he gave me full support.

After completing the detailed application form I was given an interview with the Chief Constable, Charles Box, *(below)* a kind and courteous gentleman.

He closely questioned me on the circumstances of my taking the sheet of corrugated

iron to repair our outside toilet, and clearly took the view that with my father on active war service I had taken on the rôle of head of the household whilst far too young. This was, in fact, true, as my mother was the worse for drink for much of the time. However, I sensibly withheld from the Chief Constable details of my earlier undetected escapades and he gave me his blessing to continue with my application, something I continued to be grateful for throughout my service.

In spite of my having matriculated I nevertheless had to take the written examination for entry, under the eagle eye of Inspector Fred 'Judy' Garland, with whom I quickly fell out. Prior to the examination he questioned all of us applicants, we numbered about a dozen, in the course of which he corrected somebody on a point of grammar. I cannot recall what the exact point was, but do remember that I knew the Inspector was wrong and, foolishly, I spoke up and said so. Deathly silence. I received a steely look, my name was asked (no doubt for future reference) and his incorrect 'correction' was again given, this time with no response from me.

We all had to attend a medical examination by the Police Surgeon, who also had to check that we were above the minimum height requirement of 5' 10". As I was then 5' 11¾" I had no problem with this. In due course I received an official letter informing me that I had been accepted as a Constable on probation in the Southampton County Borough Police Force as from 28 August 1952 and I attended to be fitted with my uniform. With me was another Probationer with whom I had a life-long friendship, Bill Williams, later to be the best man at my wedding.

My friend Bill Williams' attitude to life was quickly shown when we received some documentation from the officer on duty in the General Office, a portly PC Bob Lamb. He, kindly, I thought, told us where we could obtain a pair of good quality boots, and to mention his name, for which I thanked him. As we left the office Bill said "Sod him, no way are we buying boots there so he can get a backhander." so Bob's recommendation was not taken up.

Having been kitted out, our next appointment was at Court to be sworn in as Constables. There were four of us, myself, Bill Williams, Cliff Haizelden and Roy Bettany. I well remember this, my second appearance in a Magistrates Court. As we waited in the body of the court I saw a heavily bandaged prisoner in the dock complaining to the Magistrates that the officer had assaulted him whilst he was trying to escape.

He had jumped down the basement of a bombed site near Central Railway Station and the officer had jumped down after him, deliberately, he alleged, on top of him, injuring some of the prisoner's ribs. The Clerk of the Court told the prisoner, in no uncertain terms, that this was not a matter for the Court today; he would have to take it up at another time.

This no doubt had to be deferred as the prisoner, after the Court heard his previous convictions, received 14 days for shoplifting. Thus, on 28 August 1952, I officially became Police Constable 150, earning the princely sum of £9 13s 0d a week, swearing to:

"Well and truly serve our Sovereign Lady the Queen in the office of constable, without fear, favour or affection, malice or ill-will; that I will see and cause Her Majesty's peace to be kept and preserved; that I will prevent to the best of my power all offences against the peace; and that while I continue to hold the said office I will to the best of my skill and ability discharge all the duties thereof faithfully according to law. So help me God".

Prior to knowing the division to which we were to be posted, we four had to attend a 13 week training course at the No 6 Police Training Centre, Sandgate, Folkstone on recruit course No. 91, commencing Monday 1 September 1952.

REPORT OF THE CHIEF CONSTABLE.

6   APPOINTMENTS.

(a) The following have been appointed constables on probation, with effect from the dates quoted:—

Peter Frederick Dawson	31st July, 1952
Anthony Bertram Eyers	31st July, 1952
Royston Alfred Howard Bettany	28th August, 1952
James William Maxton Brown	28th August, 1952
Harold Clifford Alfred Haizelden	28th August, 1952
William Arthur Williams	28th August, 1952

Extract from the Southampton Borough Council Watch Committee Minutes 15 September 1952 *(Bitterne Local History Society)* This records my appointment, together with Roy, Cliff and Bill, as Constable.

The main entrance of No 6 Police Training Centre, Sandgate, Folkstone

The rear of the building, with my classroom on the ground floor of the right-hand wing

The dining hall, the Commandant and staff sat at the far top table

The buildings were palatial and we felt we were in a university atmosphere. The course was very intensive, covering all aspects of criminal law, traffic law, rules of evidence, liquor licensing laws, public health, betting and gaming, and more particularly police powers and limitations. The lecturers were all serving police officers with vast practical experience, all determined to instil in their recruits the absolutely correct way of carrying out the manifold duties.

Mock trials were held in a 'court room', with students giving evidence and being cross examined and road traffic and other simulated conditions were set up in the grounds using real vehicles. Sgt/Instructor Kyrke, from East Sussex Force, was a real character who continually played the part of 'George Alfred Heist', an habitual criminal, in these situations.

Students attempting to question him in a dramatised set-up were invariably met with the response "F......... off, you have no right to stop me" and similar off-putting obscene remarks. If 'George Alfred Heist' was the driver of a car in a traffic situation he would invariably appear drunk and obstructive, refusing to get out of the vehicle or produce his documents on request. His difficult behaviour, however, was instructive to us probationer constables, who gradually learnt how to overcome the problems that 'Mr Heist' took a delight in creating.

What I personally found fascinating, from my very first day in the college, was the long corridor with its many photos and exhibits of criminal cases of national interest. It also displayed the current issues of the Police Gazette, showing photos of wanted persons and details of current important crimes.

I felt privileged to have access to this restricted information and was eager to put this inner knowledge into practice. However, in the meantime we had to pass monthly examinations to prove we were acquiring the essential knowledge of the tools of our trade. To this end we had to learn by heart many sections of Acts of Parliament, called 'definitions'. To this day I can recite the definition of larceny (theft).

"A person steals who, without claim of right made in good faith, takes and carries away anything capable of being stolen, with intent at the time of such taking permanently to deprive the owner thereof".

This definition was elaborated on by an explanation of each part in some detail. A 'claim of right' could arise when somebody believed he had the owner's consent, mistakenly thought the property was his own or that he was entitled to it.

The property had to be physically taken into possession, constructive or actual. 'Capable of being stolen' did not include such things as electricity, land or plants and animals growing wild, except in special circumstances. It was also important to establish the taker's intent at the time of taking.

All these issues were explored in some depth, so at the end of the day, when faced with a decision as to whether or not a particular offence had been committed, one could rely on its memorised definition and its detailed explanations to come to the right decision. This explained the number of students, including me, seen walking around the college grounds chanting to themselves.

It was important to always bear in mind that the legal profession has the time and resources to establish such matters, with recourse to law books, but a police officer has to know his powers and limitations without such facilities, and to take the immediate correct action with confidence.

I recall with some amusement when PS Kyrke outlined the "abominable crime of buggery, committed with either mankind or any kind of animal" contrary to Section 61 of the Offences Against the Person Act 1861, punishable by life imprisonment. One of the married students asked for confirmation that this, of course, did not apply to a consenting married couple. His face when told, "No, it certainly still applies, you can get life for it" was a picture, and he sat down quickly with a worried look.

It was the same student who had previously, perhaps foolishly, asked the instructor what one did if faced with a fellow police officer found committing some very trivial traffic offence. The sergeant replied, with a very straight face "You carry out your duty without fear or favour, of course". He paused, and then said in a growling tone "But does dog eat dog?"

I soon realised that this aspect of loyalty to one's comrades, whose help was frequently needed in an often dangerous working environment, did not extend to criminal or serious matters. I quickly learnt that a 'bent copper' is despised within the organisation and warrants a more intensive and thorough investigation than any normal lawbreaker. No decent hard working copper wanted to be tarred with the same brush as a corrupt one.

On nearing the conclusion of the course a spirit of camaraderie had developed between us, although a few had fallen by the wayside. The demands of learning legal definitions, the enormous wide range of subjects to be learnt in some detail, and the responsibilities ahead of us could not be faced by a few of the younger students.

However, as these photos show, we felt and looked like the real thing. We certainly believed we were of the 'Dixon of Dock Green' mould. (In the left picture I am in centre, with thumbs in breast pockets, and standing in centre of rear row in the right photo.)

The final passing out parade was missed by me, as I succumbed to a bout of 'flu at the end of the course, but I was fit enough to take part in the group photo.

I still have strong feelings that the traditional uniform is what I and the general public still associate with a police officer, not the para-military style now more commonly seen.

I am second from the left in the front standing row, with fellow Southampton officers Roy Betteny on my right, third from the left; Bill Williams third from the right and Cliff Haizelden at the end of that row. Sgt Kyrke is sitting 4th from the left.

During my training I qualified in both the swimming life saving examination and the St John's Ambulance Brigade First Aid. The latter entitled me to wear a small silver first aid badge on my uniform right sleeve. All members of the force were qualified; some to a higher degree than most, and these became members of the Southampton Police First Aid Team, successful in many county and national competitions.

Nothing now remained but to inflict myself on the Southampton public, although I was extremely concerned that my knowledge was too sparse.

How would I deal with a real life traffic accident, with real injured people to see to?

How would I handle having to arrest two or more individuals simultaneously – come to that how would I manage to arrest one person?

How could I possibly remember all the potential legal pitfalls of "The Job" and how would I stand up to a real cross examination in the witness box?

I was only too conscious that my probation lasted for two years, during which time I could be immediately dismissed without explanation on the basis that I was unsuitable.

On our return to Southampton Bill Williams and I were told we had been posted to Shirley ("B") Division and Cliff Haizelden and Roy Bettany to Bitterne ("C") Division.

All my uncertainties as to my ability therefore came to fruition when I reported to Shirley Police Station at 5.30am on Tuesday 23 December 1952 for my first tour of early turn duty, to be let loose upon the unsuspecting citizens of Southampton.

Shirley Police Station, as it was in 1952 (Hampshire Constabulary History Society)

The rather grim-looking police station that replaced it, on the same site.

2. FIRST WEEK ON THE BEAT

"You don't know me mister and I don't know you, so we will work this sodden beat as it should be worked." This was my introduction on Tuesday 23 December 1952 to being in uniform and actually walking a beat.

PC Steve Pomeroy, far older than me and towards the end of his service, was my fellow officer and as a probationer (also called a 'nig-nog' whose 'number was not yet dry') I was not allowed out on my own. I later found Steve to be a nice bloke, but rather dour and distrustful. No way was he going to show me any of his personal 'tea holes' or other hideouts. For all he knew I would let them slip to the section sergeant or inspector, then we would both be in trouble. In any event he did not wish to share them with anybody; he had discovered them for himself and they were his personal perks.

I well remember this first time exposed to the general public in uniform. It seemed that everybody was looking at me but I felt proud when I looked down at the silver buttons and the whistle chain dangling from my breast pocket. For the next few hours we walked in almost complete silence, initially along a virtually deserted High Street, then checking the rear of the shops along a dark alleyway. This was always the first duty on 'early turn' (6.00am-2.00pm tour of duty), checking the front and rear of vulnerable premises on our beat. They had, of course, all been checked twice during the night, before and after the night duty beat officer's meal break, but we had to do it again. The purpose, apparently, was that as well as possibly catching somebody in the act, if premises were found forcibly entered CID would have some idea of the time it had occurred. For a serious break in, with high value goods taken, it was not unusual for the night duty man to be woken from his bed to check his pocket book as to when he last visited the attacked premises – no apology or overtime, of course.

I had cycled to the station from the police hostel in Archers Road, apprehensive in case I should come across an incident en route and not know how to deal with it. Few officers possessed the expensive luxury of a car or motor cycle; we all walked, bicycled or caught a Corporation Transport bus (no need to pay a fare, we were council employees). There was no option but to wear uniform, this applied to all ranks, and it was quite common to deal with incidents both going to and returning from duty. There were absolutely no facilities, as there are today, to store your uniform at the station and change at the beginning and end of the shift. In any event, it was laid down in Standing Orders that uniform had to be worn travelling to and from duty. Paid overtime just did not come into the equation.

Monday of this first week had been spent in moving home. When I joined I was living with my parents, who ran the Brewer's Arms public house in Lower Bannister Street, and had been told that this accommodation was acceptable. However, when I returned from training in Folkstone I was abruptly told that this was not possible; it was against regulations. An officer in uniform could not been seen entering and leaving licensed premises; in any case the public house was liable to regular inspection and there could be a conflict of loyalties if I still lived there.

I therefore had to move to the police hostel at 1A Archers Road, where I had a single bedroom. Meals were available, at a small cost, from the resident warden, PC Fred Gillibrand, a former War Reserve officer who no longer reached the fitness standard demanded of post war officers. War Reserve officers had been recruited, without being required to reach the normal standard, as replacement for the many officers who had been called up for active service. Only a few had been retained at the end of the war as those returning and resuming their duties meant the force was then above its authorised establishment. Fred was a pleasant character, with a fund of stories of his service during the war.

Steve and I were on early turn, 6.00am to 2.00pm, working 1 Beat, which included part of upper Shirley High Street and streets to the south west. We had reported for duty before 5.45am as arriving later than a quarter of an hour before a tour of duty was a disciplinary offence. There had to be sufficient time for us to be allocated our duties etc. as the preceding shift were not allowed to go off duty until the current shift left the station to go on their beats.

We had presented our pocket book, truncheon and handcuffs, to prove we had them available, and were given our individual 'rings and points'. This meant we had to ring in on our beat from a pillar or police box every hour, for Steve and me at 30 minutes past the hour.

This timing was spread throughout the section, with different officers ringing in at intervals of five or ten minutes throughout each hour. When ringing in we could be given a task to carry out, such as informing a householder of a hospital message, and to attend a minor incident that did not warrant urgent attention from the emergency driver. We could then nominate the next pillar we would ring in from. In that way the section sergeants (there were always two on each shift) or the duty inspector would have some idea as to where we could be found.

The purpose of the hourly contact was not only to ensure the beat was being properly patrolled, it was also a safeguard for the officer. If a scheduled ring was delayed by more than an hour, it could mean the officer was possibly incapacitated, lying injured in some dark alleyway, and a search of his beat would be carried out by all available officers.

(Hampshire Constabulary History Society)

Police pillars and police boxes were spread throughout the town, covering every beat. The pillars incorporated an internal phone, accessed by key (left) and, for the public, a speaker and microphone, activated when a small marked door was opened. Both gave instant communication with the switchboard of the divisional station concerned. The police boxes, often brick built former air-raid shelters, also contained a phone with direct access to the station as well as facilities for officers to 'make up' their pocket book.

The police box in Paynes Road, formerly Freemantle County police station. The adjacent house to the right, on the corner of Queenstown Road, was occupied by Insp. Ernie Minnett. *(Hampshire Constabulary History Society)*

The blue light on the top of the pillar, or outside the box, could be made to flash by the station switchboard operator in order to contact the beat officer. It was surprising how often this flashing light was not noticed just prior to deciding to go to a nearby 'tea hole'.

We also had to make two 'points' halfway between the rings, one before and one after the meal break. A 'point' was a nominated spot on the beat, usually a road junction or named premises. On this occasion our 'points' were 7.00am at the top of Park Street and 1pm at Foundry Lane school. This meant that the supervising officers could 'book' us at either a police pillar or the 'point'. In the event of a sergeant or inspector actually visiting the point our pocket book would be signed and the 'booking' recorded at the station. It all revolved around ensuring that officers were patrolling their beats and were sober and properly turned out. It also made certain that pocket books were contemporaneously made up.

We had to arrive a few minutes before the time of the 'point' and wait at least five minutes afterwards. On at least one of the 'points' and one of the ringing in from a pillar or box, we would be met by the section sergeant or inspector. I later realised that this was also a check on the supervising officer, ensuring that he was closely monitoring the men on patrol. However, Insp. Reg Garrett had the habit of seeing a patrolling officer from the upper deck of a bus whilst travelling around the division, or on his way to the station, then telling him later that he had 'booked' him. A pocket book entry would then be signed – so much for accurate recording.

When on parade we were informed of all incidents of interest that had occurred since last on duty, details of wanted persons, stolen vehicles, and details of unoccupied houses on our beats. Members of the public going on holiday would inform the station of the dates they were away, and who the key-holder was in the event of a problem. Officers had to visit each property at least once during their tour of duty. My pocket books for the next few years were full of such details, often as many as 20 plus during the summer months.

Parading at Southampton Central, Civic Centre police station.
(Hampshire Constabulary History Society)

We took our first meal break at 9.15am, and I state this time as being precisely when we entered the station. Our ¾ hour break was strictly monitored as duty inspectors watched our entry and departure very closely. In fact, several weeks later, after being allowed to walk my beat unescorted, I once arrived for my break four minutes early. Horror upon horrors.

The eagle eyed inspector came up to me as I entered the station and bellowed "What time is your break, Brown?" When I replied he shouted "Get back on the street, don't you dare come in too early again" and I was forced to walk several yards along the pavement before being allowed to re-enter the station. Such was the petty discipline of the time, but it was all based on the need to impress officers of the high priority of being on the street and visible to the public.

I had handed in my plastic container with my breakfast contents when I first arrived at the station. This was attended to by the reserve man, my namesake, PC Frank Browne. He was another War Reserve officer, of smaller stature than post war officers, and no longer worked the beat. His function was to cook everybody's meal in the small upstairs kitchen adjoining the canteen. He also kept the canteen clean and tidy and otherwise helped out by manning the switchboard during the telephonist's temporary absences. He was on permanent day duty but the evening and night duty officers had to provide a reserve from within their section. Only those able to cook basic items of egg and bacon etc. were chosen for this function. For some unknown reason I was never chosen.

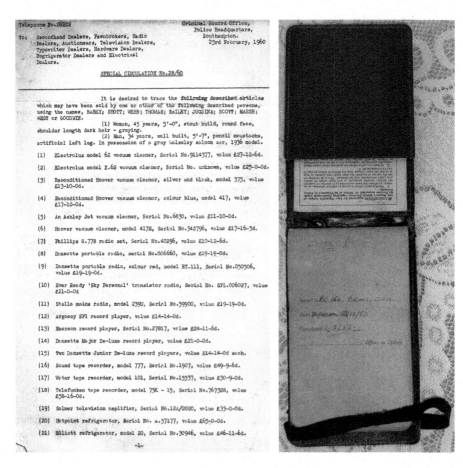

One of my first duties on that first day was the serving of 'Informations', in this case to the public houses on 1 Beat. It consisted of a single typed sheet containing details of a wanted man known to be seeking employment as a barman.

'Informations' were normally lists of stolen property distributed by hand to second hand dealers, scrap metal merchants or similar dealers likely to be offered the property. All deliveries had to be recorded in the pocket book *(right)* as this would be evidence if a dealer was subsequently charged with receiving stolen property that had been listed in an Information he had been given.

Left: a typical 'Information', in this case one delivered to all second-hand dealers, pawnbrokers, radio dealers, auctioneers, television dealers, typewriter dealers, hardware dealers, refrigerator dealers and electrical dealers.

The following day we were on coupled beats, 2 and 3, ringing in this time at 45 minutes past the hour. Coupled beats often occurred when the section was short of men, either sick or on leave, and when beats were coupled they became a cycle beat. When the section was at full strength the extra men would either be directed to take time off, or one or two would be given the 'beat' of 'main road'. This was walking up and down Shirley High Street or Shirley Road ringing hourly at the station.

Thursday was Christmas Day, and my allocated rest day. The system was that a record was kept of this holiday, so that officers had either Christmas or Boxing Day off on alternate years. On Boxing Day (you could not have both holidays off) I found we were covering six beats (with a cycle, of course) with 10 unoccupied houses to visit, the highlight of the day being called to a chimney fire.

Saturday, was equally uneventful, apart from my witnessing an accident directly in front of me when a slow moving car struck the rear of another car stationary at a pedestrian crossing. Steve made me deal with this on my own and I found my former nervousness at the thought of having to deal with such a situation dispelled immediately. I had no problem checking both drivers' documents, issuing an HO/RT/1 (official document that we all carried) for one of them to produce his driving licence and insurance at Christchurch police station and noting the damage etc.

Steve took me to one side and impressed on me that "You don't nick anybody for something petty unless you have to; it only creates a load of hassle where you can drop a bollock by forgetting to do something. Leave well alone, it's not a 'due care' so don't turn it into one." One possible offender (based on my Folkstone training) was thus let off with a verbal caution and I wrote down sufficient information in my notebook to complete the Form 17 (Accident Report) on my return to the station.

A Form17 was a single two sided sheet on which all details of a traffic accident were recorded. There was space for a sketch of the scene and precise measurements had to be taken. This was why we all carried a small piece of chalk, to mark the wheel positions of the vehicles involved before they were moved. A priority was to clear the road as soon as possible so that traffic could move freely. If there was a doubt as to the legally roadworthy condition of a vehicle then the traffic department would attend to confirm the position.

I later discovered that one of the reasons for this form being completed for all traffic accidents, with statements taken in one's pocket book and typed up afterwards, was that the insurance companies concerned were provided with this information, at a considerable cost.

I had performed my first traffic duty during that week, controlling traffic at a road junction where temporary road repairs were being carried out. It only lasted an hour but I found, to my relief, that the training at Folkstone had paid off; I gave the correct signals and everybody obeyed me.

It had been drummed into us that if the correct signals, as set out in the Highway Code, were not given, or if we were not wearing full uniform, including hat or helmet, then a driver failing to conform could not be prosecuted.

We always carried a set of white armbands when carrying out traffic control, and the photo shows me giving exactly the correct signal whilst carrying out traffic duty at The Avenue/Northlands Road junction during a funfair on Southampton Common.

I had patrolled several new beats during the week, without noteworthy incident, and now looked forward to my first tour of night duty.

3. AN EARLY ARREST

My second week began on a Sunday (when the duty week started) with my first tour of night duty, where I did not find favour with my colleagues because I was given several tours of 'Team Policing', something everybody was eager to have. This was normally only available to an individual no more than once in a week of night duty, depending on the grace and favour of a section sergeant. It was carried out in the divisional Hillman Estate, with the emergency driver, one of the two section sergeants, and a section PC. The car patrolled the division throughout the night, answering all 999 calls (hence its popularity) but also checking, at random, the front and backs of business and other lock up premises, as well as persons on foot carrying suitcases, holdalls or other property.

Notes were made in pocket books for these activities but no reports had to be made out unless premises were found insecure (Form 31). In such cases the sergeant would later trace the beat officer to find out why he hadn't found it first. A good explanation had to be forthcoming to avoid being on report. I was delighted to have been given this opportunity, but realised that I was still not yet considered capable of patrolling unaccompanied. By being with the experienced emergency driver and the section sergeant, I had no qualms over what we might have to deal with.

Our first call soon came, a chimney fire in Richfield Road. The fire brigade dealt with it, with the Leading Fireman confirming it was caused by a small accumulation of soot, so no offence had been committed. I was therefore spared from having to complete my first Form 22 – an offence report. (Form 22b was for keeping a dog without a licence.) If there had been a larger accumulation of soot, with the chimney not swept for some time, the occupier would have been reported for summons.

The rest of the night passed without incident, although I could hear the radio directing other divisional emergency cars to incidents, fights in town, traffic accidents in Bitterne etc., but nothing for us. I had anticipated we would be rushing from one call to another and had not dreamt that the night would be passed by routinely checking properties with the crew discussing the reasons why the Saints needed fresh players.

Form No. 3 **SOUTHAMPTON POLICE** — TELEPHONE MESSAGE	From P.C.Harper "B" Div. Address Tel. No.	RECEIVED Date 17.12.59 Time By 7.35p.m. P.C.169.

This evening we had a case of indecent exposure on the Millbrook Estate. Three sisters were concerned, Susan, Maureen, and Sandra Lyons, of 32, Sedbergh Road, Millbrook. We have no Police woman to interview these girls. Please could you arrange for one of your Police women to see these girls tomorrow and obtain the necessary statements.

2.

Copy to W.P.S. Cole.

Miss Rowthorn - Please attend at 4.30pm 18/11/59

I was night off the next day and the following two nights found me on patrol, with new beats, this time accompanied by a different PC. When 'the slips' were read out on parade we were told of incidents that had taken place over the previous 24 hours. These 'slips' were a typed or handwritten record, maintained on message pads approx 6" x 4", held on a ring binder, with details of all incidents taking place in the division. (Example above).

They were completed by the duty enquiry office officer, invariably a senior experienced PC who was not 100% fit for outside duty. All complaints, reported incidents, were briefly noted, with the officer dealing or attending marked on it, together with the result. We were thus fully aware of incidents and complaints on our beat; unruly youths, vandalism etc., so were able to give them some attention.

The 'slips' were filed monthly and retained indefinitely so that in the event of a subsequent serious crime or a complaint being lodged at a later date, details could be easily obtained. The divisional superintendent would request the 'slips' regularly during the day so that he was always in touch with current matters. As the Chief Constable was insistent that all complainants or those volunteering information were seen and informed of the outcome or thanked for their information, this was thus checked upon by the superintendent.

My pocket book, however, was mainly full of entries for unoccupied houses and details of vehicles seen at night. From midnight onwards the registered number of any vehicle seen travelling was noted, together with its location and direction.

Before going off duty a slip had to be completed with these details, to be passed to CID so if premises were attacked during the night they had some useful lines of enquiry. Needless to say, not every vehicle was noted, only those that attracted some attention by travelling fast or too slow.

Wednesday night was New Year's Eve and, for the first, but not the last time, I saw the New Year in whilst walking the beat and hearing the noise of revellers in the distance. However, at 11.10pm I had checked a man I found alongside the deserted Labour Exchange in Millbrook Road, but was able to confirm his excuse of urinating. This was another routine carried out at all times, checking anybody found in unusual circumstances or carrying something like a grip or case, especially at night. The approach was always polite, but firm, as it was necessary to know who they were, what they were carrying and/or an explanation of the circumstances.

All that was needed was a brief note in the pocket book, no lengthy form had to be completed or note taken of their ethnic background, as happens today. If you were happy that there was nothing at all untoward, there was no need to even take a note of their name and address. They were certainly not, as today, given a form explaining how they could complain. They had no reason to complain, it was our duty to check.

The following night, New Year's Day, found me back on Team Policing, with the first call, a garage fire in Outer Circle, coming in whilst we were still on parade. Some vehicles were damaged and the owner sustained slight burns, but then it was back on patrol with an otherwise uneventful tour. However, on the Saturday, the last of the tour of night duty, I was again on Team Policing but this time it was a more exciting tour.

It started at 1.20am with a reported break-in at the Crown Hotel in Shirley High Street, where some food had been stolen.

The former Crown Hotel (now up for sale), Shirley High Street

However, instead of me taking a statement and making initial enquiries, it was decided that I would continue the Team Policing alone, with the emergency driver, PC Jack Wallace. Both section sergeants, Jim Fibbens and 'Tiddler' Thompson (I never knew why he had the nickname.) were left to continue the investigation. It was, of course, nothing to do with the fact that the sergeants knew the licensee was extremely hospitable.

Jim Fibbens

He was later my detective sergeant when I was a detective constable at Shirley and he eventually became a divisional superintendent.

At 3.40am, just after our meal break, a call was received of a disturbance at the bottom of Shirley Road. When we arrived at the scene it turned out to be a case of extreme domestic trouble, with a smashed window and complaint of a knife being thrown at the occupier. The offender had run away into an alley at the rear of the house, so I automatically took off on my own. Jack wisely decided to remain at the front, to obtain details about what had happened.

I shone my torch down the alley and found a man crouching down, trying to hide behind a recess. I asked him to come back to the house with me, but he decided that he was better off running away again. I soon caught him and with some considerable struggling dragged him back to the house. He then became even more violent and it was noticed that he had badly injured his hand, we understood with the knife he had thrown at the female occupier.

An ambulance was called, but he continued to struggle violently and I was instructed to go with him to hospital and remain until a decision was made as to further action. I remained with the man at the Royal South Hants Hospital, and it was with some difficulty that the staff were able to deal with his injury.

He was, in fact, so violent that the Welfare Officer was called out at 6.50am and he authorised the man's removal to Moorgreen Hospital (for elderly and mentally disturbed patients). I did not go off duty until 7.30am, having been collected by the divisional car, and, after submitting my report, went home and gave no more thought to the matter.

Sunday was my rest day, with me resuming duty on the 5.00pm-1.00am shift on Monday, but some weeks later I was amazed to read on the front page of the Echo "Man was stark raving mad said PC". On reading further I discovered that this was a commit-tal hearing at the Magistrates Court where Jack Wallace had given evidence of arresting a man charged with attempted murder. It was the man I had arrested in the alley. I had played no part in the case, was not involved in any way, and yet he had been my prisoner.

I later came to realise that as a probationer I could well have said or done the wrong thing and was better left out of it, but at the time I felt strongly that I had been robbed of my first prisoner. I later saw the press report of the trial at Winchester Assizes, when the jury did not need to retire to find the man "Guilty but insane". He was then sent to Broadmoor hospital "until Her Majesty's pleasure be known".

I also attended another chimney fire, in Shirley Warren, where I received my very first "Don't you know who I am?" The offender was a local Councillor, very aware of his status, and this time I was accompanied by PC Harry Langrish as my instructing officer. The fire officer, and the occupier, confirmed that the chimney had not been swept for some time as there was a large accumulation of soot. It was therefore my great pleasure to totally ignore his exalted position and report him for summons. He received a writ-ten caution for the offence but I was satisfied that his status had not affected our joint decision.

Things then settled down into a normal routine. I was now considered fit to be trust-ed for patrol on my own, but first had to carry out a number of 'Methodical Patrols'. This was a typed sheet that set out the exact route to be taken e.g. 'Go up Shirley Avenue, turn right into St James Road, left into Darlington Gardens', and so on.

It ensured that every road on the beat was covered during an eight hour tour of duty, but was very restrictive for the officer, who could not dictate where he was to go. This system was not only used to ensure probationers knew the beats thoroughly; it was also used as a punishment by the supervising officers for those who displeased them.

At the end of my first tour of night duty I started the 5.00pm to 1.00am shift, this time working the beats on my own. This resulted in my first hospital message. It was customary for either the General Hospital or Royal South Hants (who covered casualty emergency admissions on alternate weeks) to request the police to contact next of kin to either inform them that a relative had suddenly passed away, or to attend as a matter of urgency because a patient had taken a turn for the worse. In this instance it was to inform a husband that his wife was very ill in Ashurst Hospital and he should visit straight away. This function was accepted by the police as telephones in the home were a rarity.

During this tour of 5.00pm to 1.00am I had to deal with my first sudden death, at 2, Cannon Street. Unexpected deaths, where a doctor had not seen the deceased during the previous 14 days, had to be reported to the police in the first instance, on behalf of HM Coroner. The permanent Coroner's Officer, a detective sergeant, dealt with each case, but initially a police officer has to attend to determine the position, to check if there are any signs of foul play.

I knocked on the door of 2 Cannon Street, preparing myself to show a respectful and sombre attitude, but to my surprise the landlady (it was her lodger who had died) answered the door with an outburst of "Whose going to pay his bloody rent?" Taken aback, I entered and found the body of her 76 year old tenant laid out on a filthy smelly bed, covered with a dirty sheet. On removing the sheet I saw he was dressed only in his underpants, but my attention was first drawn to what appeared to be dozens of large black warts over his chest and stomach. As I gave a closer look one of the black warts jumped.

I hastily withdrew, satisfied there was no evidence of bodily injury, and took his details from the landlady. She continued to insist I should tell her who was going to pay his rent arrears and I, wickedly, told her it would be dealt with by the Coroner's Officer. I returned to the station and stripped in one of the cells, carefully checking my clothing before getting dressed.

My first tour of 8.30am to 4.30pm, followed the 5.00pm to 1.00am shift, (with the difference that Sunday was 9.00am to 5.00pm), gave me a 'quick swing' with only eight hours between the shifts. This was common, also taking place from the 2.00pm to 10.00pm shift to 6.00am to 2.00pm early turn. Bearing in mind we had to travel home and return ¼ hour before the next shift, it gave little time to recharge one's batteries, but, again, this was accepted as part of 'The Job'.

This day shift gave me my first experience of covering the school crossings, in this case the children attending Regents Park School. Leaving Shirley Police Station just before 8.30am, I had to rush to get to the school and cover the first children crossing the road until 9.05am. Returning at mid-day until 12.20pm, then again from 1.00pm until 1.30pm and finally from 3.45pm to 4.20pm I found this a very demanding duty. Although the children were well behaved, not crossing until told, I had to maintain concentration on the passing traffic, taking care to check they had stopped on my signal before allowing the youngsters to cross. This duty lasted the entire week and from now on 8.30am – 4.40pm was not my favourite shift, although it was a good one from the view of being home at a reasonable hour.

By mid-January I found I was beginning to know the various beats and the duties that cropped up, more chimney fires, delivering messages, 'Informations' to dealers, unoccupied houses, finding premises insecure, being given found property, complaints of wilful damage etc.

On leaving Folkstone I had assumed that every day would be full of exciting incidents but, of course, life was not like that. It was monotonous walking around the streets, but I realised that I was building up an in-depth knowledge of the division, the alleyways and also getting to know a lot of local people. They would stop and chat, telling me all about themselves and petty items about their neighbours that they thought the police ought to know about – late goings and comings – property delivered at unusual hours. All these tit bits were passed onto CID, and I was enjoying the freedom of walking the streets in the early hours and late at night.

The rear alleyways of houses were especially checked after 10pm, the official reason being one might find a housebreaker leaving via the rear garden with property. The actual reason was that (a) one could indulge in a cigarette, something that couldn't be done on the street, and (b) ladies seemed to take a delight in changing into their nightclothes, or otherwise undressed in full view of an uncurtained window. Some were quite regular in their timing and were known to all beat officers (but not the supervising sergeants and inspectors.)

Whilst checking such an alleyway (purely to enjoy a cigarette.) at the rear of Shirley Road just before midnight during a tour of night duty, I heard a clanging noise coming from a nearby bombed site where several lorries were parked. On shining my torch I saw a man crouching down by the fuel tank of a lorry, with a can and rubber hose nearby on the ground. On checking I found it was not his lorry but as I was about to arrest him he pleaded with me to first check with his neighbour who he said was the driver of the lorry. He took me to the rear garden of his neighbour, where I could see a light showing, and we knocked on the kitchen door.

A very surprised driver answered, and when I asked if it was in order for his friend to be taking diesel from his lorry, he looked at me, looked at his neighbour who was now almost crying, gave the matter some thought and eventually said "Yes Officer, its not a problem, it's all in order". Although it was obvious to me that I could have made my second arrest, I nevertheless felt that I had done the right thing. I was only too conscious that I had held the culprit's future in my hand and my compassion had taken over.

Back on day duty I was given a treat, duty at the Southampton Quarter Sessions, held in the Civic Centre. It was merely to be present in the courtroom in case of any untoward incident, but it allowed me to witness cases at close quarters. Quarter Sessions was a court that tried serious cases, with a jury, if needed, presided over by a judge called a Recorder. The most serious cases were tried at Assizes, with a High Court Judge. At this time the Recorder was The Hon. Ewan Montague, the son of Lord Swaythling. He was famous for conceiving 'Operation Mincemeat', a major deception plan during World War Two. As a senior Naval Intelligence officer he arranged for alleged top-secret documents to be found on a dead body washed up on the beach in Spain. It convinced the Germans that the Allies planned to invade Greece and Sardinia in 1943 instead of, in fact, Sicily.

Although the duty extended from 10.00am to after 7.00pm, it was well worth it. My notebook records hearing cases of indecent assault, receiving stolen property, customs evasion, buggery, and an appeal against conviction for a driving offence. I learnt a lot from seeing and hearing witnesses and my colleagues being cross-examined, giving me confidence for when it was my turn in the future.

The former No.1 Court, used for cases before a Recorder at Quarter Sessions *(Taken in 2012, after police headquarters was converted into the Sea City Museum)*

The dock where prisoners stood, facing the Recorder, is in the foreground, with steps leading down direct to the cells. There was an identical system in the other two courts, with all three courts leading into the cell passage. The jury sat on the left and the witness box is on the far right, close to the Recorder.

My 2.00pm to 10.00pm tour passed without significant incident, one item being checking a man I saw going from door to door apparently selling items. His pedlar's licence was all in order, so I had yet to submit my second Form 22, an offence report. This came before the end of the month, the heinous offence of parking a motor car without displaying obligatory lights.

At this period all street lights went out at midnight and parked vehicles had to display side lights. If seen early in the evening doors would be knocked to trace the owner, whose documents would be checked and then reported for summons.

If seen late at night a Form 22 would be started, with the basic information recorded, and this would be taken over by the early turn officer who would trace and report the driver. All petty stuff, but it was the law of the land with little room for discretion on the part of the officer. If the offence was committed shortly after official lighting up time, then a verbal caution would be given, but as it was dangerous to park unseen in a dark street, especially for cyclists, who were plentiful, we felt it was justified to take action.

Another duty carried out was the service of witness notices and summons. It was another way of meeting people as they had to be served either personally or at residence, and signed for. It also, of course, reduced administration costs as we were walking around the area anyway.

My expertise in completing offence reports soon developed, with such matters as stopping a lorry with an expired road fund licence, cyclists seen failing to stop at a halt sign or pedestrian crossing when it was in use, cycling without lights, all heady stuff of national importance. Still, it gave me useful practice in report writing and taking statements in my pocket book. Such statements had to be typed up when report writing in the station, on a battered old typewriter where, if making a mistake, one merely backed up and overtyped by banging hard.

On my next tour of night duty I narrowly escaped receiving my first misconduct report. I had been allocated my one rest day in the middle of the week. Consequently I was on duty all night, followed by part of the next morning in bed, then trying to sleep that night, badly as it turned out, then up all day again before returning once more to night duty. As a result in the early hours of the next morning I was very tired indeed.

On checking the T.A. Blighmont Barracks in Millbrook Road, I discovered the front doors were insecure, and entered, finding the interior doors all firmly locked. I then sat down on the inside steps, just for a brief rest, but suddenly woke up when my helmet fell off and rolled on the ground. I had fallen asleep, missing my next 'ring' from a police pillar by 15 minutes. I forget the excuse I gave, but it was a narrow squeak, saved only by my helmet falling off.

I also dealt with more sudden deaths and my first 'domestic trouble'. This was very common, spouses or parents would see you on patrol and rush out to tell you their problems. You would also hear shouting and screaming from properties or be called to them. I initially felt strange giving fatherly advice to persons much older than myself, but such advice was always listened to and accepted gratefully (at least, most of the time.).

One particular 'domestic trouble' springs to mind, showing the practical, if almost unlawful, way in which situations could be dealt with. Neighbours had reported screaming coming from a house in Cannon Street, and I attended, accompanied by Insp. Johnny Summers. We found the front door unlocked and hearing continued screaming from inside, opened the door and walked along the passage into the living room. We saw a man, very much under the influence of drink, with his fists clenched in front of who was clearly his wife, showing her bloody and battered face.

We restrained him, dragging him away from the woman, who at once cried out "Leave him alone, he's my husband". The man then gave us some violent verbal abuse, in the course of which Insp. Summers, who was not of large stature, went directly up to him, pushing out his chest right up against the man, forcing him along the passage towards the open front door.

The man retreated, and directly he reached the outside pavement Johnny said "You're now in a public place – you're under arrest for being drunk and disorderly" and we both escorted him to Shirley Police Station where he was placed in a cell and later charged once he was sober.

It was an interesting experience for me, as I had realised that no offence had been committed whilst in his home, especially when his wife clearly would not prosecute for assault. It was, as far as I was concerned, natural justice that he should pay for his behaviour. More importantly, it was the only way to protect her.

Several minor traffic accidents were dealt with, some of which I witnessed, and in one case reported somebody for driving without due care and attention. I had decided to ignore the advice given by PC Steve Pomeroy, my first beat tutor, not to do any more than necessary as you could forget something. I felt happier actually doing what was laid down for me. It was also pleasant to be able to sit in the station, out of the weather, report writing. However, there was always a sergeant or inspector looking over your shoulder to check what you were doing, anxious to get you back out on the street at the first opportunity.

I was now beginning to feel confident in what I was doing and no longer felt that everybody was looking at me walking along in uniform. Another treat came when I was seconded to 'A' division for the day, helping to line the route for the university 'rag day'. It gave me a full front line view of all the floats and activities, and I was being paid for it.

My 21st birthday came on 18 February and when I asked PS Stan Dunn, the Clerk Sergeant, for eight hours time off, with only five hours 'in the book', time off was refused. When I said I would no doubt soon be working overtime and gain the other three hours the point was made that I could possibly die before then and Stan would have lost out. Such was the attitude of the time. What turned out to be particularly galling was the fact that on that day, working the 8.30am-4.30pm shift, the section was fully manned so I was not even allocated a beat, merely 'Main Road', walking up and down Shirley Road and Shirley High Street, reporting to the station on the hour.

By now I had discovered my own 'tea holes' on the various beats, the first one being the petrol filling station on the corner of Millbrook and Paynes Roads, managed by Ted Haresign and his wife. At this period motorists were not allowed to fill up their own vehicle, this had to be carried out by an attendant, who also collected the cash. I became very friendly with this couple, who were from the north, and as well as tea always readily available in the back office, they were a useful source of information regarding suspicious vehicles they serviced.

The junction of Millbrook and Paynes Roads *(Bitterne Local History Society)*

The photo shows the junction as it used to be, with the filling station in the centre, now all swept away by the construction of a diverted and enlarged Millbrook Road.

I became very familiar with the division's streets and alleyways and my pocket books (they lasted around 2 months before needing replacing) were showing how my aptitude for the work was bearing fruit. I was now used to taking statements in my pocket book, following my training of 'start at the beginning, go on to the end then stop'. This applied to statements not only of traffic accidents but witness statements, all having to be typed up at the station to be submitted with my reports.

I thus also learnt to be a proficient two finger typist, an accomplishment that remains to this day. When a pocket book was nearly full it had to be checked by a sergeant or inspector, who would then give a consecutive number and sign the replacement.

My first experience with 'Dell Duty' took place during this period. Cover for the match itself, at the Southampton Football Club in Archers Road, with the 'The Saints' team, was given by five officers on 'special duty'. Officers were either on allocated rest day or a night shift and were thus paid for being on duty in their own time.

One officer was stationed at each corner post and one at the players' entrance during the match. These were the only police officers required to be in the ground.

There were usually 12 to 15 officers from both Shirley and Central Divisions on duty, normally the 2.00pm – 10.00pm shift, and they were allocated to various points around the football ground. One position, for Shirley Division, was the junction of Hill Lane, Howard Road and Archers Road.

Two of us would take up positions about an hour before the match, turn off the traffic lights at that junction and one perform traffic duty to control mainly cyclists whilst the other controlled hundreds of pedestrians.

I well recall being on duty on one occasion, with hordes of pedestrians streaming towards me along the pavement of Howard Road, when one individual some distance from me stepped off the crowded pavement onto the road. Although I was then only just turned 20 I called out and indicated he should get back onto the pavement. He did so immediately, of course, because I was a uniformed police officer and thus had authority (and respect).

Ten minutes after the match started those on duty were permitted to enter and watch the match from the rear of one of the stands, leaving about ten minutes before the end of the match to resume our former positions.

The 'Saints' football ground *(Eric Gadd)*

There was never any significant trouble inside, with the occasional drunk being gently but firmly ejected by the stewards, to make his own way home. There were, of course, no seats in the stadium, it was standing room only.

Several decades later, in 2001, when I was a well known local historian and author, I made an outside broadcast with Radio Solent, talking about how we policed 'The Dell' in the 50's.

C/Supt, Graham Wyeth, then took me on a conducted tour of the new stadium in St Mary's, showing me the cells, the control room with its battery of CCTV cameras and explained how several hundred officers and stewards now controlled the crowds. Graham then made an outside broadcast, talking about the modern methods of policing the football ground. The comparison between the two structures, and the policing methods, were startling.

Inside the new stadium and with C/Supt. Wyeth in the Control Room

One case I dealt with that February 1953 took me back to my childhood misdemeanour. Five boys were seen stealing 'Waggonwheels' biscuits from the back of a delivery van and one of them had been caught by the driver. 12 biscuits, total value 4/- (20p) had been taken. I soon traced the other four youngsters, aged 7 to 11 years.

My pocket book contains the written statement of the driver, with details of the boys, all of whom were reported for summons in the presence of their parents. I could not refrain from submitting a covering report requesting they be dealt with by way of caution from the Superintendent, and this was agreed. I could only hope that their future turned out as well as mine.

I now looked forward to completing my probation with a faint hope that perhaps I would, in due course, become a detective.

4. ON PROBATION – 1953

Checking the rear of premises at night was something that was not particularly enjoyed. We not only had to have the key-holder called out if premises were found insecure but also if an unusual light was seen. It was amazing how often staff left premises without checking that all means of entry were secure, or left lights on where they shouldn't. On your own, on a dark and windy night, hearing all sorts of noises, checking places like the large Labour Exchange in Millbrook Road was daunting. But it had to be carried out because if the Team Car found it insecure and you had failed to discover it, you were in serious trouble.

What used to be the Millbrook Labour Exchange

I well recall one particular night, an especially wet, dark, windy one, checking the Labour Exchange on my own. Having gone along the lengthy side of the building, I had to enter a narrow covered passageway leading to a small cul-de-sac at the rear where there were some ground floor windows that had to be checked. This was always important because it was the most vulnerable part of the building.

As I left the alleyway, with my truncheon in my hand (this was always a necessary thing to do as it was a most remote area and I always felt vulnerable myself) a cat jumped off the alleyway roof above me, onto the ground in front of me. I yelled out, absolutely terrified, and if I could have caught the equally terrified animal, well, I don't know what I would have done, (but perhaps I do.)

It was not unusual for a cat to leap out whilst checking the rear of premises, making you jump with fright. This was no doubt the reason why a certain inspector hated cats. I once cycled along Foundry Lane with him when we saw a cat jump out in front of us; to my horror he quickly drew out a short rubber truncheon from his pocket (not the standard issue) and threw it at the cat (luckily he missed.). It turned out this was his hobby on nights.

On the other hand, I once welcomed the attention of a stray dog whilst on night duty. The small fellow latched onto me whilst I was walking along Shirley High Street in the small hours, and followed me for the remainder of my shift, not leaving my side. I found him agreeable company, talking to him as though he was my own pet, but when it came to returning to the police hostel in Archers Road at 6.00am I had to pedal very fast in an attempt to lose him.

I thought I had succeeded along the lower length of Archers Road, but when I went up to my room, after breakfast, I heard a whining from the courtyard below, and there was my friend from the night. Fortunately he was unable to wait until I woke up many hours later and had gone when I got up. However, I did miss him.

In March I attended a two week long course at the Training School, Hulse Road. This was an in-depth review of recent legislation, criminal and traffic law and local by-laws. I was also shown over the fingerprint and photography department, run by DC Basil Ballard in the Civic Centre, with an explanation of how they were classified.

The Training School, Hulse Road (currently up for sale)

The training course was interrupted several times by my having to attend court for minor cases I had dealt with. We had to attend court for every case, no matter how trivial and regardless of whether or not a guilty plea was anticipated. This was acceptable when we were on a tour of 6.00am to 2.00pm; it was a break from patrol, but a nuisance when on other shifts. Space was provided on the Form 22 Offence Report for "dates to avoid", but this was frequently ignored. The needs of solicitors were always treated as a priority; those of police officers were considered unimportant.

For serious criminal cases, where the offender was to be committed for trial at Quarter Sessions or Assize, all witnesses had to attend the magistrates' court to give evidence on oath. They were thus available to be cross-examined by the defending solicitor, who would have a copy of the depositions and thus be fully aware of the prosecution's case. The defence could be reserved so prosecuting counsel would not know of a line of defence until the last minute.

This always struck me as unfair and unbalanced. It was also a real problem having a committal that lasted several days prior to a trial that lasted even longer. It seemed a farce to me as Magistrates invariably had no option but to commit for trial, although in theory, rarely in practice, they could dismiss the committal. In such cases the alleged offender had not been dealt with, so could once again be arrested and brought before the court if further evidence came to light.

I attended a further local training course in April, where I was given an explanation of charge sheets and enquiry office duties, with a visit to the cells and Information Room by PS Kinchinton.

Part of the cell corridor and one of the cells.
(There were 17 male cells, two female cells and one padded cell.)

This was followed by an explanation of hackney carriages (the control and licensing of taxis) and diseases of animals by PC Denison (his full time duties); the Warrant Office for an explanation of procedures relating to Informations and Summons by PS Ralph Farrindon; the General Office for talk on records held by the force, Forms 22 and pay and finally the duties of the Traffic Department with PS Bill Moore.

PS Bill Moore – he retired as Traffic Superintendent.

The following day I attended the usual morning CID conference, followed by a discussion of local bye-laws by Insp. Fred 'Judy' Garland (my 'friend' from initial induction days); talk on divisional Clerk Sergeant's duties by PC Budd; detailed explanation of the CRO by DC Archie Davies, covering his files, indexes of individuals, street names, stolen property, wanted persons, nicknames, stolen motor vehicles etc. The training concluded with a talk by the Aliens Officer of powers under the Aliens Order and the procedures to be followed as well as a talk by the Coroner's Officer, DS John Jefferis.

The Criminal Record Office (CRO) *(Hampshire Constabulary History Society)*
DC Archie Davies is checking his large table of index cards, with PC Des Barnes, Cadet Howard Willis and PS John Creighton in the background.

Archie had a simple but very effective system to locate a file. Every crime file, minor or major, including murder, was allocated a consecutive number, starting with the year, and filed in the large series of shelves. Index cards were then typed or handwritten with the name of the loser/victim and offender, showing the file number. Someone with a long list of convictions would have all his crime file numbers listed on his index card. That way it was quick and easy to locate everything relating to an offender.

Soon after I had another treat, duty covering a Speedway Championship event at the Bannister Court Stadium. I initially was stationed in Hulse Road to prevent parking, and then had free admission to watch most of the events before leaving to carry out traffic control at the Stag Gates junction when the stadium emptied. I found I was really enjoying some of these 'perks' of the job.

By the end of June 1953 I had completed my first six months service and looked back with some satisfaction. Although I had dealt with many trivial matters they had added up to give me confidence and some useful experience. Such trivia as reporting motorists for failing to give precedence on a pedestrian crossing or parking within 45 feet; domestic arguments, usually resolved; finding vehicles with an expired road fund licence; drivers with expired driving licence; youths using abusive behaviour outside shops warned as to their behaviour, invariably with a good result as they knew I would be on the beat again; premises found insecure or showing an unusual light, cyclists without lights (never seen cycling on the pavement.); cars failing to stop at halt signs or red traffic lights, all minor but nevertheless good experience at report writing and dealing with the public. This was one aspect I found especially enjoyable, contact with so many nice people as well as the unlawful ones. People would report all manner of helpful facts worthy of passing onto CID, things they would never bother to go into a police station about, but "Just thought I'd let you know about......" because I was readily available.

Some things were not so common, like finding a stray horse walking along Shirley Road one evening, and after contacting the station for help to be told "Just take him along to the Pound on the Common, it's OK to leave your beat." I'm not sure who was more scared, the horse or me. I also found that individuals would come up with all sorts of excuses when found committing an offence. One that I recorded, after seeing a cyclist riding straight through a Halt sign without stopping, was "I can't read or write and didn't know it was a Halt sign".

It was surprising how people managed to find me walking along when they had found some property and found it easier to give it to me instead of taking it to the station. I was very conscious of the fact that it had been drummed into me that more officers had been dismissed over property than anything else (with 'romantic' attachments being a close second.). It was therefore extremely important to immediately record the full details in my pocket book, including the details of the finder, and to hand it in and enter everything in the property register directly one returned to the station.

My friend PC Bill Williams had a most unpleasant experience over found property. Two girls once let slip in front of their parents that they had found a large sum of money in the street. When asked what they had done with it they said they had given it to a policeman walking along the same street. The parents then went to Shirley Police Station to ask if the owner of the cash had been traced, otherwise they would have been able to claim it for the girls. Records were searched but there was nothing recorded about the cash having been handed in. Statements were taken from the girls, and from the time and place mentioned the only police officer they could have seen would have been Bill.

When questioned he denied all knowledge of being handed any money. His pocket book was seized and he was suspended from duty whilst DI Bob Masters investigated the matter. Bill was intensively questioned but continued to deny all knowledge of the matter. Things were looking decidedly serious for him, when further questioning of the girls revealed that, in fact, they had spent the money but were too frightened to tell their parents. They had seen Bill on patrol but admitted they had not, in fact, mentioned the find to him at all. They were cautioned for their behaviour, but Bill

maintained a hearty dislike of Bob Masters, who later became Assistant Chief Constable, for the rest of Bill's service.

Detective Inspector Bob Masters

The Prevention of Crime Act, 1953, came into force on 6 June, prohibiting the carrying of offensive weapons in public places without lawful authority or reasonable excuse. I soon exercised my power of

search under this act and took possession of a 'flick-knife' I found on a youngster playing on waste ground in Shirley Warren. He was only 11 years old and I thought there was little purpose in detaining him or taking any action other than removing the knife. I was satisfied he had no real idea of its danger and I still have the knife after all these years.

At the end of June I had my first experience of the much sought after "Bassett Patrol". This was a daily 3.00.pm-11.00pm duty in an unmarked Hillman Estate, with a sergeant, driver and a constable, covering the Upper Bassett area of Southampton. This area was full of high value detached properties and the unoccupied houses would be checked whilst the owners were on holiday. It was, of course, a pure coincidence that the Chief Constable also lived there. The patrol would also be on the look-out for suspicious vehicles or individuals that might possibly be involved in breaking into properties, the majority of which had high value contents. The duty was invariably a relaxing break from foot patrol and was allocated to officers from all divisions on a roster.

A change in night duty patrol came about that June when a decision was made to leave all street lights on throughout the night during Coronation Week. It first seemed strange to have the streets lit during the night, being so used to complete darkness throughout the tour of duty.

My personal life was about to change dramatically the following month, when my pocket book records me having eight hours time-off on Friday 3 July 1953, followed by a Saturday rest day and then my full quota of two weeks annual leave. This had been arranged early that year to allow me to marry my childhood sweetheart on 4 July.

Before my marriage could be confirmed I had to submit her full details, date of birth etc., and get official permission to marry her. She had to be properly checked to ensure she had no previous convictions, or warnings for soliciting, if so I would have to either resign or not marry.

Our rented top flat in Graham Road also had to be visited by an inspector to ensure it was suitable, before it was agreed that I would now receive a rent allowance, to cover the rent of £1. 15s a week. I now had the added responsibility of married life and looked forward to resuming duty as a more mature officer.

Our wedding day, with my best man, PC Bill Williams, alongside me.

I had originally arranged to have the photographs taken by one of the Force photographers, who worked in the fingerprint department, but he was unfortunately unavailable on the day. Luckily, family members turned up trumps.

On my return to duty from annual leave another 'perk' arose, on 22 July, when I was detailed for duty at Central Railway Station for the arrival of HRH Princess Margaret, where I had a very close view of her.

This was followed a few days later with a full day attachment to the CID, attending their morning conference and being briefed by the detective inspector on the outstanding cases being dealt with. This was most certainly what I had joined the police force for and I immediately determined that this would be my destiny.

My determination was strengthened that same month when, on night duty team policing, a call was received at 11.45pm of a 'smash and grab' at Burton's shop, Shirley High Street. A car was seen at the scene, driving towards town, and its registration number taken by residents opposite. A 'hue and cry' was immediately put into operation. This code meant that all operational vehicles took up predetermined positions at locations around the borough perimeter, at all main exits from the town, as well as some touring the area in an attempt to locate the vehicle. As a result it was soon found abandoned at the cattle market near Terminus Terrace, with its radiator still hot. Although the Shirley team car was not involved further that night, I thought of the enquiries that would be carried out by detectives, examining the scene and the car for clues, and wished that I could be one of them. However, this was not to be and I continued with my routine patrols with nothing of significance taking place for some considerable time.

One of the normal routines on 'early turn' was the changing of the unilateral parking signs along Shirley Road. These were large metal circular plates, hinged in the centre to form half circles, mounted on a pole and scattered along both sides of Shirley Road. The principle was that when the bottom half was clipped at the top, it showed 'No Parking', and when dropped down 'Parking Allowed'. By having no parking on each side of the road on alternate days, it avoided complaints from shopkeepers that access to their shop was restricted every day. It was the 6.00am to 2.00pm officer's job, armed with a wooden stick with a hook at the end, to cycle along both sides of Shirley Road, clipping and dropping half sections to change the sides of the road that prohibited or allowed parking. We looked something like the lamplighters of old, getting the hook to enter the appropriate slot with ease. The problem was that when they were dropped they made a very loud clanging noise, sufficient to wake up residents sleeping over their shops, but they never complained because 'it was a police duty'.

Shirley Road c. 1950 - prior to Unilateral Parking *(Bill Moore)*

One of my early arrests occurred that August. Whilst walking from the station to my beat I passed waste ground in Shirley Road, an old bombed site opposite Jenkins & Pursers. The site was very overgrown but I noticed a figure lying down in the long grass. Curiosity has always been one of my strong points, especially when on duty, so I strolled across to check the position. Several children were playing a short distance away and as I approached from behind the figure I saw it was a man with his trousers down to his ankles, fully exposed.

On seeing me he cried out, got up, hastily dressing himself, but his intention was absolutely clear. I arrested him and at the station, when charged with "lewdly and wilfully exposing your person etc." and given the usual caution, he replied to the charge, and this was duly recorded on the charge sheet, "I've got TB and my doctor told me to get as much fresh air as possible."

My notebook records an entry when I turned up for normal 5.00pm-1.00am duty, to be greeted on arrival with "Take 8 hours time off, you're not needed." None of us were on the phone so I didn't know anything about it until I arrived. No compensation whatsoever for having to travel to and from Shirley Police Station or for the day to have been ruined.

My notebook also records the fact that I was warned to attend a church parade outside Bitterne church in October, starting at 11.00am. However, I was forced to report sick that day because of severe stomach pains, following a few weeks later by an operation in the Southampton General Hospital to have my appendix removed.

I was sorry to have missed this parade; it would have been an opportunity to show off my uniform, marching with my colleagues in front of my family.

Previous page: Shirley Division marching outside Bitterne Church, with the long vanished Red Lion Cut and Albert Terrace in the background. *(Janet Holloway).* **Superintendent Gordon Baker is leading, with Inspectors Reg Garret, John Quinlan and Alan 'Gunner' Payne behind him. Behind Reg Garret is PS Frank Holloway in front of PC Ken Holmes, behind John Quinlan is PS Tim Blake in front of PC Bob Smith and behind 'Gunner' Payne is PS Jim Fibbens in front of PC Pete Adams.**

Insp. Alan 'Gunner' Payne, pictured in the parade above, was, to say the least, an eccentric. I have fond memories of him at 6.00am on early turn, startling us on parade with strange outbursts. Two in particular stay in my memory. He had the habit of gesticulating, stabbing his hand towards us with the forefinger and little finger outstretched and the centre fingers doubled over as he bellowed at us. An incident I recall was placing his hand on top of his head, waggling it side to side, saying "You see a chicken with drooping comb". Then, doubled over, he slapped his hand repeatedly against his backside, saying "Dirty end, dirty end". He then jabbed his hand at us asking the question "What's wrong, what's wrong?" We all looked at him blank, none of us daring to speak, when we received the shouted answer "Epizootic lymphangitis", before he stormed out of the Parade Room back to his office. It was something that stuck in our minds, I still recall the disease after all these years, but it was much later that I discovered that 'Gunner' was wrong, the disease only affects equine animals.

Another one that sticks in my mind is being shouted at "You see a load fall off a lorry, what do you say to the driver?" – stabbing his hand at each of us in turn. We mumbled replies such as "Can I see your driving licence?", "Are you the owner or the driver?", but all being told in no uncertain terms that we were wrong. He then shouted "Does your firm supply you with a rope?" before striding back to his office. In this case it was something we all remembered to ask when dealing with an offence of insecure load.

One minor incident worthy of mention took place the following March. I was on night duty and directly I arrived at the bottom of Romsey Road, at 10.20pm, near the junction with the newly constructed Tebourba Way, I saw two cyclists travelling away from me, towards the junction. As they reached the junction a large Humber Snipe saloon drove out of Tebourba Way and turning sharply into Romsey Road, on the wrong side of a traffic island directly into the path of the two cyclists.

I glanced at the traffic lights and saw that the car had driven through a red light. As I did this one of the cyclists, a Miss Jonquil Crowe, 17 years, swerved to avoid the car, lost her balance and fell onto the road. I stopped the car, discovering that the driver was a 27 year old RAF Lance Corporal from the RAF Station at Lyneham, Chippenham. The driver of another car, that had followed the Humber, got out and gave me a statement describing the erratic driving of the Humber along Tebourba Way, prior to it turning into Romsey Road against the red light. I therefore reported the driver for summons for careless driving and failing to conform to the traffic light. The girl's companion, Ian Whitford, 18, later gave me a statement corroborating the incident, as did a pedestrian who I had seen standing at the junction. When the driver eventually appeared at court he was fined £5, 15 shillings costs and licence endorsed.

The points of interest out of this routine incident are (a) The girl was the daughter of PS Jim Crowe, (b) Ian Whitford later joined the Force and served as a PC with me in Shirley and (c) the three passengers in the Humber Snipe were survivors from the *Empire Windrush*, a ship that had been used for large scale immigration from the Caribbean. The ship had sailed from Japan in February with wounded United Nations veterans of the Korean War, but after sailing from Port Said an engine room fire broke out. There were no means on board for fighting the fire and many survivors were rescued, still in their pyjamas, and taken to Algiers where they were cared for by the French army and Red Cross. The ship later sank and the survivors were taken by British ships and Shackleton aircraft to the UK, hence those in the Humber being driven by an RAF member.

I had by now attended a number of traffic accidents, many involving injury, some serious, and became accustomed to performing some initial first aid until the arrival of an ambulance. This attendance at an RTA (Road Traffic Accident) obviously increased over the years, but I never overcame my strong feelings of sympathy, and sometimes helplessness, for the injured, especially if they were children.

One accident that I actually witnessed sticks in my mind. I was on 'Main Road' duty in Shirley High Street when I saw a man step out from the front of a stationary bus opposite as a car was in the act of overtaking it. The car made a very good emergency stop, but this caused an elderly lady sitting in the back to be thrown forward violently. The back of the empty passenger seat in front of her folded over and she fell across it. However, her legs were under the front seat, with the result that both of them snapped. She was in absolute agony and in a state of severe shock. It was impossible for me to help her out of the car and I could do little other than reassure her whilst awaiting the arrival of an ambulance. It proved extremely difficult to assist her out of the car without causing further damage to her legs, but with the assistance of the ambulance driver we managed it with a minimum of extra pain.

It is worth mentioning that at this time ambulance drivers were just that, drivers, with the same first aid qualification as me. Paramedics had yet to be invented and I recall almost punching an ambulance driver. A woman had slipped up in Woolworths in Shirley High Street, and when I attended I found her sitting on a chair, in extreme pain, with one foot at right angles to her leg, suffering from an obvious severe fracture. We made her comfortable but when the ambulance driver arrived the first thing he did was to try to straighten her foot to place a splint on. She screamed, I shouted, and the ambulance driver had my fist stopped short just inches from his face. Common sense then prevailed and she was carefully assisted into the waiting ambulance.

One of my first 'sixth senses' occurred in June, when I stopped a 16 year old youth in Millbrook Road during the afternoon. I had stopped and checked a large number of individuals, usually during the night or early hours, but there was something about the youth that made me suspicious, I have no idea what it was, but I felt he warranted a thorough check.

When asked for his address he said he lived at 31 Alban Road. I immediately knew this to be false, there is no such road in Southampton, and it did not take me long to discover that he was an absconder from Redhill Approved School, Surrey. He was accordingly arrested and taken to Shirley police station. He was the first in a long line of successful checks that helped give me the later nickname of 'Lucky Jim'.

My next arrest, in July, also came as a result of a check. At 11.20pm I saw a cyclist travelling along Millbrook Road, swerving more than was needed. When I stepped into his path to stop him he immediately fell off the machine onto the road. I then realised that he had been drinking, but he was sober enough to answer my questions. He was a Glaswegian assistant cook on *RMS Queen Mary*, but when I asked how he came by the cycle, bearing in mind he was from Glasgow, he couldn't give me a satisfactory answer. I arrested him on suspicion of theft and drunk in charge of a cycle, and whilst I was dealing with him at the station a lorry driver called to report his cycle stolen from a yard in Commercial Road, a short distance from where I had stopped the cyclist. Of course, he identified the cycle as his and at court the following morning the Glaswegian received a conditional discharge with 15 shillings cost.

My next offenders, that August, were two small boys, brothers aged 10 and 12. They had been cycling along Aldermoor Road and when they saw me cycling along on my beat, dropped the bike and ran away. They were soon caught and it turned out that the cycle had been stolen earlier that day. Both boys were under the care of a Probation Officer for previous thefts, and I was saddened when the case came before the Juvenile Court because although the elder brother was placed on Probation for a further two years, his younger brother was sent to a Remand Home. I could not help but compare it with my situation at the same age.

I then had a break from police duties in early August, two weeks Army Reserve training in Aldershot, the final part of my National Service. To my surprise the army had cottoned on to the fact that I was now a police officer, so it was spent as a Military Policeman, but as a lance-corporal instead of sergeant. I found it interesting, as army powers over soldiers were far greater than civilian ones - they could be detained on a whim.

My final offenders, on 27 August, the day before my own probationary police service came to an end, committed a misdemeanour of a very rural nature. Whilst on patrol in Brownhill Road in the late evening, I saw several boys playing in a field of wheat adjoining Aldermoor School. They were carrying several sheaves of wheat through a gap in the hedge, leading into a copse. I followed them, saw they had piled the sheaves up into a heap, and when I asked what they were doing I had the reply "We're making a den Mister". I knew the field was owned by Farmer Tuffin so took the boys names and addresses before getting in touch with him.

He was most upset about the incident. He had made a large stack of sheaves ready for collection and on checking found that between 400 and 500 had been disturbed, with 100 removed to the adjacent copse, causing some damage. I then saw the youngsters at their homes, in the presence of their parents, and reported them for wilful damage. I had not thought the matter too serious, the damage amounted to £5 (about half an average weekly wage) but the four youngsters, all aged 12, were taken to Juvenile Court where two were fined ten shillings, with 6/3d costs, one placed on 12 months probation, but to my dismay one was sent to a Remand Home, because of his previous offences.

One evening that winter I attended a St John's Ambulance Brigade refresher course at the Civic Centre, after which I walked back through West Park to return to the police hostel in Archers Road. I was in uniform, but with a civilian raincoat on top. As I passed behind the Cenotaph I saw a man crouching down, in the dark, doing something to the flower beds. I went up to him and saw that he was holding several plants in his hand, with the appropriate empty spaces in the flower bed. I told him who I was and he readily admitted unlawfully removing the plants, apologising profusely.

I felt I had no option but to arrest him, and took him to the police headquarters, where I told the station sergeant, PS Peter Turner, what had happened. He took the man into the charge room and returned some time later to say "The man you detained is a customs officer. It is entirely a matter for you, but if you wish to charge him he will lose both his job and his HMC pension. If you are happy to leave the matter with me I will deal with him, and you need put nothing in your pocket book. But if you want to continue with it I will accept a charge and you will need to complete all the paperwork. It is entirely your choice." I did not need to give the matter too much thought and told the sergeant that I was more than happy to leave the matter in his hands. On reflection I believe I made the right decision, although many will no doubt disagree.

The rest of my second year was mainly concerned with dealing with traffic accidents, reporting motorists for various traffic offences, including driving without due care, domestic troubles, mainly husbands and wives fighting, and what seemed to be millions of checks on unoccupied properties whilst the owners were on holiday.

I found it interesting when I worked the beats that took me to the division's borders. Tanner's Brook was the western extremity of Shirley division, and I could see much activity there. It was a rural area, with some farms and country houses, with a County officer living in a police house in Wimpson Lane, but there was talk of it being taken over by Southampton Council.

As the months progressed I saw a massive council estate in the course of development, to the west of Tebourba Way, which had been constructed alongside the Tanner's Brook borough boundary. It was fascinating to see the area completely changing in character, with massive tower blocks rising on what had been fields.

By 1954, when the borough was extended as far as the River Test, to include Redbridge, four new beats were created on the new Millbrook Estate, 11 to 14, and the divisional strength was also increased. The northern border of the division, Lordswood and Coxford, also had some character. It was bordered by Farmer Tuffin's fields, regularly occupied by gypsies – not the travellers of today, but genuine gypsies with their decorated horse drawn caravans.

We were instructed to move them on, firmly but politely, and I was frequently amused by the range of excuses they gave to avoid being moved. "Wife's in the Unit Sorr", 'Orse gone lame Sorr" were typical examples. I was also often offered a cup of tea, brewed in an empty paint tin hung over an open fire, which I always politely refused. They were wonderful characters, rarely causing trouble, making wooden pegs for sale, and I became quite friendly with them.

However, I had heard there was once a disturbance involving the gypsies. They had caused trouble in the nearby Bedwell Arms, Nursling, just outside the borough boundary, in the course of which a chamber pot was thrown at them. The public house was thereafter always referred to as 'the flying piss-pot'. Some months later gypsies also became involved in a serious disturbance in the Griffin public house in Anglesea Road. A crowd of them were fighting in a crowded bar with locals and it had got out of hand. PC Dennis Barrett was the emergency driver, and grabbing several officers who were report writing in the station, he attended. The fighting was such that Dennis had to use his stick, and eventually order was restored with several prisoners taken to the station and charged with assault.

Half an hour later a report was received that a man was in the emergency ward of the Royal South Hants hospital, suffering from injuries after having been struck by a car in Shirley Road. He had made his own way there. Den Barrett attended to obtain details but on seeing the man said "You are the first one I hit. It wasn't a car that hit you, it was me", and, after some treatment, another prisoner joined those in the Police Station.

It was during this period that I narrowly escaped my second misconduct charge. I had visited my close friend from my boyhood, John Bocock, and his wife whilst on the Maybush beat. Their home in Coxford Road was one of my private 'tea-holes' and on this occasion John was interested in seeing my handcuffs. For fun I put them on him, but to my horror when it came to removing them my key failed to work. No matter how much we tried, the handcuffs were clearly faulty and we had no option but to spend some considerable time cutting them off with a hacksaw.

I then had the problem of explaining this to my sergeant, Vic White, as I needed them to be replaced from the store. The only thing I could think of, on the spur of the moment, was that I had tried them on my wife for a joke. This explanation was accepted, but I thought that several of the sergeants later gave me funny looks and I believed I once heard the word 'bondage' used.

PC Derek Lowe attracted much attention that September when the Daily Order announced that he had obtained the degree of Bachelor of Law, LL.B at London University. As far as I am aware Derek was the only member of the Force to possess a degree. All officers, including the very senior ones, had worked their way up through the ranks purely on their police ability, not via an academic qualification.

Changes in the size of the Division on 1 April 1954 resulted in Supt. Gordon Baker transferring from Shirley to be Det/Supt Headquarters CID and being replaced by C/Insp. Hugh O'Connor from Portswood A-sub Division as Superintendent, Shirley Division.

13 May found me on duty at the Girls Grammar School, Hill Lane, supervising the ballot box for the Municipal Elections, being delegated to escort the box and Presiding Officer to the Civic Centre and remain in the Counting Room whilst votes were counted for Shirley Ward. I found this an interesting experience, seeing how the piles of votes changed and the excitement of the candidates as the outcome became more and more certain.

At the very end of my probationary period, 24 August 1954, the Chief Constable saw me and told me he was now satisfied I was suitable to be retained in the Force. I was now a fully fledged Constable, only able to be dismissed through serious misconduct, and I looked forward to what I blissfully assumed to be a further 28 years service.

5. OUT OF PROBATION – 1954

Now a fully established constable I found that one of my first duties, whilst making a routine call from a pillar, was "Please call at 77 Kingsley Road and tell the occupier that the nurse who lodges there has left her gas fire on and it needs to be turned off". Another request was "Please tell Mrs X, of Outer Circle, to take her husband's false teeth when she next visits him in Winchester Prison".

These and many similar routine and mundane calls helped to pass otherwise boring tours of duty and, in fact, served as a useful service to the public. It certainly helped to establish good relations with the police and as a by-product brought us into contact with people who were much more likely to pass on useful information about the activity of others. One of the things I found so enjoyable with police work was the contact with people, good and bad. Being on foot, with all the time in the world to chat (unless one was late for a 'point' or routine call) made the time pass quickly.

I was now trusted enough to give spells of meal relief cover to the station enquiry office and switchboard whilst on night duty and, **once only**, to act as section cook.

I reflected on the previous two years whilst on probation. The first thing that had struck me was the general use of obscene language amongst officers. I had been used to this in the army, conforming to what was the norm myself, but had somehow expected something different from those who upheld the law. Because it was an arrestable offence in the public domain, and generally enforced, I had assumed police officers would be above it. It was, however, in common use within the police station, but not in the hearing of woman officers or the civilian typists in the general office.

I recall, with some amusement, standing next to my friend PC Stan Stevenson whilst we were looking at the newly posted duty roster, setting out the following week's leave days. I saw my allocated rest day and moved away, being replaced by PW Norma Pledger. Stan stabbed his finger at the roster, turned round to where I was standing and said, directly into Norma's face, "Look, f.....g Friday again." She immediately moved away, giving him a withering and offended look in the process, leaving poor Stan looked very embarrassed. The reason Stan was upset was that Friday was the weekly pay day, paid in cash, and Stan had to travel from Woolston to get his cash – badly needed as no-one had cash reserves to spare. Nobody had a bank account at this period; that was yet to come.

Another thing I discovered, and the reader will come across it in this book, is the often macabre sense of humour that officers have. It is probably a defence mechanism against the sometimes horrific incidents that have to be deal with. I well recall attending a suicide where an unfortunate individual had placed his shoulders on the railway line in front of a passing train near Central Station. I personally recovered the severed head, to be taken to the mortuary with the mangled body, singing aloud as I carried it by his hair "With 'is 'ead tucked underneath 'is arm", to the amusement of my fellow officers. Looking back it is not something I am proud of, but it was nothing unusual for the period.

Once, during a tour of night duty, PC Wally Tate had brought a barrister's wig and gown to the station. I don't know where he obtained it, or for what purpose, (possibly a stage production) but during our meal break he decided to hold a court appearance for an Irish drunk someone had brought in earlier. Those of us on duty took off our tunics, to act as jury members, and Wally dressed up and sat in front of the parade room bench, whilst the prisoner, still drunk, was brought in from the cells to stand in front of him.

Wally then told him he had been convicted of murder and would be hanged by the neck the following week. The poor man staggered back to the cells, visibly shaken, but was quickly brought back to the 'court' to be told that there had been an appeal and he was to be released. He was then allowed to leave the station, rather less drunk than before, and was seen rushing along Shirley Road, still bemused but as though the devil were behind him.

My patrols were still full of routine matters; dealing with traffic accidents took up much of my time, and such things as reporting a youth for setting off a firework in the street (he was only cautioned), vehicles causing an obstruction, parked without lights, covering school crossings, reporting (or often only cautioning) people for petty traffic offences, serving summons or witness notices and delivering 'Informations' to dealers.

My experience was now increasing rapidly and I was beginning to subconsciously recognise body language when interviewing suspects or those merely checked as a matter of routine. Police officers tend to develop a sixth sense when observing the actions of others, and a check will often produce a surprising result.

One such was whilst keeping observations one evening from a doorway on the roof at the rear of the Regent Cinema in Shirley Road. I did this whenever I was on this particular beat during an evening as it overlooked the cinema's car park. It also gave me the opportunity of a sly smoke. There was a cycle shed in the car park, and this particular evening I saw two youths walk past the entrance. One stopped, entered the car park and disappeared from view in the cycle shed for several minutes.

I carefully came down the fire escape into the car park and when he reappeared stopped him to ask what he was doing. He said he was looking for a friend's cycle but gave a different description to that given by his friend, who I questioned separately. I then searched the boy, aged 16, and found a cycle battery and bulb in his pocket. I checked the parked cycles and found a machine with a missing battery and bulb. Both youths, the other was aged 14, admitted a number of previous similar thefts and were reported for summons. When they appeared at Juvenile Court they were both fined £1 and their mothers Bound Over for two years in the sum of £20., i.e. no further action taken unless they committed a further offence.

In September 1954 my wife and I moved home, into a two bed-roomed semi-detached house, "Romilly", in High Firs Road, Sholing. It was bought for £1,650, with a monthly mortgage repayment of £8. 8s 0d. We had to find a deposit of £165, which took a year to save, and my wife's income as a shorthand typist was not allowed to be taken into account. The same house in 2012 could be sold for in excess of £165,000, so to keep pace a probationary constable's weekly wage would now need to be in excess of £900 a week.

"Romilly", High Firs Road, Sholing

That October saw Sgt Jim Fibbens appointed Det/Sgt in Shirley Division, something that became important to me some years later but didn't seem important at the time.

My first off-duty arrest came that November. My wife and I were returning home from town by bus, getting off in Bursledon Road just after 11pm. After we crossed the road I looked back and saw a woman walking across the front of Donkey Common. As she walked, in the glare of oncoming car headlights, I saw that her raincoat opened to reveal a flash of white thigh. I pointed this out to my wife as it looked as though the woman had no skirt.

We both stopped, the woman also stopped, as she saw we were looking at her, and suddenly turned and walked into Donkey Common, along a small pathway. At this time of night Donkey Common was pitch black and the path led directly into very dark and dense undergrowth. I felt that something was very wrong so crossed the road and hurried along the path towards the woman, calling out as I did so "Don't worry, I'm a police officer."

Donkey Common

I received a very gruff reply of "It's all right Officer" and realised that the 'woman' was, in fact, a man. I caught up with him and saw he was wearing a headscarf wrapped around as a turban, heavy make up, pair of brass ear-rings, high heeled shoes, a long black raincoat and carrying a handbag. I pulled the raincoat open slightly and it confirmed he was not wearing a skirt but only white panties, silk stockings and suspenders. His woman's jumper showed a large 'bust', giving every appearance of a well built woman. I told him he was under arrest and took him to the police pillar at the top of North East Road, directly adjoining Donkey Common, where I used my key to open the telephone section and contact Bitterne police station direct, informing them of the situation.

As I was doing this I saw that the man was removing his high heeled shoes; he then suddenly broke away and ran swiftly down North East Road. I dropped the phone, soon caught him (I was extremely fit in those days) and dragged him back to the pillar to await the arrival of the Bitterne police car. He was taken to the station and questioned by Insp. Newbury and PS Peter Turner, when it transpired he was a 43 year old married man living nearby with his wife and two children. When searched it was revealed that underneath his jumper was a brassiere filled with two water filled balloons. He was also wearing home-made black rubber underpants underneath his panties, giving an initial impression of not having male genitalia.

After questioning it transpired that he was in the habit of dressing in his wife's clothing, unbeknown to her and after she had gone to bed, but as no offence had been revealed he was taken home. It must be emphasised that at this period homosexual behaviour was a serious criminal offence and my arrest had been based on the fact that he could have been importuning passing traffic en route to Portsmouth. Transsexuals and cross-dressing was relatively unknown at this time and I had no experience whatsoever of such behaviour.

My next offenders were three 10 and 11 year old tricksters. Whilst on patrol in Millbrook Road during late morning I saw three young boys talking to a Co-op delivery milkman who then handed them some cash in exchange for milk tokens (made of plastic and used by the Co-op instead of cash) and a note. I casually spoke to the milkman who said the note was from their mother who wanted the tokens exchanged for a few shillings cash because she had changed from Co-op to Frays Dairy. There was, however, something about the boys' behaviour that aroused my suspicion, so I noted their names and addresses before allowing them to leave.

The milkman then checked his cash and accounts whilst I was there and found that he was short of exactly the amount given to the boys. I therefore took a statement from him and checked the address alleged to be that of the mother, finding it to be false. I went at once to nearby Freemantle School where I saw the headmaster, giving him the names and descriptions of the three boys. He easily identified them and had them brought to his study where I asked them where they had obtained the milk tokens. They admitted they had stolen them from the Oxo tin kept on his van earlier that day, and had written the note alleged to be from one of their mothers to obtain the cash refund.

I later saw all three at their homes, in the presence of their parents, and reported them for summons for 'larceny by means of a trick'. I was, however, saddened when they eventually appeared before the juvenile magistrates. Two of the youths were placed on probation for 12 months, but the third boy, who was the seventh in a family of nine, was sent to the Remand Home for three weeks because of a previous conviction. I was once again reminded of my own appearance many years ago, and the outcome.

In early December I experienced my own private 'domestic trouble'. I was on 2.00pm-10.00pm duty and my close friend PC Bill Williams suggested we had a drink and a chat at the police club in Hulse Road before we cycled home. By now we had sold our house in High Firs Road and moved in to my wife's former home in South East Road, because her father was seriously ill with terminal Hodgson's Disease.

The police club wasn't a police authority club; it was a private one, owned by the Southampton police officers, who paid the sum of sixpence (2½p) a week to remain members. Licensing hours for public houses were 10.30am to 2.00pm and 6.00pm to 10.30pm, but the hours in the police club were far more flexible. Consequently Bill and I met there not long after 10.00pm, both having 'rung off duty' from our beat pillars, and each bought the other a drink. We were then joined by PC Sam Passmore, who was celebrating something; I think possibly just getting engaged. He therefore bought Bill and me a drink. so we, of course, each had to also buy a round back.

I was therefore very much under the weather and the time had passed considerably. I was not unduly concerned about getting home so late as I took it for granted that my wife would assume I had got involved in an incident taking me over my normal finishing time. Of course, nobody possessed telephones then so I had no way of contacting her anyway.

When I eventually left I was most certainly a good case of 'drunk in charge of a bicycle' and recall weaving over Northam Bridge, in full uniform and my helmet, hanging from my handlebars, calling out "Merry Christmas" to any startled individual walking by. On arriving home I was surprised to see the ground floor living room light on, threw my cycle in the sideway and staggered indoors, to be greeted by my wife, mother and father-in-law, all looking very worried. My pregnant wife burst into tears and ran upstairs, leaving me bewildered.

It turned out they became worried by midnight, and on going to the nearest telephone box and contacting Shirley police station were told I had rung off at 10.00pm and had not been involved in an incident. As a result officers were detailed to check the route I would have taken home in case I was lying somewhere injured. I had to phone the station and explain, but my domestic situation was, to say the least, very frosty for some time.

My new home in South East Road, adjacent to the Primitive Methodist Chapel

Christmas 1954 saw me on 2.00pm-10.00pm duty both Christmas Eve and Christmas Day, with a quick swing to 6.00am-2.00pm on Boxing Day. I couldn't really complain, I had been off sick for this period the previous year having had my appendix removed, and as I had no children it was not an issue. However, my wife was pregnant with our first daughter so I was hopeful that in the ensuing years I would always have at least one of the two festive days off.

Early in the New Year, whilst on night duty and at the start of Team Policing, we had a 999 call to Shirley Road where we were told that the occupier, a general dealer, had been regularly missing tinned goods from his cart left in his yard at Beatrice Road. He had kept observations on the yard and caught a friend leaving with a bag full of goods. He had stopped him and found seven tins of peas and 2 tins of luncheon meat, stolen from his cart. I took a statement from him in my pocket book and DS Jim Fibbens went with me to the home of the man we had detained, where further tinned goods were found. I thought I would be the officer in the case, but to my dismay DS Jim Fibbens took the case over and charged the man with the thefts, which he admitted. I resolved that if I became a sergeant I would ensure that my junior officers had that experience themselves.

The following week I experienced my first struggle with a suspect. I had by now checked numerous individuals whilst on patrol, without a problem, but this night I did have a problem. I was on 5.00pm – 1.00am duty in early January and at 12.50am checked a man in Wimpson Lane. He was carrying a bundle of clothing and told me he was returning home from the Docks and lived at 36 Wimpson Lane. However, when asked to produce any documents to confirm this he showed me a National Insurance card with a Northampton address.

As I was not satisfied with his explanation I started to search him. As I did so he started to struggle violently, attempting to strike me and run away. I had great difficulty in restraining him but managed to pin him down and get a passing motorist to dial 999 for assistance. This soon arrived and he was taken to Shirley police station, where it was then revealed that he had been a voluntary patient at Knowle Mental Hospital and had left of his own accord. No offences came to light and he was taken home to his parents who lived locally. This was my first experience of a 'difficult customer' but meant I was more aware in future of a potential problem when stopping people late at night.

If the Force had any doubts about my honesty, in view of my juvenile conviction, this was dispelled when I checked a car parked on the forecourt of Hendy's Garage. The window was partly open and I was able to open the door, having seen a carton of 1,000 cigarettes on the front seat and £80 in cash (the day's takings) on the back seat. The owner was traced to the nearby Railway Hotel and I was duly thanked. This was the first of many similar incidents, with business properties found insecure and the contents, often with large amounts of cash still in the till, found late at night or in the early hours. I always ensured that the station was contacted by the property's internal phone and another officer attending to confirm the amount of cash etc.

It was around this time that I was told an anecdote involving the officer detailed as permanent gaoler at police headquarters. He was a nice person and a good copper but before being given this duty had to once appear in the witness box having charged someone with 'using obscene language in a public place'. He told the magistrates that the defendant had told him to "F.....k off". When asked to confirm that this had been said direct to the officer, he replied "Yes your Worships, three f.......g times". Laughter in court. It was also said, on good authority, that when he was first appointed gaoler he was told to exercise the prisoners, but instead of using the internal enclosed exercise yard leading from the cell passage, he took them for a walk around the parks. Amazingly they all happily returned with him but the episode passed into local folk lore.

Another well known anecdote concerned PC Ken Spiller, one of my close friends on my section. Ken had been called to a complaint of a noisy party in St James Road, but on calling at the house concerned received verbal abuse from the occupier, a private-hire taxi driver. The noise continued unabated and the door was slammed in Ken's face. This was well before the days of environmental officers, so nothing could really be done as it took place on private property. Ken was extremely upset and frustrated.

69

However, three weeks later the taxi driver called at Shirley police station and asked to see the officer who had dealt with the complaint, when he was available. He returned when Ken was next on duty and said "I'm sorry about what happened, can you please accept my apology and all is forgiven?" Ken agreed, and the taxi driver no longer received phone calls during the late evening or night (depending on when Ken was on duty) from individuals with differing voices, asking to be collected from bogus addresses. The taxi driver had worked out why he had been receiving so many false calls.

Night duty in February found me arresting my first 'drunk and disorderly'. I was approached in Shirley High Street by a woman who said "Would you please see me home?", because she was frightened of a nearby man. The man, who was staggering along the pavement, then attempted to catch hold of the woman's arm. The woman told me he was a neighbour who had been continually annoying her so I told him, politely, to go away and stop annoying the lady. I could see that he was drunk and had difficulty in supporting himself. He again tried to catch hold of the lady so I took him by the arm and firmly led him away some distance, telling him, not so politely this time, to go away "or else". To my annoyance he again returned to the woman, shouting at her and yet again trying to take hold of her arm, so I arrested him and took him to the station where he was placed in a cell and later charged. I was allowed to go off duty at 4.00am for court, and the man, a 57 year old Dock Checker, appeared that morning and received a conditional discharge. Of course, I was back on duty as usual that night.

Early March saw me taking part in the Police Athletic Association National Cross-Country championship at Ludlow, representing Southampton police. I was away for three days and in order to take part had to take my weekly leave day, together with eight hours time-off plus one day leave granted by the Chief. Sadly, I came 73rd out of a field of 159, my previous excellent athletic ability ruined by excessive smoking and exercise limited to slow walking or cycling on the beat.

My personal life took a dramatic turn on 28 March 1955 when my father-in-law, who I was extremely fond of, died. He had been ill for several months and my wife, who was an only child, needed my support, as did my mother-in-law who had been 100% reliant on her husband for all household decisions. I found that I suddenly became the head of the family, organising my father-in-law's estate, taking it to probate, and helping to arrange the funeral. Because of the circumstances I was allowed to bring forward my week's Annual Leave, on compassionate grounds.

When I returned to duty I performed my first tour on the newly created Millbrook Estate, working 14 Beat. The previous 11 Shirley Beats had been increased to 14 as a result of the Borough boundary being increased both east and west.

My life changed again in May, 1955. When I returned home after my 2.00pm to 10.00pm shift on Saturday 14 May and discovered that my pregnant wife, Marion, had been taken to the General Hospital that evening because her labour pains had started. Late visiting was strictly not allowed, but as I was on 6.00am to 2.00pm duty the following day I visited her that afternoon, finding that nothing had yet happened. I was then told to leave as the labour pains had started in earnest. No way were husbands allowed to be present during a birth; such a thing was unheard of.

We were not on the phone so had to phone up late that evening to discover that Amanda, the first of our two lovely daughters, had been born at 9.45pm. The following morning I was again on early turn and, luckily, was given 9 & 10 beats to cover. It just so happened that the General Hospital was on these beats, so I was allowed to enter just after 6.15am, my uniform giving me a real advantage, to see my wife and the delightful little creature that was to be one of the lights of our life.

On my return to duty I realised that I had suddenly matured a lot. The nature of police work and my domestic circumstances had completed my manhood and I now thought of myself as a family man and an experienced police officer with a lot to offer. I once again looked forward to completing my service.

6. GAINING EXPERIENCE – 1955

Now well out of my probation, and having had a satisfactory interview with the Chief Constable, I felt extremely confident about carrying out my duties. I had by now dealt with numerous 'domestic troubles', handing out advice to people often old enough to be my parents. Many cases involved a minor assault, resulting in slight bruises or red faces. The victims were always advised that if they wished to take the matter further they needed to apply to the Magistrates Clerk for a summons for common assault, as minor injuries were not a police matter. I had also dealt with many minor traffic accidents where lengthy statements and details had to be obtained and reports submitted.

I had experienced problems in my early days of service, by discovering that I had failed to ask the right questions or make the correct checks when taking statements. This meant going back to see somebody again or visit the scene, often in my own time. I therefore was far more experienced in taking down statements, taking my time to think about just what was required in each case and to write out statements in a logical and chronological manner.

Members of the legal profession, it seemed to me, lived in a sort of bubble, where witnesses or accused persons dictate statement in a fluent and logical way. In fact, a police officer has to guide both witnesses and accused persons through their statements. Left alone they will often want to start at the end instead of the beginning, and to introduce all manner of irrelevant matters. Even an accused person under caution needs guidance on what to say and how to say it. It is not a question of putting words in their mouth, they have to fully understand and agree before anything is written down, but their version has to be written in the correct way.

Probationers were also always encouraged, in fact directed, to submit offence reports, no matter how minor, to show (a) that they were out and about doing their job and (b) became proficient in dealing with the paperwork. This I had done, to the discomfort of many otherwise law abiding members of the public. Many had only received a caution and those going to court receiving such small fines as £1 or £2. Those fined were invariably such matters as cycling without lights; parking a car at night without lights (all street lights went out at midnight, so this was important). A Daily Order of the time reminded us that parking lights (one white and one red) did not apply to Southampton, only London, and all parked cars had to display full obligatory lights during the hours of darkness.

I therefore now concentrated more on trying to detect crime, rather than dealing with the petty traffic offences where the offence was so often unwitting as opposed to deliberate. I was, however, dragged by PS George Mansell into what I regarded as a ridiculous alleged offence.

It involved Beirne's Second Hand Shop in Shirley High Street, next door to the Regent Cinema.

The Regent Cinema and Beirne's second-hand shop *(Dave Goddard)*

William Beirne had plastic imitation human stools in his shop window, with the caption 'piping hot', and George Mansell considered this to be indecent. He therefore instructed me to accompany him to the shop where I had to corroborate his evidence of advising Mr Beirne to remove the "imitation excreta displayed in your shop window as they are of an indecent nature". Mr Beirne, not unreasonably I felt, declined to do so and was thus reported for summons. Nothing came of it, of course, and I felt somewhat embarrassed by the entire episode. George eventually became a Divisional Superintendent so it didn't do him any harm.

George was also the subject of a practical joke whilst still a sergeant. He asked PC Ken Spiller, my close friend and a practical joker, to get some string for him from Surridge Dawsons, wholesale newsagents. in Millbrook Road, whilst he was on nights. He needed some to string up his runner beans. Ken was in the car for 'Team Policing' that night, and it was the regular practice for the car to visit Surridge Dawsons in the early hours to be given a bundle of free newspapers for the police station. They took delivery of large bundles of newspapers tied up with string. Instead of waiting until the early hours to visit Surridge Dawsons, Ken, on the instructions of his duty sergeant, went there early that night and collected a massive pile of loose string.

He then sat in the police car, in between calls, tying the loose strings together into one long piece. He and the sergeant than went to George's home in lower Shirley and quietly and carefully tied the string to George's door knocker, then to his front gate, side gate and front fence, so that his front garden was a massive criss-cross of string.

George, who was on early turn the next morning, was forced to climb out of his front ground floor window to cut the string and open his front door. He was none too pleased with Ken but could not take the matter further as it had been arranged by his fellow sergeant.

PS George Mansell (later Divisional Superintendent)

Ken Spiller was also part of another joke that we played on a night watchman, Frank, who was looking after road-works in Millbrook Road throughout the night. He was known to us beat officers as "Cup of 'Ot?" as that was his usual opening phrase when he saw us.

His little warm hut, with a lit brazier outside, was a welcome break from the beat and his cup of hot tea always went down well. Frank was a Spiritualist and his experiences in his church were always of interest. We also knew that his father had died some years ago.

One night Ken and I were both night duty team policing, in the divisional Hillman Estate, and arrived in Millbrook Road during the early hours. We parked in a nearby lay-by, turned on the Tannoy speaker and Ken whispered "Frank, Frank, this is Dad".

Ken's voice echoed eerily over the empty street and the next thing that happened was the sound of bolts being closed on the door and the inside light going out, then silence. Ken repeated the phrase; then we waited for some time before turning on the engine and slowly creeping away.

The following night I called on Frank, who told me, excitedly, that his father had spoken to him the previous night. It was definitely his father because he recognised his voice. In retrospect it was perhaps a cruel joke, but Frank was none the worse for the experience, in fact he was more than happy about it.

That April saw me carrying out my first duty on The Common for the fairground, reporting every hour to the mobile police office near the Cowherds public house. I found it interesting, walking among the crowds to 'show the flag' and watch the various stalls. Only minor incidents took place, none of any consequence, and it was a real change from walking around a Beat.

I was disappointed not to have been chosen when a National Emergency was declared 4 June because of a rail strike and an inspector, two sergeants and 32 constables went to London to assist. The Daily Order for this stated that officers had to arrange for their wife to collect their pay on Fridays. The emergency came to an end 16 June.

July 1955 saw another successful check of an individual. I frequently stopped people, especially during the hours of darkness, and eventually realised that I had sometimes failed to ask the right questions or take the correct action. I had once checked a man late at night in an alleyway where he said he had gone to urinate. I obtained his details, having found no trace of him having urinated, and allowed him to leave. I later discovered that he had convictions for housebreaking and I had failed to search him. Had I done so I would almost certainly have found housebreaking instruments and he would have been arrested and charged accordingly. I therefore now paid much more attention to such things.

In this instance it was a mid-week afternoon and I was making a routine call from the police box in Shirley Recreation Ground. I saw a man, of the vagrant type, lying on the grass nearby, and asked him for his name and address etc. He gave me a name and address in Bowden Lane but I was unhappy with the way he answered so took him to the police box and rang the station. I discovered he was wanted on warrant for failing to pay a £5 fine the previous October, so he was arrested and taken to Shirley police station, charged and appeared at court the following morning, when he was sentenced to a month's imprisonment.

Vagrants and those found begging were treated differently at this period. Those sleeping rough were often on the run as wanted persons, so were always checked out thoroughly. I must admit, however, that once I was satisfied they were not wanted or had not committed any offence, I was quite happy to let them remain sleeping where found. Those found begging, however, were not allowed to continue and were liable to be arrested or, at the very least, made to move on, preferably to another town. The object was not to annoy the public, who were often disturbed by beggars and sometimes intimidated by them. In modern times it seems that as long as you have a dog and something to sell, you can remain undisturbed by the police.

I had heard an anecdotal story, possibly with some truth in it, that pre-war the Chief Constable had placed two of his biggest officers on plainclothes duty for a week, with the instruction to 'clean up the town of its vagrants and beggars, there are too many and becoming a nuisance, I don't care how its done'. The two officers, whose names I was given, had forthwith frightened the town's many vagrants and beggars with threats of violence if they did not depart the town at once, in some cases using some physical violence towards them. I had heard that a vagrant sleeping on a pile of newspapers had woken up to find them on fire, and another had been hung by the arms from the upper window of a bomb damaged house and threatened to be dropped if he did not leave Southampton immediately. Whether these stories were true or not, the general idea of moving them on persisted in my time. We had a zero-tolerance policy for such things.

We then heard a not anecdotal story from one of our colleagues on my section. He told us how that winter he had stopped a woman cycling without lights in Hill Lane in the early hours. After some conversation warning her to take care in future, for her own safety, he went onto the adjacent Common and was followed by the woman. Before he knew it she had dived under his cape and performed oral sex, to his great surprise but delight.

We couldn't stop laughing at the mental picture of our friend, who was well built and very good looking, standing there in full uniform and helmet, with a woman buried under his cape. Several of us then realised that we had also stopped the same woman cycling without lights and that she was obviously attracted to police officers for sex and had struck lucky with our colleague, who was single.

August saw another two weeks Army Training at Aldershot and this completed my Army Reserve commitment, although I remained liable for call up in the event of a national emergency.

Police Regulations were amended 5 September 1955 to reduce our working week from 48 to 44 hours. This was achieved by an additional rest day taken every two weeks. Annual Leave was also extended to 17 days and paid overtime (never actually known.) to be 5/9d (approx. 29p) an hour.

My interest in mainly criminal matters continued; persons found committing minor purely traffic offences, such as leaving their bicycle on the wrong side of the road contrary to the unilateral parking signs or parking their car without lights in the early evening, were all given verbal cautions.

I had several successes with petty criminal matters, such as youngsters stealing a cycle lamp and others for stealing from cycles in the Regent Cinema car park. The latter gave me my first successful detailed questioning of suspects. I caught two 13 year-olds attempting to steal a cycle lamp from a bicycle in the car park, but by seeing them separately, in the presence of their parents, it gave me the opportunity of playing one off against the other. The result was admissions of several earlier thefts and the recovery of further cycle parts. I found that I really enjoyed tricking them into confessions, each one not knowing what the other had said, and it was the forerunner of many similar questioning of suspects in the future.

My first shoplifter soon followed. I had seen a woman running after a man in Shirley High Street and when she caught him up he paid her some cash and then walked away. I spoke to the woman, a shop assistant, and she told me she had seen him take two tins of beef and walk out without paying, but after she stopped him he paid her for them. I caught up with the man, a J.I. Thornycroft shipyard worker, and when I searched him found further tins he had failed to pay for. Arrested, charged and appearing before the court the following morning, he was fined £2.00.

Within two days I had to deal with thefts whilst off duty. That evening, in my garden at home, I heard a noise in the grounds of the adjacent Chapel. Looking over my hedge I saw three youths in the act of forcing open a tin of biscuits. I went round and on seeing me they ran away but I caught one and discovered they had broken open the store shed at the rear of the nearby grocer's shop in South East Road and stolen some stores. It didn't take much to discover who the remaining two lads were, all aged 16, and they were taken to Bitterne police station, where I obtained full admissions. When they eventually appeared at Juvenile Court one was placed on Probation for two years and the remaining two had to attend the Attendance Centre for 12 hours.

Routine patrols were enlivened by a week of plain clothes duty keeping observations in cinema car parks – all without success – and then came my first attempted suicide. A woman had slashed her wrists because she thought her husband was leaving her and I was called to the house by her doctor. I was present when her doctor bandaged her wrists and although this was still a criminal offence I took no action other than obtaining a statement from her, under caution, and submitting a report. I found I was not upset by the sight of blood or the injury and was very sympathetic towards her. No further action was taken.

December 1955, on a tour of night duty, found my routine checks paying off again. It was my personal habit, when on 1 Beat at night, at the very southern end of the division, to check the unattended railway carriages that were regularly parked on the railway lines. Access was possible from Saxon Road and the lines were not electrified at this time. I frequently found persons sleeping rough there and they were always worth checking. On this particular night I checked two vagrants sleeping in a carriage, taking their details for a later check on my return to the station. I allowed them to carry on sleeping as it was a very cold night and they were causing no trouble.

When I left, walking along the waste ground adjoining the railway, I saw two youths, aged 18 and 17, cycling across the railway bridge that connected Saxon Road to the waste ground. One of them was carrying a complete cycle wheel. I stopped them, queried why they were carrying another wheel and received the reply "I had a puncture and borrowed a front wheel from a friend in Millbrook".

This did not make sense to me, so I searched them both, finding various cycle accessories, bulbs, batteries and lamps. I detained them and took them to the police box in Paynes Road, from where I phoned the station for transport. While waiting for the divisional car I asked one youth why he had the spare cycle battery and he said he had bought it that day. However, I saw that his machine was fitted with a dynamo lighting set, so no battery was needed. Both were taken to Shirley police station where they admitted the articles had been stolen that night and that they had taken accessories and machines recently.

They were taken to their homes at 2.45am, (one lived in a houseboat near Cobden Bridge) their parents seen and a large number of articles and several cycles recovered. Both were reported for summons, after I was delighted to spend several days in plainclothes getting the recovered articles connected with theft reports and seeing the losers, ending up with 12 offences identified, nine of them "Taken Into Consideration" when they appeared at court. Both were placed on probation for two years, but one, the main offender, was remanded in custody for two weeks whilst Borstal Training was considered. I was very satisfied with the outcome and revelled in making enquiries out of uniform, as though I was a real detective.

December 1955 saw an increase in police pay. £475 on joining, £535 after three years, £550 on reaching four years up to a maximum of £640 on completing 15 years. Policewomen received £50 less.

In early January 1956 I was detailed to spend two days, on 2.00pm-10.00pm shift, checking parked cars showing expired road fund licences and my pocket book records many pages of such details. The idea was that no offence was committed during the first 14 days of expiry, providing the tax was renewed on or soon after the 15th of the month. Details were submitted to the local vehicle taxation office so this could later be checked. Such duties did not appeal to me; dealing with crime was what I wanted.

Dealing with a sudden death on top of a Corporation bus at Maybush Corner that month gave me my first duty of breaking the sad news to a wife, now an unexpected widow. I found this an emotional thing to do, but hopefully broke the news sympathetically and gently, having first approached the next door neighbour, who accompanied me. I was often surprised at the initial reaction when doing this over the years – some partners merely say "Thank you" at the news and show little or no other reaction, as though it were an everyday occurrence. Others burst out crying and sometimes scream in horror, so it was always essential to be accompanied whenever possible; shock can certainly take people in different ways,.

The same month brought me another distressing incident. A 16 month old boy had pulled a tea pot full of boiling tea off the kitchen table, resulting in severe scalds to his chest and throat. PS 'Paddy' Furlong and I attended, rendering initial first aid until the arrival of the ambulance taking him to the Children's Hospital. The parents had called us from the newly constructed police box at Millbrook Roundabout and an ambulance has therefore been called whilst we attended.

By this time the Shirley Divisional Superintendent, Hugh O'Connor, had been replaced by Supt. Bill Moore, a real gentleman who was admired by us all. He very much a 'hands on' officer and my notebook records him attending a sudden death I dealt with in Waterloo Road.

A woman recluse had not been seen for some days and some food delivered and left at her front door had not been collected. I attended initially with PS. Vic White and PC Tony Webb and we forced the front door open after repeated knocking had no response. We found the premises to be disgustingly filthy, something I found repeated many times during my service, and in this instance we found the elderly occupier dead at the foot of the stairs. By now I was accustomed to seeing dead bodies and it no longer disturbed me.

She had clearly sustained severe head injuries to the back of her head, and the fact that one of her shoes was lying near her body suggested it had come off and caused her to fall down the stairs. Rigor was present, as I discovered when my fellow officers suggested I check on that by gently and carefully lifting her head. What I had not realised, however, that their idea of a joke was that they had known that the back of her head was saturated with blood, consequently my hand also became covered with her blood, to my great dismay. Another example of police sick humour. Because of the situation CID were called in, and with Supt. Bill Moore, a former detective, all were satisfied that there was no other forcible entry and that death was due to her accidently falling down the stairs. This was confirmed by the verdict at the subsequent Inquest.

PS Vic White, who was responsible for the rather gruesome joke, was, in fact, a great section sergeant, as I discovered some months later. I was then on a 2.00pm-10.00pm tour of duty and had already been 'booked' on my point by Vic White when I came across my father, an ex-War Reserve police officer who had served with Vic during the blitz. Vic had received the BEM for his heroism in rescuing some residents from their severely bomb damaged home, at great risk to himself, and my father had been present. This particular evening, a warm summer one, Dad said he was going to have a drink in the Swan Inn, Park Road, on my beat, so I decided to join him. I left my helmet and tunic in the boot of Dad's car and was happily supping a pint at the bar when, to my horror, I saw PW Norma Pledger enter the bar, in uniform, closely followed by PS Vic White. They were checking public houses and Norma looked at me in absolute disbelief. I just froze, looking in the mirror behind the bar as they both walked past me and left the pub, without saying anything other than "Good evening Landlord" as they did so.

I just could not believe that my section sergeant had missed me, and my disbelief was confirmed the following afternoon when I reported for duty. Vic White casually announced to the shift that he and Norma had enjoyed the previous evening checking pubs, seeing former War Reserve officers and their families out enjoying themselves. He took me aside after the parade and warned me not to be silly again, but from that moment on I absolutely worshipped him and would have backed him up if he had been in trouble, whatever the circumstances.

My return from a week's annual leave in June saw my first significant criminal investigation. It started when I was on night duty Team Policing with PS Vic White. We received a call to Outer Circle, in Coxford, when it was alleged that a 49 year old man, known locally as "Dirty Gertie" had sexually interfered with some young boys.

We went to the address and saw the man concerned, who strongly denied carrying out any indecent behaviour, but my interviewing technique had much improved and I continued to question him, pointing out that I knew the identity of the boys alleged to be involved. He then admitted that some indecency had taken place, saying it had been carried out by the boys when they were in his house, but with no involvement on his part.

No further action was taken that night, but I was instructed to report in plain clothes the next day to continue my enquiries into the alleged offences. This I happily did and spent the rest of the week interviewing a number of young boys, taking full detailed statements and building up an unanswerable case against "Dirty Gertie". The sordid story that emerged was of the man, who lived alone, encouraging local lads, aged between 14 and 17, to spend an evening at his home indulging in mutual masturbation and buggery between the boys and the man, who was the willing passive recipient. Another man, aged 20, was also involved and I spent some considerable time taking detailed statement from the young boys, all of whom had to be convinced that because of their young age they were not responsible for what took place, even though they were more than willing to take part. I eventually ended up with a comprehensive dossier, bundle of statements, with times and dates, including the fact, and this aroused smiles in the station, that Germolene was used as a lubricant instead of the orthodox Vaseline because it was considered more hygienic.

Both adults were arrested and interviewed under caution at Shirley Police Station. They initially denied committing act of indecency, but when faced with the evidence I had obtained changed their minds and both made statements of full admission. They were released on police bail and I submitted a full report, with the statements, for a decision to be made as to the charges to be brought. This was then put out of my mind as, to my great surprise, I was instructed that on the following Monday, 18 June 1956, I would be attached to the CID at headquarters as 'Aide to CID', something that every officer experienced during his service.

7. AIDE TO C.I.D. AND A MURDER – 1956

The principle behind the two months attachment to headquarters CID was that (a) officers gained an insight into the workings of that department and (b) they could be assessed as to their suitability for later transfer as a detective. Those on attachment would be accompanied by existing senior detectives to 'learn the tools of their trade'. In my case, however, being accompanied did not take place much in the early days because of what happened on my second day.

My first day was exciting for me, attending the regular early morning conference where the overnight crime was discussed and new incidents booked out to officers. It took place at 9.00am punctually, with every headquarters detective present, plus a detective from Shirley, Bitterne and Portswood. The system was that both Shirley and Bitterne divisions had a detective sergeant and several DCs based there, with some DCs based at Portswood station, whereas headquarters, based in the Civic Centre, had a large number, about 17 or 18 officers, together with several detective sergeants and a couple of detective inspectors.

The reason the entire CID strength was available for the conference was the shift pattern they worked. There were three shifts: Day shift - 9.00am to 5.00pm; Ordinary 'Split' shift – 9.00am to 1.30pm, returning at 6.00pm until 9.30pm; and Late 'Split' turn – 9.00am to 1.00pm, returning at 8.00pm until midnight. It can thus be seen that every officer had to report at 9.00am regardless of when he had reported off duty the previous day. Without exception every single shift resulted in officers remaining on duty well after their official finishing time, often several hours after. As with the uniform branch, there was no paid overtime or even, in the case of CID, time off in lieu. They were paid £1.10s 0d a week 'detective expenses' in addition to a plain clothes allowance, and this was supposed to cover both having to buy drinks in public houses whilst seeking information (a hardship for many) and any overtime.

Directly after my first morning conference I was attached to the Aliens Officer (name I cannot recall) for an in-depth explanation of his duties. During his explanation a call was received from the Immigration Officer that a Norwegian seaman deserter had been detained, so we went to collect him, brought him back to PHQ where he was charged under Article 9 of the Aliens Order 1953. He was then placed in a cell to be taken to Liverpool the following morning.

After lunch I went to the Royal South Hants hospital with the Coroner's Officer, DS John Jefferis, who showed me a number of post mortem reports, explaining the meaning of the medical terms. We then went to the public mortuary in Western Esplanade, where I was present during three post-mortems carried out by Dr Richard Goodbody, Pathologist. This was my first experience of the initial horror of seeing a dead body sliced open from the base of the neck to the pubes, with the internal organs removed and examined. This was followed by the hairline being cut round at the back of the head, the scalp and hair pulled across the front of the face, and the noise of a saw cutting through the skull to remove the top and expose the brain, which was also removed. However, I remained relatively unmoved by this unreal experience, my main cause of concern being the awful putrid smell when the body was opened.

I was somewhat almost amused when Dr Goodbody, a lighted cigarette dangling from his mouth, pointed out a set of cancerous lungs and said "Look at the state of those, it's a wonder he could breathe at all". A total of three bodies, two male and one female, were opened in front of me and the experience certainly hardened me to the sights I was to see in the future.

The following day brought a dramatic change to the morning conference. "You're on a murder squad, Brownie," greeted me when I reported for duty, to a packed CID office, headed by the newly promoted D/Supt. Bert Gibbons.

At 9.30pm the previous evening the second-hand shop at 51 St Mary's Road, owned by the well known colourful character 'Ma' Levene, was, most unusually, still open with goods left on the pavement. Mrs Lillian Levene was then found lying in a deep pool of blood, with two scarves pulled tight around her face to apparently gag her and a massive gash in her throat.

The scene outside 'Ma' Leven's shop the day after the murder *(Hampshire Constabulary History Society)*

Following the Murder Squad briefing from D/Supt. Bert Gibbons I joined the team of officers making door to door enquiries in the neighbourhood and my notebook soon became full of details of those interviewed, with statements taken from some that were highly relevant.

D/Supt. Bert Gibbons

DC's Basil Ballard and Geoff Hayes, the Force photographers and fingerprint experts, were among the first to examine the murder scene to check for fingerprints or other potential evidence. (Teams of forensic 'scenes of crime' officers had yet to be invented)

DC Geoff Hayes and DC Basil Ballard, in the foreground. Behind them, left to right, are DC John Porter, DS Jim Fibbens, DS 'Perce' Amess and DC John Whale. (Photo taken at a CID Dinner, some years later)

They found relevant fresh left thumb impressions at the scene and these were photographed and copies sent by patrol car to New Scotland Yard for checking against their records, but they could not be connected to anybody on file. One thumb print was on the cash box that had been forced open, and the other on a chest of drawers upstairs. The prints were identical.

The chest of drawers, showing powder marks following its examination for fingerprints. *(Hampshire Constabulary History Society)*

I was privileged to have a first-hand view of how a major enquiry was handled at that time. Details of those interviewed, addresses, descriptions, anything likely to help the enquiry, were all indexed by DC Archie Davies on handwritten cards, filed in alphabetical order, and with all statements chronologically numbered and cross referenced.

My initial enquiries on the first day were checking the crews of the late ferries to and from the Isle of Wight and Hythe, to see if anybody had attracted their attention by their behaviour. In the afternoon I questioned several antique dealers in Northam Road, showing them a photo of an initial suspect that had come to light from other officer's enquiries, and took a statement from one, with a description, of somebody who had called at his shop trying to sell a pair of ladies shoes.

I was then booked out to investigate an allegation that a man had tried to force his way into a house a few weeks earlier, demanding to purchase an old vase the occupier had, saying he was interested in buying antiques. This turned out to have taken place several months earlier, there was no forceful entry and the man was confirmed as a genuine antique dealer from Portsmouth. This was typical of the many mistaken allegations made during the course of any major investigation, which is why investigating the really important ones can be delayed, and individuals, with hindsight, can later accuse the police of not following them up immediately.

As were all members of the squad, I was fully occupied on duty without a break until late at night, following up enquiries into a number of different suspects, until they were eliminated. My notebook was crammed with names and addresses of persons interviewed, whilst I worked 12 to 15 hour tours of duty over the ensuing five days, along with all other members of the squad. I found it all very exciting and the long hours worked did not matter at all.

Enquiries centred on a dark skinned man as a suspect and a decision was made to take the thumbprints of all such men in the town. I soon became involved in this, and joined other officers issued with fingerprint forms and basic fingerprint equipment to take on door to door enquiries, each allocated his own section of road. I soon became expert at taking a rolled thumb impression and completing every form with the name, personal details and description of each individual, as well as their account of their movements the day of the murder.

Over the next two days several hundred men had their thumb prints taken, nobody objected when asked, but we had been instructed that if there was a refusal to make immediate contact with a senior officer for a decision on detaining the person and obtaining a court order to take a print. This did not arise; there was a large immigrant population in the district and when informed it was to assist in a brutal murder enquiry all were only too willing to provide their thumbprint. I was also amazed at the number of times I had to write "Singh" for a surname, ensuring that the forenames were clearly printed.

During the routine 9.00am CID conference on Saturday 23 June, Basil Ballard informed us that he had identified the thumb print. It was that of an Indian, Gurdial Singh, living in lodgings in a bungalow in Mortimer Road, Woolston.

Immediate enquiries were made of his landlady, but he was not at home. Armed with his description, I was initially sent to keep watch on the Floating Bridges arriving from Woolston.

Gurdial Singh *(Southern Daily Echo)*

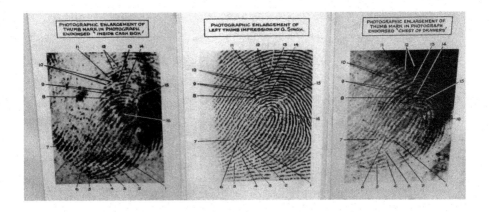

Photographs of thumb print on the inside of the cash box (left), that of Gurdial Singh's left thumb (centre), and on the chest of drawers (right) *(Hampshire Constabulary History Society)*

I later returned to the CID office to complete my reports, and at 4.30pm the office phone rang to say that Gurdial Singh was believed to be visiting a friend in Sedburgh Road on the Millbrook Estate. DI Frank Baker and DS Alf Proops were present and I saw them immediately leave for the Millbrook address, where they arrested Singh. He was later charged by DI Bob Masters, the officer in the case.

He eventually appeared at the Hampshire Assizes, found guilty and sentenced to death. He appealed against his conviction and sentence, but this was dismissed, and he was scheduled to hang on 30 January 1957. However, on 29 January a reprieve arrived from the Home Secretary and he was committed to life imprisonment. He was eventually released in accordance with normal guidelines and is understood to have then returned to his native Punjab.

What had never been reported was that on Saturday 30 June, prior to Gurdial Singh's trial, I went with DS 'Len' Smith to an address in Sandown Road, Shirley, Southampton. It had become known that Singh had been lodging at that address the month previous to the murder but moved because the elderly landlady had suddenly died. There was an obvious suspicion that he may have been involved in her death, but enquiries of neighbours and of the deceased's relatives did not reveal anything that involved him.

DS Len Smith (he retired as Superintendent)

The fact that the lady had been cremated put paid to any further investigation into the cause of death, but although a suspicion remained, the case could not be taken any further.

The thrill of being caught up in a successful murder enquiry remained with me for a long time, but I was soon engrossed in dealing with further criminal investigations, not always accompanied by a more experienced detective.

(For a more detailed account of this murder enquiry, see my book "*Southampton Murder Victims*")

8. AIDE TO C.I.D. – CONTINUED – 1956

During the Lillian Levine murder investigation, because of the massive influx of enquiries and leads to be followed up, I had been given numerous enquiries to carry out on my own. It seemed that my results, and consequent paperwork, were more than satisfactory, as explained to me by D/Supt Bert Gibbons. No doubt this was the reason that although I was sometimes accompanied by detectives, I was frequently given crime complaints or incidents to deal with on my own. However, I was frequently assisted in the interviewing of prisoners or dealing with complicated paperwork by my detective colleagues.

It was during this period that I received a salutary lesson. Whilst travelling along Northam Road to headquarters one morning, on the top deck of a bus, I saw a young man walking on the pavement carrying a large amount of sheet lead on his shoulder. This appeared worth checking, so I got off at the next stop, by which time he had turned into Britannia Road.

I soon caught up with him and asked for an explanation. He was quite unconcerned and pointed to a lorry parked further down the road, explaining that he was assisting a builder renovating a shop in Northam Road but the lorry had broken down. The builder was away trying to get assistance with the lorry and he was therefore forced to carry material back and forwards.

He appeared quite genuine to me, so I merely noted his name and address, primarily because I was worried that if I was late for the 9.00am CID Conference I would need an explanation. However, during the conference the duty officer received a telephone call, informing us that the steward of the Working Men's Club in Northam Road had reported discovering lead stolen from the roof. Without thinking I blurted out that I had checked someone carrying lead on my way to work that morning. DC Norman McDonald hissed at me "Shut up you fool." and everyone looked at me as though I were the village idiot, which, of course, I was. The name and address, naturally, was false and, even worse, I had failed to check the lorry and take note of its registration number. I was forgiven this mistake, down to my inexperience, but never again did I accept anything at face value and all my future checks were much more thorough.

My first solo case occurred the first day I was on duty after the murder investigation had concluded. A man called at the CID office to report that four hub disks had been stolen from his parked car, left on a bomb site in Onslow Road the previous week and he had just seen them on another vehicle parked in Mount Pleasant Road. The hub disks could be identified because of various marks known to the loser. I was sent down, with the loser, to investigate. I located the vehicle concerned and traced the driver, who initially said he had bought them from an unknown man. He was arrested and taken to the CID office where, on further questioning, he admitted having taken them from the car. He was then charged and bailed, appearing at the Magistrates Court the following morning when he was fined £10.00.

That morning, after court, I dealt with four nine year old boys for shoplifting from various stores in the town, with a large quantity of toys stolen and recovered. Mindful of my own youthful discrepancies, at the conclusion of my enquiries I took them, with their parents, to the CID office, had a word with the duty Detective Inspector, who verbally cautioned them, having first shown them the inside of a cell. The parents then took the children and toys back to the stores, making the children apologise for their actions.

I was on late turn that day and, with another officer, made enquiries at boarding houses in the lower town, enquiring after three men wanted by the Metropolitan police for murder. We had been given full descriptions and warned that they were in possession of firearms, but there was no suggestion at all that we should also have been armed in case they were located.

Over the ensuing weeks I was given a number of reported petty thefts to investigate, the vast majority of which were impossible to solve, but I enjoyed the freedom of being allowed to carry out enquiries in my own way, unsupervised and trusted to do the best I could.

I also had the experience of carrying out a successful routine roadside check with another officer, DC John Baker. We were in London Road, on our way to a routine enquiry, when we decided to check two young men walking towards us. John recognised one of them as CRO (having a criminal record) and his companion gave us what was clearly a false address, so both were taken to the CID office for questioning. The one John recognised was on licence from Borstal and enquiries showed the other was wanted on warrant in London for False Pretences. He was therefore detained and later collected by the Met.

Some days later I became involved in another arrest for the Metropolitan police. A 14 year old lad was known to be arriving at Southampton by boat from Jersey and was in breach of a probation order. I was given his description and had no problem in identifying him and taking him to PHQ to await collection by the Met.

This was followed by another shoplifter, a woman arrested in Edwin Jones store by the store detective for stealing items of clothing. It was a straightforward case, with the store detective knowing the procedures as well as I did, making everything simple. We all went to PHQ where I charged and bailed the woman, who, however, pleaded not guilty the following morning but was convicted and fined £5.00

A more interesting arrest came about when Weymouth police gave details of a man who was wanted on warrant and known to be the radio officer on a yacht moored in the Solent. It was arranged that I would be taken to the yacht by the crew of the police launch to make the arrest. This went without a hitch. He was arrested, collected by Weymouth police and we learnt that he received three months imprisonment. I really enjoyed the boat experience.

It seemed I was having a spate of arrests for other forces, as DC 'Mac' McCarthy and I also visited Weymouth Terrace that week to execute a warrant for Dorset police, arresting a man wanted on warrant for GBH. I was pleased with the result of my next investigation as it confirmed I had the ability to extract confessions from guilty individuals.

A complaint had been received that 100 feet of lead piping had been removed from an empty house, 11 Brunswick Square, in the course of demolition. It had come to light when the adjacent householder found her water supply had been cut off. This had occurred some time between 11.00am and 12noon the previous day and I was booked out to investigate. I visited the scene and saw that floorboards in the passage had been removed, giving access to a water pipe underneath, and noticed that a copper pipe appeared to have been newly sweated onto the lead pipe. The occupier of the adjacent house told me that she had seen three workmen working next door at the material time. I saw that three workmen from the electricity board were working at another site in Brunswick Square and asked them if they had worked in the empty No. 11 the previous day. They admitted they had worked in the building but denied all knowledge of the missing lead pipe. I took their details and then went to the Southern Electricity Board office where it was confirmed that the men had legitimate work to be carried out at No.11, making the electricity safe.

Brunswick Square – after No.11 was demolished. *(Bitterne Local History Society)*

I saw one of the men again that evening, at his home, questioning him again, this time pointing out that the three of them had been seen in the house at the material time the lead was removed. I led him to believe, without actually saying so, that I had already seen his two colleagues and they had admitted everything.

He then admitted they had been responsible. It was therefore very easy to obtain identical admissions from the other two and all three made full statements of admission. They were told I would be making further enquiries.

When asked they had said the lead pipe was sold to a dealer in Orchard Lane, so, this time accompanied by DC McCarthy, we went to the premises to recover the stolen property. However, the owner denied having bought the lead pipe, although informed we had been told by the thieves that he had done so. We then said we wished to search the premises, receiving the reply "Not without a warrant." I replied "Then I will remain here while my colleague gets one", whereupon he changed his mind and allowed us to go through the premises. No lead piping was found, but I went to the rear garden, where I saw a caravan, which I entered, opened a cupboard full of stacked paper, pulled it out and found the pile of lead piping. 'Mac' later dealt with this himself and charged the owner with receiving stolen property.

I later charged the three SEB workmen with the theft; they were bailed to appear at court three days later, when they were further remanded for a week and then each fined £5.00.

Later that July I continued my enquiries into the indecency offences involving "Dirty Gertie" and he and the other 20 year old were charged with various offences of buggery and gross indecency. I found it strange that when 'Gertie' was charged he replied "I would like to have my legal advisors", but when they were contacted they said they did not wish to attend but would do so when he appeared at court the following morning.

Both men were then bailed by the court and appeared the following month, when they were committed to the forthcoming Assize. Unlike today, I had to give evidence and sign a deposition, together with the other witnesses, before the magistrates authorised the two being committed, on bail. I had always thought it unjust that the defence thus had copies of all the prime evidence, whereas the prosecution did not know the possible lines of defence until immediately prior to the actual trial. This injustice no longer applies.

I then had a most pleasant experience - my first visit on board a cruise ship. A first class passenger on the *SS Orcades* reported her £100 bracelet stolen from her cabin, so I accompanied DS Fred Williams on board when we obtained a full description, questioned the bedroom steward and searched the cabin, all without success. This was my very first experience of such a luxury ship and I knew full well that I would never be in a financial position ever to take a cruise myself. (However, at the time of writing, my wife and I recently took our 40th cruise.)

My pocket books for this period contain many entries of attending forcible entries of shops, offices and houses, invariably accompanied by another detective, and I gained valuable experience on the correct action to be taken. Scenes of Crime officers had yet to be invented and it was incumbent on every detective to possess both black and white fingerprint powders so he could dust for fingerprints at such scenes. Any found meant calling in Basil Ballard or his staff to take a photograph of the mark(s) but for the detective to obtain elimination prints from those having legitimate access.

More youngsters were reported for minor thefts whilst I was an Aide, most being placed on probation or receiving small fines and I was booked out to a number of petty offences, none of special significance.

To my delight I again had to board a cruise ship, the *RMS Rangitata*. A stowaway was reported by the ship's agents; he had been found on board after the ship had left New Zealand. I went on board at 6.20am, saw the stowaway detained, arrested him, took him to PHQ, charged him, completed the charge sheet and paperwork and he appeared before the magistrates at 11.15am to receive 28 days imprisonment. I was told by DS 'Paddy' O'Sullivan that this work was of a good enough standard for me to be transferred to the CID some time in the future and that he would recommend me. I was delighted.

DS Patrick 'Paddy' O'Sullivan

Just before the end of my tour of duty with the CID I was given the job of locating a man wanted for indecently assaulting a 5 year old girl. I traced him to the Church Army Hostel in Carlton Place, but he had already left. I discovered that he may have gone to Bolton, and on checking with the police there found he had already been arrested for a similar offence committed there. The Southampton offence was TIC'd (Taken Into Consideration) and he received a sentence of six months.

It should be explained that having an offence 'taken into consideration' was a useful tool I later used when interrogating a suspect after they had already admitted an offence. I would point out that if they had committed other offences now was the time to get them cleared up.

No matter how many crimes they had committed, I would only charge them with, at the most, three offences, and the rest would be listed on 'other offence' forms, signed by the prisoner. It meant that the court would take these offences into consideration when they passed sentence, but the value to the prisoner was that they could never be charged with them again. However, I would point out that if they failed to tell me of other crimes and they came to light at a later stage, and I would ensure they did, I would be waiting for them at the prison gates when they were released to re-arrest them. They would have to appear at court all over again, with a conviction already behind them. If not sent to prison the same applied, they would be arrested and dealt with again. This frequently worked and the divisional crime detection rate figures would accordingly be improved.

My final incident at PHQ was attending the Thornycroft workshops in the Old Docks with DC Bob Shergold. We had received information that a man was behaving suspiciously there but when we attended found the man was clearly very mentally disturbed. He was detained and taken to the CID office, when it was discovered that he was a certified mental patient who had escaped from an institution. Arrangements were made for his collection and return.

My attachment to CID as Aide was now finished and I returned to uniform duty at Shirley in August. I had found the experience invaluable, with many of the detective officers having their own ways of working that I found fascinating.

One, however, who shall remain nameless, was a great thief-catcher but embarrassing to be with. I accompanied him on various enquiries, in the course of which, one evening, he said "Do you feel like a meal?" I agreed and we entered George's Café in the High Street where we enjoyed a very pleasant meal.

I had assumed he was treating me, but to my horror when the waiter presented the bill he just said "Tell George I came in with a colleague, it's all right, we don't have to pay", showing his warrant card before we walked out. I was most unhappy about this, but he told me that he knew many café owners who all gave him, and his friends, free meals because of offences he had cleared up for them.

He did the same when we entered the Magnum Club in St Mary's Road frequented by known "queers" (as suspected homosexuals were then known). Charles, the owner, allowed us both to enjoy free drinks while we were there, something that my colleague clearly expected and enjoyed to the full, whereas I sipped mine and made it last. What made this visit even more embarrassing was the fact my colleague made a great play of announcing his name and occupation in a loud voice, slapping people on the back, obviously enjoying himself. We made no enquiries whatsoever; the visit was clearly purely social. This officer was the only one I knew who exploited his position in such a way but I forgave him because he had the wonderful ability of getting people to confess, and I learned a lot from him about how to question suspects.

Another, a detective sergeant, had a great reputation for taking two or three detectives out for a drink after a successful enquiry but never buying a round, always deciding the visit should end when it was his turn.

I had made many new friends during my attachment, but now had to return to the real world of walking the beat.

9. BACK ON THE BEAT – 1956

It felt strange to be back in uniform again, but this was short lived as the following week I was detailed for 'plainclothes obs'. ('obs' was the usual term for maintaining observations) Complaints had been received of a 'flasher' (indecent exposure) from the window of a building in the grounds of Follands Aircraft Works in Winchester Road and I was detailed to observe it during the material times, accompanied by a probationer, PC 180 Moffatt.

Our first evening of keeping observations turned up trumps within 15 minutes. We both saw a man in the window, visible from the roadway, where women were passing by, with his lower body naked and clearly masturbating in full view of passersby. PC Moffatt and I entered the building, located the man, a labourer employed by Follands, and arrested him. He initially said "I didn't do anything", but en route to Shirley police station said "Will I go to prison for this?" and admitted the offence. He appeared at court a week later and was fined £10, more than the average weekly wage at the time.

I was given some more periods of 'obs' the same month. Millbrook Sailing Club, a small building at the end of a long landing stage in the New Docks, was regularly broken into, so it was decided that officers would be placed inside the closed and empty club for a period in the evenings. I carried this out several times, without result, but a certain un-named PC, who we will just call 'Bill', startled Jim Fibbens, the Shirley detective sergeant, when 'Bill' reported to him at the start of the 'obs'.

Jim noticed that 'Bill' was clutching a wrapped paper bag in his hand and asked what it was. To his amazement 'Bill' said "Pepper Sarge, if they break in they'll get it in their face". 'Bill' was put very much in his place. One must, however, bear in mind that we had no radio or other means of communication, and the clubhouse was in a very dark and remote area at Millbrook Point.

'Bill' was a smashing lad, but very naive. This was borne out by the fact that on an early turn when his wife, a very attractive girl, was pregnant, 'Bill' asked another officer, who had an unwarranted reputation as a ladies man, to wake his wife up for him. The officer, who was working the beat where 'Bill' lived, was given the front door key and asked to go into the house and wake her up, because their alarm clock was broken. I'm delighted to say that the officer's reputation was not justified as he merely called out from the bottom of the stairs, but the temptation was certainly there.

'Bill's reputation was further enhanced when he arranged with his neighbour to call him at the station should his wife go into labour whilst 'Bill' was on duty. The neighbour was one of the rare householders with a phone, something no junior police officer had. It was arranged that she would bang on the wall if in trouble and the neighbour would go round, give assistance and phone Shirley police.

Accordingly, a few weeks later, at 5.00am, the neighbour was woken up by a banging on the wall, rushed next door to be greeted by 'Bill' who calmly said "Just thought I'd check and make sure that the banging on the wall would wake you up." The neighbour, as one would expect, was a most unhappy neighbour from then on.

My next incident was the real start of my nickname 'Lucky Jim'. I had already carried out several successful stop and check cases, but this one took place at 11.30am in a crowded Grove Road. I saw a man walking towards me, dressed in overalls and carrying a large grip. As he approached some sixth sense made me stop him. I do not know whether I subconsciously recognised his body language, or what, but I politely asked him what he was carrying in the grip. He told me it contained clothing.

I asked him if I could look inside and he replied "Why, its only old clothes" but I, still politely, took the grip from him and opened it. I saw it contained a very large quantity of loose tobacco, and on asking for an explanation was told it was Navy tobacco, given him by a naval friend to take to someone in hospital. I was not satisfied and therefore took him to the police box in Paynes Road to check his story, whereupon he said "Oh dear, I didn't know you would take it this far. I'd better tell the truth. I took it from the tobacco factory where I work."

I then walked with him to Shirley police station, where I asked him to remove his overalls so I could search him. He refused to do so, rather aggressively, so I told him very firmly that either he removed it or I would get assistance and do it for him. I explained that he was a prisoner and as such must be searched in case there was further evidence to be found or weapons that could be used against me. He therefore very reluctantly removed his overalls and I realised why he had refused.

He was dressed completely in feminine underwear, black brassier filled with cloths, girdle, panties, and black silk stockings. There was no offence in being dressed in this way, but with DC John Webber assisting me, we went to his lodgings in Shirley Warren where I had my first knowledge of the fetish world. We found a suitcase full of photographs of men and women dressed in heavy rubber clothing and rubber masks, sometimes handcuffed or otherwise chained up, together with letters addressed to "my rubber masked slave" and similar headings.

But what initially puzzled us was an obviously home-made contraption that can only be described as a baby's metal napkin. It was made of heavy duty aluminium, consisting of two wide strips of metal hinged at the back, so they could be fastened at the front, around the waist, with a third wide strip, also hinged at the back, which could be swung underneath and between the legs to also fasten at the front. This third strip had a large elongated hole at the front, to give access to his private parts, but the back of this strip had a 6" wooden rod incorporated into it, with the result that this rod would enter the backside when fitted. It was a 'do-it-yourself' buggery kit.

Again, no offence was committed regarding this material, but it opened my eyes to a side of life about which I had no previous experience. He was charged with stealing the tobacco, identified as coming from the British American Tobacco Company where he worked, appeared at court the following morning, when he was remanded on bail for a week and then fined £20 or two months.

Life continued as normal for some time, with my duties taken up with what were now routine matters such as sudden deaths, road traffic accidents, unoccupied houses, school crossings and the like, as well as several housebreakings or shopbreakings, where all I had to do was advise the occupiers to await the arrival of CID. Night time Team Policing duty was also my most interesting tour of duty, attending various break-ins, thefts, fights, domestic troubles and the like.

I found that I was now increasingly being instructed to report in plainclothes for various observations, something I always welcomed, and although nothing ever came of them, I felt it was an indication of things to come. The observations would take place after series of break-ins occurred at different areas within the division, in an attempt to catch offenders in the act, but it was rare that they were successful.

A break from routine was looking for a reported army deserter, who I traced to one of the addresses supplied by the military police. He was only 24 years old and gave no trouble when I arrested him and took him to Shirley police station where he was collected by the military police. I should perhaps mention at this stage that I seldom handcuffed prisoners during my police service; it was rare that I felt the need to. I was always confident that I could walk with them, close and slightly behind them, to the nearest police pillar or police box to obtain transport.

In November, 1956, I had my first experience of the Assize Court in Winchester, with the Judge in his crimson robe and long wig, a most imposing affair. It was when my 'Dirty Gertie' case was dealt with. 'Gertie' pleaded guilty (my paper work was 100%) and was sentenced to 18 months for buggery and three lots of 12 months for Gross Indecency, all to run concurrently. The 20 year old charged with him was placed on probation for two years.

One of my prisoners was a well known local drunk, Stanislaw Biegalski, 41, who appeared before the court with monotonous regularity. It became my turn to arrest him one night, to my annoyance, as I was on leave the following day and had to appear at court to see him fined his usual £2.00 Appearing at court for every case one dealt with, whether or not a guilty plea was anticipated, was accepted as part and parcel of the job, but it was an irritation as there was frequently absolutely no need to be present. The convenience or otherwise of the officer in the case was something that never appeared to be taken into account.

In January, again on Team Policing, we received a call to a lorry on fire in the goods yard of W.L. Page in Princes Road. The fire brigade attended, with DCO Tickner in charge and extinguished the fire, which they determined started in the cab upholstery because of an electrical fault. The clutch pedal had worn away the insulation on the battery lead, causing a short circuit running back to the rear of the driver's seat.

This was an example of the usual drill, whereby the fire service was on the same radio frequency as the police, so they heard us being sent to the scene, as well as receiving the '999' call direct. It was always a friendly race to see who could arrive first. We attended every single fire call, no matter how trivial it seemed at the start, as one never knew how things could develop. This does not happen today.

Whilst walking my beat I was informed by a driver that a wallet had been stolen from his car, left unlocked in Bourne Road, and he had seen several children playing around it at the time, giving me their description. I made a few door to door enquiries and soon had one of the boys, a nine year old, identified. I saw him at his home, in the presence of his father and he readily admitted taking the wallet, which was handed to me. I reported him but no further action was taken, other than a verbal caution from the Superintendent.

My personal idea of checking the railway carriages off Saxon Road paid off again when I found a 23 year old man, with a number of convictions, sleeping rough with a 16 year old girl who had run away from her home in Jersey, Channel Islands. I arrested them both and took them to the police box in Paynes Road, from where they were taken to Shirley police station. The girl was subject to a Care and Protection Order, so was detained until collected by her parents.

Later that February, 1957, I was in the station having my meal break when William Bierne, son of the owner of the second-hand shop in Shirley High Street, phoned to say a man had offered him a bicycle for only £4 and it was worth considerably more. He thought it might be stolen. As I was readily available I ran to the shop, spoke to the man, who had a new condition high value machine, and as I was not satisfied with his explanation walked with him (and the cycle) to the station. En route he said "I will tell you the truth. I pinched it in Portsmouth last night." Portsmouth police were informed and collected him that evening – once again I felt there was no need for handcuffs.

I then had my first, and last, lost prisoner, and the first and last occasion of using my whistle. I was carrying out my usual practice, when on 7 Beat, of keeping observations from the rear roof of the Regent Cinema, and saw two youths enter the car park and rummage through the saddle bags of the cycles parked there. This time they heard me coming down the stairs and took off. I chased them along Carlisle Road, throwing my torch at one when I got closer, but they were too fast for me, having had a head start. I then tried to blow my whistle, hoping that a passerby would assist, but found I was out of breath and nothing came out.

My next drunk, found staggering along Romsey Road, was a 21 year old seaman, stationed on HMT Dilwara, Portsmouth. He was charged later that morning and collected by an officer from the ship. His wage, as the ship's butcher, was £9 a month and he was subsequently fined ten shillings (50p).

Further promotions were announced in March, among them my not so favourite officer, Fred 'Judy' Garland, BEM, from C/Insp to Supt. 'C' Division, fortunately a Division where I lived but never served in. Russel Tribe, BEM, took over Shirley Division at the same time.

In April, whilst on 5.00pm – 1.00am tour of duty, I was given plain clothes duty for several days, keeping observations in various parts of the division. One was watching a suspected brothel in Millbrook Road, where I noted down descriptions of women and men seen entering the premises.

Another was observing a sack of metal that had been found hidden against a fence at Millbrook Point, just outside the New Docks. I struck lucky as I saw it collected by two youths, aged 12 and 14, who were easily detained. Enquiries revealed they had climbed the dock fence and broken into a store in the New Docks, where they found the metal. They had placed it in a sack by the fence before climbing back. It was too heavy to take at the time, so they had gone home and returned with a cycle to help carry the sack, just after I started the observations.

I took them to Shirley police station in the divisional car, their parents were contacted and the boys reported for summons. They later appeared at Juvenile Court and each fined £1.00.

My spell of plainclothes duty ended with observations at the rear of my favourite cinema, the Regent, as well as on the car park at the rear of the Atherley Cinema. Both were negative but always interesting as one never knew what might happen.

The Atherley Cinema, the car park entrance is on the left. *(Dave Goddard)*

My 'Lucky Jim' nickname proved itself again one afternoon when I stopped a 15 year old boy walking along Winchester Road. I had no idea why I chose to question him, but when he gave me a Basingstoke address I became suspicious when he couldn't explain why he should be in Southampton. I took him to the station, where he confessed to having absconded from an Approved School in Essex. He said he had hitch-hiked to Plymouth, then Basingstoke, where he broke into a house via the back door, when he stole some clothing and cash. I found that gentle questioning came easy to me and he readily admitted what he had done. He was detained until the arrival of an escort from Basingstoke.

A Sunday lunch-time found me once again arresting our local drunk, 45 year old Polish Stanislaw Biegalski, in Shirley Road. This time he had fallen on the pavement and struck his head, so I had to first call an ambulance for him to be taken, under escort, to the Royal South Hants hospital and have five stitches inserted before being returned to Shirley and placed in a cell. The following morning he received his customary £2.00 fine.

I continued to check the railway carriages, regularly finding vagrants sleeping there, all checked but not wanted for any offence. It was my practice to walk along the train corridor very carefully, not showing my torch until I saw a carriage occupied. It was therefore a surprise both to me and the two couples I found in a carriage, all four actually in the final stages of intercourse. No offences were revealed but it was an eye-opener to me that some could perform in each other's company.

My next arrest took place following my return home from 5.00pm – 1.00am duty, having rung off from my beat at Redbridge. I was cycling to catch the Itchen Ferry to Woolston and just before reaching the bridge I saw, in the dark, two figures walking along Albert Road. On seeing me they stopped, so I also stopped, whereupon they both ran away, accompanied by a small dog. I cycled after them and saw them both enter a house, slamming the door almost in my face but with the dog left outside, scrabbling at the door.

I knocked very hard on the door, with no reply, so although I had no idea why the two had run away from me, I, in desperation, tried my own front door mortise key in the lock, and to my amazement the door opened. I then found the woman occupier, fully dressed, who said she had not heard me knocking. Her explanation for being dressed was that she had no night clothes and always slept that way. I then saw a woman's red coat covering something in the passageway, and on lifting it saw a very large quantity of sheet lead. The woman could not explain it, but when I searched the house I found she was the only occupier. I went to the nearest phone box, called for assistance and the lead was removed to the Civic Centre police station.

I was instructed to report in plainclothes the following morning and, accompanied by DC John Porter and other officers we returned to the house to arrest the occupier, who we knew had a long criminal record and was prone to violently resist arrest.

Officers covered the rear of the terraced house and when I knocked on the front door I looked through the letter box as I did so. I saw a man running down the passageway and, after some delay, his wife opened the door to let us in. We searched the premises, but there was no trace of the man I had seen running down the passage. However, the rear living room window was wide open, as though someone had escaped through it, but the outside officers confirmed that nobody had left.

We again searched everywhere but the mystery was solved when I lifted a large upturned metal bath that was on the floor in front of the open window. We had assumed it had been placed there to assist someone leaving that way, but, in fact, it covered several loose floorboards. I lifted one, and lo and behold, there was my prisoner, lying in the gap between the floorboards and the foundations. He was lifted and owing to his extreme violence had to be forcibly restrained. This was the first time I used handcuffs and it was very difficult, taking three of us to hold him. He was charged with stealing or receiving the lead, property of person or persons unknown, and remanded in custody whilst DC John Porter and I made enquiries.

We found he had sold a large quantity of identical lead to a scrap metal dealer over the previous few days and discovered that it had come from houses in the course of demolition further along Albert Road. The man continued to deny all knowledge, but in view of his long record was committed from the Magistrates Court for trial, in custody, eventually appearing before Ewan Montague, the Recorder, at Quarter Sessions, when he received a sentence of 12 months.

My next drunk was a woman, calling herself an Artist, who had been evicted from her lodgings in Bridlington Avenue. She was shouting and refused to move on when I asked her to, so was arrested and taken to police headquarters and placed in a cell as too drunk to charge. She appeared at court the following morning but as she became very abusive to the magistrates was remanded for three weeks, in custody, to Knowle Mental hospital. She was later placed on probation for two years, with a condition of hospital residence for 12 months.

The next night of Team Policing brought some excitement. The radio reported a car having just been stolen from outside the Key & Anchor public house in Millbrook Road.

We were not far away and attended within minutes, finding the car abandoned in Cracknore Road with two soldiers, army sappers, not far away. They were detained and whilst being taken to Shirley police station we heard that another car had been taken from Lakelands Drive.

The Key & Anchor
(Dave Goddard)

This car was stopped in Redbridge by a traffic car and found to contain three more army sappers, so all five were held in custody. They all came from Marchwood and I charged my two with taking and driving away without consent whilst PC Sibley charged the three he arrested in Redbridge. When they later appeared before the magistrates they were fined sums of between £10 and £27 and disqualified from driving for either two or three years.

The same week, whilst on the beat, I became involved in 'Teddy Boys' fighting outside the Salisbury Arms. It was quickly dealt with, PC Frank Bloyce and I separating the antagonists, but Frank found that one of them had an offensive weapon, a piece of wood, so he was arrested. ('Teddy Boys' were young men who wore clothes in the fashionable Edwardian style, sporting velvet trim collars, drainpipe trousers and chunky brogue shoes. Some formed gangs and gained notoriety following violent clashes with rival gangs).

Although Teddy Boys caused trouble in many towns along the south coast, it was very limited in Southampton. Primarily because we were very heavy handed with them, absolute zero tolerance, any sign of a disturbance and they were told to break up and move on, or else. 'Or else' meant being arrested for breach of the peace, drunk and disorderly or any other offence that came to mind.

It was this year that saw a new Magistrates Courts Act, changing the procedure whereby it now became possible to accept a 'guilty' plea for absent defendants on a summons for a summary offence, meaning that witnesses were then not needed. Up to then every case was treated as though defendants were going to plead 'not guilty' and all witnesses, including the police officer in the case, had to attend court. This was a great relief as I had so often had to waste time in court, following night duty, and not be needed.

During this period of returning to beat work, after Aide to CID, I had dealt with numerous 'domestic troubles', which seemed to act as a magnet for me; many traffic accidents, some with minor and some involving serious injury, where my First Aid training proved invaluable; many, many unoccupied houses; many school crossing patrols, numerous routine delivery of messages etc. etc., but all this now came to an end.

I was then delighted to be told that PC 'Jock' Adamson and I were being transferred to police headquarters to man the CID enquiry office, the first step towards becoming a detective. I therefore started my first shift, although still in uniform, on Monday 16 September, 1957.

10. THE CID ENQUIRY OFFICE – 1957

The large CID Office was on the ground floor, at the northeast part of the Civic Centre, with its own external access. The key used to open police boxes or pillars also fitted this door, so I had no problem gaining entry. Inside the office door was a long counter, with a flap allowing officers to enter the room, and the duty enquiry officer sat behind the counter; this was my first office job.

I found this a most instructive tour of duty. Behind me were a dozen or so desks, each allocated to an individual detective, and at the far end of the room was a small enclosed room where suspects could be temporarily held whilst being interviewed. There was also a side door which led directly into the cell passage, so prisoners could be spoken to in their cell. They could only be taken from their cell with the permission of the duty station sergeant, and they had to be signed for.

Opposite was the Detective Superintendent's office and further along the side corridor the offices of the duty detective sergeants and inspectors. At the end of the main corridor was the police reception office, where members of the public initially made their enquiries. If it was a criminal matter, such as reporting a theft, they were directed to the CID office to see the duty CID office PC.

Every crime had to be allocated to an individual detective, so statements were given to the duty DS or DI, who would place them on the in-tray of an officer's desk. All telephone enquiries also had to be dealt with, enquiries from other forces, reports of crimes, shoplifters detained etc. and the appropriate reports submitted.

It was a busy office and I not only developed my typing skills and telephone manner, I learnt a lot from listening and talking to detectives. I also helped by remaining with suspects whilst the officer in the case left the room, sometimes chatting to them and obtaining useful information.

The station sergeant once amused himself one evening by sending down a very large 'busty' woman to me in the CID office. With a very serious face she informed me Rasputin kept raping her and she wanted something done about it. I was alone in the office at the time so carefully remaining my side of the counter I gently asked her for her name etc. She started to tell me, then suddenly jumped up and down, calling out "He's doing it now, he's doing it now." Thankfully DS Jim Glass, hearing the noise from his office, came in and rescued me. I later went up to see PS Joe Cass and thanked him very much.

We worked two shifts, 8.00am to 4.00pm and 4.00pm to midnight, and my first shift was the late turn. I had to deal with all enquiries, take statements from losers or otherwise deal with their problem. It was on my late shift on 18 September, 1957, that I returned home to find that our second lovely daughter, Wendy, had been born at home at 8.45pm that evening. We now had two wonderful daughters, who have both proved a real joy throughout our lives. Our family was now complete.

Overall my time in the CID office was an interesting experience, lasting three weeks, coming to an end on 15 December 1957 when, to my great delight, I was transferred to the CID as a detective and posted to Shirley division.

I had replaced DC Frank Beasley, who had retired in October, and my two CID colleagues were DCs Trevor Lobb and John Webber, both experienced and helpful colleagues.

I then realised that during my time in the CID office I had been quietly assessed by senior detectives as they observed how I dealt with sometimes difficult phone calls, interviewed complainants and the way I took statements.

11. SHIRLEY C.I.D. – 1958

When I reported for my first tour of duty at Shirley on the Monday I was allocated a desk by DS Jim Fibbens and given two fine brushes and my personal jars of black and white powder, to carry out my own search for fingerprints. I was also given two or three small plastic bottles to hold paint fragments or other samples. That was the sum total of my scenes of crime training. I had watched other detectives carry crime examinations when I was an Aide to CID, also seeing DC Basil Ballard or one of his team (DCs Ron Ledgerwood, Geoff Hayes and John Parris) take photos of prints found at the scene, so felt confident in being able to carry a fingerprint search myself.

Basil, who had examined many thousands of fingerprints in his time, was officially recognised by the courts as a 'fingerprint expert' as the number he had searched had passed the qualifying number required to be treated as such. This was particularly useful as his court appearances avoided the expense of calling a Scotland Yard expert.

Basil could always be recognised by his habit of smoking cigarettes in a long cigarette holder, something unusual.

DC Basil Ballard
(Hampshire Constabulary History Society)

My first housebreaking investigation took place almost immediately. I was sent to Raymond Road, broken into during the Sunday evening, and took a statement giving a description of the stolen jewellery and cash box. I used my fingerprint powder for the first time, discovering a clear impression on the attacked window frame. This was later photographed by Basil Ballard.

I took elimination fingerprints from the occupiers, also visited two painters who had worked in the house recently and took elimination prints from them. Basil later told me he had identified the print as that of one of the painters, who, of course, had legitimate access.

I then visited all the Shirley dealers, giving them details of the missing property and also made door-to-door enquiries during the afternoon, being told of different men seen in the area during the material time. It was then back to the station to complete a 'crime complaint' and crime report, plus a circulation to all stations, giving details of the break-in and stolen property.

Before completing any 'crime complaint' form we had to first check with the divisional detective sergeant that it was in order to do so. The 'crime complaint' book had consecutive numbered pages, carbon copy duplicated, and this formed the basis of the divisional crime statistics.

Petty crimes that had no possible chance of success, such as a lamp stolen from a bicycle or small items from an unattended vehicle, would not be 'crimed'. Statements would be taken and given to individual detectives so that in the event of a prisoner admitting them, they could then be 'crimed' and used on 'taken into consideration' forms, thus enhancing the detection figures. This was a common practice in all stations as there was some competition between the detective sergeants.

My tours of duty were also very different; working the same 'split' shifts I had found at headquarters when I was an Aide. The slight difference was that the Late Turn, 8.00pm to midnight, was not worked as often in divisions, but there were alternate weeks of days and 'Ordinary', the 9.00am to 1.30pm, returning at 6.00pm until 9.30pm. The same as at PHQ, no shift ever finished on time, the heavy case load plus intensive enquiries on individual cases meant carrying on well past the allocated finishing time.

All this was fully accepted as part and parcel of detective work; after all, we were receiving an additional £1. 50s a week.

It was January 1958 when I made my first visit to HM Prison, Winchester. A prisoner I had dealt with for a theft, and who was serving three months, had asked to see me. My first impression of the visit was the lengths I had to go through to gain entry, even though the visit had been arranged. Showing my warrant card was initially not enough; I had to wait in an ante room whilst the prisoner agreed to see me.

My second main recollection was the distinctive smell, a combination of urine and disinfectant, once I got into the main section. All he wanted was to confess to being responsible for breaking open the electricity meter at his home and regretted not having it taken into consideration when he was dealt with. He realised, as a result of a visit from his wife, that I had made enquiries into the theft and he was worried that she could be held responsible. I was able to reassure him that no further action would be taken against either of them, and thus made another future informant.

In this January DS Jim Fibbens was at the Police College for six months and was temporarily replaced by DS Arthur Offer, a very nice officer, gentle but firm when dealing with problem individuals. Now I was a working detective I discovered another difference to being in uniform. Previously, when I became involved in a lengthy enquiry I only dealt with that one case, often assisted by a detective to ensure my paperwork was correct. Now I had a number of simultaneous cases to handle, some of them complicated.

March, 1958, saw me giving evidence outside my normal area. It was in the middle of my annual leave and I had to attend Windsor Magistrates court to give evidence in a case of unlawful sexual intercourse. I had interviewed an 18 year old at his home on the Millbrook estate at the request of the Metropolitan Police, regarding him having sex with a 13 year old girl at Romney Island. He was placed on probation for two years and I was allowed one day's leave in lieu of the court appearance, no other compensation.

In April the Chief Constable notified us that the cycle allowance officers had been receiving, the princely sum of three shillings (15p) for a six day week and 2/6d (12½ p) for a five day week, would cease. This was replaced by the issue of 36 police bicycles, six allocated to the CID. Needless to say, CID officers rarely used their allocated bicycle as it was too readily identifiable.

When DS Jim Fibbens returned from the Police College that June he was immediately promoted to uniform Inspector, remaining at Shirley. DS Arthur Offer was then replaced by DS 'Perce' Amess, who had been running the Vice Squad for some time.

I was present in the Shirley CID office a few weeks later when Alf Cullen, then Deputy Chief Constable, decided to carry out an inspection of Shirley Police Station. Poor Perce was asked what was stored in the cupboards at the top of the cabinets in the CID office. He didn't have a clue, never having had need to check them, and when they were opened out fell a huge pile of uncompleted crime reports and un-crimed witness statements for minor offences.

None of the documents were Perce's doing. They had accumulated over many years, stored by various detective sergeants to keep their crime statistics down but still available should somebody admit the offence. I think Perc managed to convince Alf Cullen that they were not his fault.

I now found that my caseload gradually built up as further crimes were given to me to deal with, so that I dealt with several crimes simultaneously. As time went on my personal caseload increased tremendously. The procedure was that every crime, no matter how trivial, had to be booked out to a detective, even stolen vehicles, including bicycles. My In and Pending trays built up very quickly.

Once a crime was detected, or a decision taken that nothing further could be done, the crime report, with the attached statements and result of my enquiries, was written up, passed to the DS and onto Archie Davies in the CRO (Criminal Record Office) for filing. If a subsequent prisoner admitted offences that had been filed as unsuccessful, they were rapidly recovered and either subject of a charge or TIC (Taken Into Consideration).

Young DC150 Jim Brown in the door-way of the former Shirley Police Station

The crime that I attended on my second day was a very common one; theft of cash from gas or electric meters. Virtually every home was fitted with pre-payment meters, irksome when the gas failed or the light went out and one had to scramble to find a shilling or two to put in the meter. They were usually attacked when the house was forcibly entered, with the proceeds always available to the housebreaker by merely forcing open the lock on the coin container. However, the householder sometimes felt the need to break the lock when short of ready cash. The contents were the property of the gas or electricity board and such thefts were always reported by the collector for the police to state whether the theft took place during a forcible entry or by the occupier.

As the occupier had to refund the money if they were responsible for the theft, I sometimes stated on my crime report that it could not be ascertained whether or not there had been a forcible entry. I did this, knowing, and sometimes getting an admission, that the occupier was responsible, as that way I built up a useful team of informants, grateful for not having been prosecuted. This proved very useful over the years and I had no compunction with covering up such a petty crime, for the greater good of worthwhile information on more serious crimes.

My next crime may interest the reader because of its nature and the amounts involved. A car salesman reported that he had sold a 10hp Opel to a man for £20 on hire purchase terms. This arrangement kept the ownership with the dealer until the terms were completed. A deposit of £9 had been paid, leaving a balance of £11.00, plus £5 charges, giving a total of £16.00 to be paid by means of the HP Agreement.

A total of £5 had been repaid, in £1 weekly payments, but the payments had stopped and all attempts to get the man to pay had been unsuccessful. The dealer then discovered that the car had been sold to Kingsley Motors and was in the process of being broken up. I therefore had no option but to see the buyer and charge him with larceny as bailee. The man elected to go for trial at Quarter Session where he pleaded not guilty and was acquitted on the grounds that the car was un-roadworthy and he was unaware of having committed an offence.

In common with other detectives, I formed a good relationship with second-hand dealers, one in particular being George Handley in Romsey Road. He phoned me at the station one morning to say he had bought a watch from a 15 year old boy whose address he knew and thought it was worth much more than he had paid. I saw George, recovered the watch and saw the boy at his home. It did not take me long for him to admit he had entered a house in Imperial Avenue and taken it from the kitchen. I reported him for summons and when he appeared at Juvenile Court he was sent to an Approved School because of his several convictions.

I next found I was assisting a uniformed officer, PC Peter Halford, with a case. He had caught three 15 year old boys in possession of a motor cycle stolen from the rear of the Regent Cinema (my old haunt). I helped him interview them and take statements, under caution, and they admitted several offences of taking and driving away other motor cycles and vans. They subsequently appeared at Juvenile Court when one was placed on Probation for 2 years and the other two sentenced to 12 hours at the Attendance Centre. The above had all taken place during my first week as a detective at Shirley, together with several shop and housebreakings, one of which involved the police dog being called but failing to pick up a scent.

I had also taken part in several periods of observations, with DC Trevor Lobb and DC 'Spud' Murphy, in areas where there had been a series of break-ins, as well as being given crime reports for a number of petty larcenies. I now began to realise just how busy a life I was going to have. Attending break-ins, dealing with shoplifters, keeping observations in an attempt to catch offenders in the act, report writing, assisting uniformed officers, this all became my normal working life and I loved every minute of it, in spite of the long hours.

Some individual cases may be of interest to the modern reader because of their political incorrectness. One such was a theft from a house in Wilton Avenue. Two young boys had called at the house with one asking to use the toilet. After they left the woman occupier found that a watch was missing from her bedroom and believed that the boy was responsible. I made enquiries along the road and found they had knocked on several doors asking for 'bob-a-job' work.

From their description I suspected they attended Shirley Warren School so went there the following day and saw the headmaster. He checked the attendance registers and found that two boys answering the description I gave him had failed to attend the day of the theft. He sent for them, one at a time, and the first readily admitted having called at houses in Wilton Avenue, saying that his friend had come out of one house with a watch.

The second boy (both were 10 years old) was sent for and he initially denied any knowledge of a missing watch or calling at the house and asking for the toilet. However, when pressed, he admitted having entered the house. At that point the headmaster interrupted my questioning, told the boy to hold out his hand and gave him two strokes of the cane. "That is for lying about not entering the house. Now answer the police officer's questions" he said.

The unfortunate lad then freely(?) admitted stealing the watch, later handing it over to me after he was taken home. It should be noted that corporal punishment in schools was the norm, as was interviewing juveniles without their parents being present. After all, we only wanted to get to the truth of things. Thankfully the 10 year old only received a verbal caution from the Superintendent.

Young housebreakers then had to be dealt with. Two 15 year olds were seen by a neighbour climbing a fence into the garden of a house in Birch Road and enter through an open bathroom top window. As usual, the gas meter had been forced open and the contents taken. Both boys were known to the neighbour so I saw them at their home, with their parents.

They not only admitted breaking into the house in Birch Road but also a series of identical break-ins in the area Both were charged and appeared at Juvenile Court the following day, when they were remanded on bail for three weeks. One was then sent to an Approved School and the other to 12 hours at the Attendance Centre.

November was fully occupied with various petty offences, some detected others not, and I was also busy assisting uniformed officers with enquiries after they had arrested various individuals for miscellaneous offences, all of which took up much of my time. Although not the officer in the case I was nevertheless responsible for the paperwork being completed correctly, with the caution in the right place.

The caution that applied at this time "You are not obliged to say anything unless you wish to do so but what you say may be put into writing and given in evidence" was extremely important as its absence could lead to an admission being rendered inadmissible. Lawyers love a loophole, regardless of the guilt of their client. It could lead to an acquittal, even though the person charged could be seen to be clearly guilty. It was basically a warning to keep quiet. The wording has now been changed, warning that if you do not mention something that you later rely on in court, it could harm your defence. In other words, there is now an invitation to say something.

All we ever wanted was to get to the truth of the matter, as much concerned not to charge an innocent person as we were to charge a guilty one. The British legal system is an 'accusatorial' one, whereby the prosecution must prove the guilt 'beyond all reasonable doubt'. Unlike the French 'inquisitorial' system, where all the facts must be established to get to the truth, the British system is not concerned with the actual guilt or innocence, only whether it can be established within a laid down legal framework and rules of evidence. Any breach of the rules can give a defending lawyer grounds for asking for an acquittal.

The rules of evidence stated, and I give it in full: "As soon as a police officer has evidence which would afford reasonable grounds for suspecting that a person has committed an offence, he shall caution that person, or cause him to be cautioned, before putting to him any questions or further questions relating to that offence."

It was always a matter of opinion as to whether the 'reasonable grounds' for giving a caution had been reached and that is why detectives, who were far more experienced in the rules of evidence, needed to be involved with uniformed officers when questioning prisoners. A caution given too early could result in a suspect declining to answer further questions, and one given too late could give grounds for a successful appeal.

I must be honest and say that when it came to writing up an interrogation a decision was made as to when the caution should have been given, as opposed to when it was actually given, or whether indeed it had been given at all. Modern technology, with the videoing of interviews, does away with all these earlier police misdeeds, all made at the time with the honest interests of true justice at its heart. We did not feel that we were doing anything that was immoral, merely ensuring that wrongdoers did not evade conviction because of an avoidable technicality. In no way could it result in an innocent individual admitting something he had not done.

I was issued with a new pocket book, the standard larger and slimmer size one with a blue cover, only issued to CID. I now really felt that I had properly arrived as a detective. My first entry related to a call from another second-hand dealer, William Beirne, son of the former owner, next door to the Regent Cinema.

A 30 year old man was attempting to sell him a typewriter which William suspected was stolen. I attended and questioned the man who gave his name as Peter John Robertson, 42 Burgess Road. When I said I intended searching him to establish whether he had given a correct name and address he said "I'd better come clean, I've given you a false one. I pinched the typewriter from Udalls in West Quay Road." I then cautioned him (yes, I actually did.) and when taken to Shirley police station he readily admitted a number of other thefts from the same premises. He was therefore handed over to DC 'Paddy' Phillips, the thefts taking place in his area. The man was later sentenced to four month's imprisonment.

Another enquiry that involved the CID was assisting the uniformed branch in dealing with fatal accidents. I was detailed to assist PC Jack Pead who was dealing with the case of a man killed by a lorry in Wimpson Lane. My help was primarily involved in ensuring that the correct enquiries and reports were prepared for HM Coroner. The weeks continued with me making a number of arrests for minor thefts and attending the scene of numerous houses, shops or offices being broken into. None of my enquiries into the breaking offences came to anything, but the result of one reported break-in pleased me enormously.

The offence had taken place at Durafencing Ltd, in Millbrook Road, near Millbrook Railway Station, where a cash box had been stolen. Their office was a wooden hut adjacent to the main road and entry was by smashing a pane of glass in a rear window to open it and climb through. However, when I examined the attacked window I found fragments of glass on the ground outside but no sign of glass at all inside.

I also saw that the outside window ledge, over which an intruder must have climbed to gain entry, was very dusty and this had not been disturbed. It seemed to me impossible that entry had been gained in this way, so I questioned the staff at some length.

One man, a clerk, had been the last to leave the attacked building and I took a statement from him in which he stated the cash box had been in the office when he left. The manager had opened up that morning, finding the smashed window and the cash box, with cash, missing.

The junction of Paynes Road and Millbrook Road in 1960.
(Bitterne Local History Society)
The photo not only shows the timber Durafencing office and window that was alleged to be the point of entry in the lower left hand corner, but also the filling station at the junction, managed by Ted Haresign, my first 'tea-hole' on the beat.

Although I was satisfied that one of the staff had faked a break-in, I was unable to get anywhere. However, whenever I was in the area over the next few weeks I called at the premises and asked a few more questions. I then strongly suspected the clerk who had locked up, but he did not change his story.

A break through then came some months later when the Corporation decided to drain Cemetery Lake on Southampton Common to clear out rubbish. An empty cash box, neatly wrapped in brown paper was found in the lake and this was circulated to divisions as possibly being the proceeds of crime. I recovered the cash box, had the

Durafencing manager call at the station and he identified it as the one stolen from his office. I then arranged for the clerk to visit the station and see me.

I showed him the cash box and said, "It has just come to light that a man of your description was seen to throw this cash box, neatly wrapped in brown paper, into the Cemetery Lake, so I had the lake drained and the box recovered. The man can be identified and there are fingerprints still recoverable on the paper. Have you anything to say?" I made this completely untrue statement with a straight face, and to my delight he replied "I'm glad this is now over, every time you called at the office my stomach turned over. Yes, it was me, I'm sorry". I felt more than justified in tricking him this way but my written evidence had the man confessing directly he was seen at the station. This put him in a good light and he was only fined £10 for the theft, but I was delighted to have cleared the matter up.

Arrests for minor crimes, break-ins at premises throughout the division, sudden deaths and enquiries for other forces, all took up my time and my case load constantly increased. Matters were then enlivened by a strange case of suicide. A call was received of a suicide at the rear of a butcher's shop in Shirley Road. The position was that private flats were at the rear of the building and the woman occupier of the top flat had gone downstairs at 11.00am and found the ground floor flat door ajar.

She looked in the room and saw the occupier on the floor, apparently dead, with his head on a cushion just outside the open door of the gas oven. She immediately told the butchers and they dialled 999 for an ambulance and the police.

I attended the scene, arriving the same time as the ambulance, and on checking the body I found it was still warm, with no sign of rigor mortis. He was, however, clearly dead and the body was taken away in the ambulance. I then checked the scene for a suicide note and noticed that all the gas taps on the oven were in the off position.

As a matter of routine I checked with the upstairs woman occupier and the shop butchers, wishing to know how many taps had been switched on, but they all denied having touched the oven. I had not touched it and had not seen the ambulance staff touch it, but went to the ambulance station and spoke to them. None of them had touched the oven.

I was then faced with the situation of a suicide who had managed to turn the gas taps off before dying. It did not make sense. I saw the upstairs occupier again and she told me that her husband, an Irishman, worked at Fawley and had left home at 7.00am that morning. He would be returning that evening. She also explained that a gas meter on the ground floor of the house served both flats and it had run out that morning. Her husband had placed sixpence in the meter before going to work.

I returned to the station and saw DS Arthur Offer, who had replaced DS Perc Amess on sick leave, and explained what had happened. We were both concerned so arranged to be present when the male occupier of the upstairs flat returned from Fawley, hoping he could resolve the mystery. Up to that point we were treating the death as suspicious and were busy all day taking statements from all involved, including friends and relatives of the deceased. We treated it as a potential murder.

DS Arthur Offer

'Paddy' duly returned from Fawley and was seen by DS Offer and myself that evening. Unbelievably, he told us that when he left for work he saw the ground floor door ajar and the light on. He looked in the room and saw the deceased lying on the floor, head face downwards on a cushion in front of the open oven door. The Irishman then said "He was snoring quite normally. I saw that the oven gas tap was turned on so stepped over him and turned it off. There was only a faint smell of gas. I shook his shoulder to see if he was all right and he stirred a bit and then carried on snoring normally. I then placed sixpence in the meter, had my breakfast and looked in again when I left for work but he was still snoring."

The poor man obviously was unaware of the effects of coal gas poisoning, with the absorption of carbon monoxide slowly killing the downstairs tenant. I attended the post mortem the following day, when carbon monoxide poisoning was confirmed. The matter was subsequently dealt with at an inquest, where I gave evidence at a Coroner's Court for the first time. It was clear that had an ambulance been called at 7.00am the man would almost certainly have survived.

By this time I had acquired a BSA 350cc motor cycle and this greatly assisted travelling to and from Shirley on the split shifts, especially when returning home late at night.

DC Brown on his trusty machine, at the side of Shirley Police Station.

My sometimes strange sense of humour was put to the test one afternoon when I was returning home on my motor cycle during a split shift. As I travelled up Lances Hill, Bitterne, with a scarf wrapped around my face as protection from the wind, I noticed a police Wolseley traffic car behind me, driven by PC Norman Chalk, my regular snooker opponent at the police club. I couldn't resist looking behind me, giving them a 'V sign', and immediately opening the throttle.

As I reached 40mph along Bitterne Road, taking the right hand fork into Bursledon Road, I increased my speed to around 50mph and turned into Middle Road, which was devoid of traffic. I then increased to 70mph, hearing the traffic car's warning 'gong' as I did so, which I ignored. After turning into South East Road I pulled up on my nearside and looked round to see Norman striding towards me, notebook in hand and with a grim look on his face. After all, I had obviously and deliberately taunted them.

When he reached me he burst out "Do you know the speed you were doing?" and I removed the scarf from my face and said "At least 70 Norman." He was taken aback and said "I've a bloody good mind to do you, you bugger." to which I replied "In that case I won't let you beat me at snooker again". He then burst out laughing and said he would get his own back at the first opportunity. I somehow don't think that serving officers today would get off so lightly.

Investigating a number of similar housebreakings in the Stratton Road area led me to strongly suspect a 22 year old youth who I discovered had left his home in that road following domestic problems with his parents. By tracing and questioning a number of his friends I discovered that he was sleeping rough somewhere in Shirley but I could not locate him. I circulated him as wanted for questioning and he was eventually found in town, arrested and taken to PHQ, where I interviewed him. My interviewing technique had by now developed considerably and it did not take long for me to take down his voluntary statement, under caution, in which he admitted a total of 15 housebreak-ings in the Shirley area.

When the case was dealt with at Quarter Sessions he was placed on probation for three years, partly because I told the Recorder how the youth had readily admitted everything and had co-operated fully with my enquiries. This was something I had promised the youth and I always honoured promises (or threats) made to suspects.

Confessing to crimes and making full statements about them is something that the legal profession appears to believe comes about purely because the defendant wants to confess. The truth is that everybody, almost without exception, initially tries to avoid prosecution and will lie to avoid being caught. The prime reason they eventually con-fess is either because they know the evidence is overwhelming and the police possess it, or because they become aware of some benefit in admitting it. The law of evidence states that voluntary confessions must be "obtained without fear of prejudice or hope of advantage exercised or held out by a person in authority". Police officers, CID offic-ers in particular, knew that to offer bail or other advantage could make such a confes-sion inadmissible, but I instinctively knew that I had to get across to a suspect that it would be to his advantage to confess.

My method was to let him know, before making any written record of an inter-view, that (a) I believed he was responsible and would work ceaselessly to obtain the evidence, during which time he would have to remain in custody and (b) if he was honestly remorseful and wanted that to get across to the court, he needed to tell me the truth. I would only suggest to him that he could be bailed, once the matter had been cleared up, if I knew that to be possible. A long record could make that out of the question, so I would not even mention bail in such a case.

I would also let him know that if my valuable time was saved, because I was always very busy, I would be appreciative and help him as much as possible, telling the court how I had been helped. On the other hand, if he was indeed responsible and made me spend much time and effort in establishing it, I could only tell the court how obstruc-tive he had been. Saying that, plus sometimes lying about how much evidence I actually had, as well as a friendly and helpful manner, usually did the trick. I never attempted to be confrontational, as that never helped, but would be very firm if met with aggression.

I can say, with complete honesty, that I never charged anybody without knowing for absolute certain they were responsible. The only exception to that is when faced with a situation where it was the word of the suspect against the word of the victim, such as in assault cases. In these instances it was left to the court or jury to decide.

My style of questioning stood me in good stead when later interviewing a man I had arrested for stealing a fountain pen. The circumstances were that he had called at a shop in Shirley Road asking to look at expensive pens. During the course of examining a tray of pens he asked to see other makes but left without making a purchase. The assistant then found that one of the expensive pens was missing. I then received information from two local dealers, William Beirne and George Handley, that they had purchased expensive pens from a man of the same description. They gave me the pens and I spoke to DC Archie Davies in the Record Office, giving him the man's description, distinctive black curly hair and a swarthy complexion, and he gave me the name of a man known to be such a good shoplifter.

I obtained his photo and, with 14 other similar police photos, showed them to William and George, who both, without hesitation, picked out the man suggested by Archie, who gave me access to the man's file, showing his last address. When I visited his home and told him of the photo identification, he admitted having stolen the pens, and when I said I knew of other offences he readily gave me a long list of thefts from various stores, telling me where he had sold them. I was able to recover many of the items, including jewellery, get them identified and charge him with the thefts, many others being taken into consideration. Because of his long record he was sent to Quarter Sessions for sentence but, again my evidence of his co-operation being given, he was placed on probation for three years.

In May 1959 I did my first tour of night duty at PHQ. The system was that all detectives, on a roster, did a week of night duty based at the Civic Centre. They had the sole CID car for their use (an unmarked Hillman Estate fitted with a police radio) and were thus available to ensure the correct initial action was taken when a crime was reported.

They would not necessarily deal with offenders themselves, the uniformed officers would become the officer in the case, but the detective would assist with interrogation and initial action at the scene of a crime.

On my very first night I had returned from a patrol and went into the Information Room at midnight to talk to the officer on night duty. I was thus there when he took a call from PC Ernie Waterman saying that he had disturbed three men at the rear of Bates the Chemist, in Above Bar. They had jumped from the roof and ran away in the direction of East Park Terrace.

I immediately ran out of the Civic Centre, went across to Commercial Road where I could see the silhouette of three figures walking through the unlit West Park. Without thinking, I entered the parks ahead of them and when they reached me stopped them and said who I was. I told them that three men had been disturbed nearby a few minutes earlier and I was taking them to the police station for further enquiries.

Perhaps because I was very direct and confident, or perhaps because I didn't think clearly, but they went with me to the CID office without any problem or other difficulty. I then saw they had a quantity of fresh cut grass on their shoes and a lot of dust and dirt on their sleeves and shoulders. I phoned the main office for uniformed assistance and was joined by some officers, including Ernie. The men were then detained while Ernie and I went back to the rear of Bates the Chemist.

We saw that the intruders had jumped from the roof onto a pile of rubbish and freshly cut grass clippings, and there were fresh foot impressions in a nearby flower bed. The shoes of two of the men fitted the impressions exactly. The three, all aged 18, were then interviewed and two of them made written statements, under caution, admitting that the three of them had been on the roof in an attempt to break in, but the third denied any involvement. Even when served with a copy of the statements made by the other two he still said "Nothing to do with me. I don't know what you are talking about."

All three were charged by PC Ernie Waterman with being found on enclosed premises and later appeared before the magistrates when they were each fined £20.00 However, the third man, who had denied being involved but who was convicted, was remanded in custody to appear at Maidstone Borough Quarter Sessions. He had appeared there the previous November for various offences and had been Bound Over. He remained in custody and appeared at Maidstone that June for sentence, when he was sent for Borstal Training for his original convictions there.

I later had to submit a report to the Under Secretary of State at the Home Office about the matter because he had alleged at Maidstone that the grass on his shoes were because he had walked through the parks, that he had not been with the other two when they went onto the roof, and that he had been hit by a police officer. I was able to refute all his allegations, confirming that he had never complained to me about being struck and that throughout my dealings with him he had been insolent and pugnacious. This was my first experience of somebody making false allegations against the police in an effort to discredit them and avoid a conviction. I was always very careful after this to ensure that everything I did was properly recorded and open for inspection, with corroboration from others whenever possible.

I next suffered the frustration of seeing a clearly guilty person avoid prosecution because of the age of the victims and my inability to obtain an admission. It arose following a complaint from a parent. I took a detailed statement from a seven year old boy in which he described how a 44 year old man living next door invited him into his house, where he touched the boy's penis and gave him three pence. The neighbour then asked the boy to return with a girl, and when the boy returned with an eight year old girl the man put his hand up her skirt and touched her private parts, giving her three pence and telling them not to say anything.

A policewoman took a statement from the girl, which corroborated everything the boy had said. I interviewed the man, putting the detailed allegations to him, but he vehemently denied any indecency, although admitting that the children entered his house and that he had given them money. Although I had no doubt whatsoever of the man's guilt, because of a lack of other evidence and the children's ages, it was decided that no further action could be taken. This rather upset me but I had to accept that you win some and lose some.

Life continued, with a steady stream of premises broken into, shoplifters, petty thefts, and a regular supply of prisoners from second-hand dealers William Beirne and George Handley, as a result of stolen property being offered to them and me being informed. Such things became a matter of routine. I also dealt with a number of suicides, mainly as a result of coal gas poisoning, and a number of sudden deaths.

One sudden death initially appeared suspicious, also upsetting for me as I had two young daughters. It was that of a baby boy, 72 days old, found dead on a pillow one morning. When I examined the body I saw a number of sores and ulcerations on the buttocks and scrotum, and had them photographed at the mortuary by DC Basil Ballard. However, further enquiries of the family doctor confirmed that he had treated the baby earlier for nappy rash and that this was the cause of the ulcerations. I was pleased that the parents were exonerated but upset at seeing the little helpless body.

My next sudden death was the first where the body had not been discovered for some time and as a result was covered in maggots. I saw many in the future, but this was the first time I had seen, and smelt, such a revolting occurrence. The man had his head in the oven, the room was full of buzzing flies and the head and upper body were a writhing mass of maggots. It was difficult to search the body, the smell was overpowering, but it had to be done and I overcame my initial revulsion to carry it out properly.

I was amused to read a Daily Order in June, stating that the wearing of chin straps was discretionary between 1 May and 30 September, but must be worn down at all other times. June also saw the retirement of D/Supt. Bert Gibbons, a real gentleman, and he was replaced by newly promoted Det/Supt. Bob Masters. I had a great deal of respect for Bob Masters; he was extremely efficient and a good leader, always leading from the front.

The first of many future frauds came my way when I dealt with a 36 year old man who had borrowed blank cheques from a friend and then presented them for goods at various shops. He was charged with false pretences and forgery, receiving six months imprisonment at the magistrates' court. This was a very straightforward fraud, but complicated ones were to come my way in the future.

I then had an accident on my motor cycle whilst returning home at lunchtime before recommencing the evening shift. It was raining and as I approached the Six Dials junction a woman ran onto the pedestrian crossing in front of me as I had almost reached it. I braked violently, the machine slid; I lost control, and ended up with a fractured wrist. The emergency driver who attended was PC Bryan Davies and he called for an ambulance and arranged for the recovery of my machine. It was the first time I had appreciated the action of the emergency services. My left arm was encased in Plaster of Paris and I remained on sick leave for the remainder of the day, returning to normal duty the following morning.

Bryan earned a more than justified promotion in later years, reaching the very senior position of Assistant Chief Constable of Hampshire.

ACC Bryan Davies leading a march past at Winchester *(Hampshire Constabulary History Society)*

Within a few days I temporarily regretted not being in uniform. A 19 year old man had gone berserk at his home in the Millbrook Estate, with his relatives fleeing the house as he threatened them with a bowl of boiling water. Police had attended but were warned that he would react violently at the sight of a uniform. As the only available plain clothes officer I was detailed to attend the scene and see what I could do.

When I arrived there was a large crowd of sightseers in the road, two police cars parked outside the house with several officers looking at me in expectation. I thanked them profusely for asking for my assistance and gingerly entered the house via the front door. I was expected to detain the unfortunate youth. The ground floor was deserted and when I reached the bottom of the stairs and looked up I saw him standing at the top, looking at me with a wild look and holding a large bowl that had steam rising from it.

We exchanged looks for only a few seconds, when to my great relief he threw the bowl down the stairs, giving sufficient warning for me to jump out of the way, and ran into a top bedroom. Before I could make up my mind what to do next, and I was apprehensive in going up the stairs into the unknown, I heard shouting from outside. I returned to the front of the house and saw that he had somehow (I have no idea how he got away with it) opened a bedroom window, climbed out, caught hold of the gutter and lifted himself onto the roof, from where he proceeded to rip off the tiles and throw them down. To my great relief the fire brigade attended and with the help of their escape ladder managed to reach the man, calm him and assist him down the ladder. An ambulance had also attended and he was seen by a doctor and taken direct to Knowle mental hospital.

My next incident was one where at one stage I genuinely feared for my life. It started with a straightforward arrest of a seaman in the New Docks. He had stolen some cigarettes on board a ship, the *MV Lapwing*, and was caught by another member of the crew but struggled and broke away, managing to get ashore. The crew dialled 999 and I attended in a Wolseley traffic car driven by PC Norman Chalk. I still had the plaster cast on my arm at this time.

**PC Norman Chalk with his beloved Wolseley, being inspected by
Chief Constable Alf Cullen *(Hampshire Constabulary History Society)***

We found the man, drunk, at the Dock Gate, as he was about to be checked by the dock police officer. Other crew members had followed and pointed him out. After talking to them I told the man who I was and told him he was being arrested for stealing the cigarettes.

He was placed in the back seat of the Wolseley but as I sat beside him he suddenly leaned forward, caught hold of my tie and tried to butt me in the face. With some difficulty, and much assistance, we managed to handcuff him but as he was so violent and in a restricted space we could only cuff him with his hands in front, not behind his back.

During the journey back to the Civic Centre he again became extremely violent, trying to grasp my throat with his outstretched and handcuffed hands. His hands were only inches away from me. He also had his legs stretched out, forcing them against the back of Norman's seat, so severely that we afterwards found it buckled and damaged.

Norman was most unhappy about this. I, however, was more than unhappy as I had great difficulty in making sure that the man did not get hold of my throat. I was absolutely frightened of what might happen as he was very strong and in a drunken rage. Luckily, my left arm, in its plaster cast, was rigid and I managed to force it against his neck, keeping him away from me, but he still attempted to strangle me.

I then clenched my right fist in front of him and said "Stop it, or I have no option but to belt you one." He then bellowed and tried even harder to get hold of my throat with his hands outstretched, so I punched him in the face as hard as I could. This further enraged him, so I had to continue punching, to the extent that my arm became tired, and his face and our clothing were covered in blood. By the time we arrived at the front door of the headquarters police station the man was semi-conscious and I was absolutely exhausted.

The front entrance of the Civic Centre police station, police headquarters.

Norman and I managed to pull the man out of the car and dragged him, with his trousers slowly coming down to his knees, inside the front door and past the reception desk where the Station Sergeant was talking to a woman customer. I was in a terrible state myself, hair everywhere, shirt out and covered in blood, and I walked past the sergeant, helping to drag the prisoner, nodding as I did so, with Norman helping me, past the counter and into the corridor leading to the cells.

I could see the woman had a look of horror on her face, and I imagined she was thinking "It's true what they say about police brutality." Little did she know that I was the one being brutalised.

The man was charged with the theft of cigarettes and wilful damage to the police car. I did not charge him with assaulting me as I felt I had given more than I received. He appeared before the magistrates the following morning and received two sentences of three months, consecutive, making a total of six months. I felt satisfied with this. He was also committed to the next Quarter Sessions for sentence, as he was in breach of an order, but no additional sentence was imposed by the Recorder.

The reader may feel that punching a prisoner in the face as hard as I could shows me to be somebody who deserves to be accused of police brutality? As I have, hopefully, explained I had little option at the time. On the other side of the coin there are two instances that come to mind where I have perhaps shown a gentler side.

One was where I had arrested a man at Christmas time and felt sorry for him; he was a reasonable person down on his luck. I knew that his wife and children had little or no money for the festive season so my wife and I bought some toys to take to their children and she made some turkey sandwiches and a slice of Christmas cake, to take to my prisoner in the cells.

Another instance was where I had arrested a man at the beginning of a Bank holiday period, when he would not appear before the magistrates for a remand until after the holiday. This meant he had to remain in police custody for three consecutive days in not ideal conditions. He also was a reasonable person so I saw the station sergeant and arranged for my prisoner to be released into my custody for further questioning. To my prisoner's great delight and surprise, I took him out of the station and walked with him to the Brewer's Arms public house, run by my father, for a drink, having first explained that if he attempted to escape I would almost certainly injure him in the process of recapturing him.

He fully appreciated me buying him a drink before taking him back to PHQ but the station sergeant was none too pleased as he had initially failed to find me when checking on the position and later realised what I had done.

I should also explain that at this time the Southampton Docks were owned by the British Transport Docks Board and policed by the British Transport police.

They were basically a private police force but nevertheless fully trained and qualified police officers, with full police powers. However, the docks were still part of Southampton and as such the ultimate responsibility of Southampton police.

What this meant in practice was that day to day policing was carried out by the BT police, but all incidents on board ship were dealt with by us. Thus thefts, murder, deaths, stowaways etc. on board ship were dealt with by us from the outset. The BT uniformed branch, who also policed the railways, were mainly occupied with manning the dock gates to ensure that goods were not removed without a dock pass, and checking premises within the dock estate.

The docks CID were extremely efficient in dealing with thefts of goods in transit, having a detailed working knowledge of the paperwork involved and the various shipping companies and their agents. Thefts in the course of transit could be a tricky matter to deal with as the point of theft had to be established as far as possible and the paperwork could be complicated.

We had a very good working relationship with the BT police, with a BT detective attending the PHQ morning CID conference to keep up to date with crime generally. We fully recognised their expertise in dock matters, but it was also a fact that when it came to really serious crime, such as murder, grave injury, or a large scale theft, then a Southampton detective would take over and work closely with the docks CID to resolve the matter. There was never a conflict over this and officers worked closely together towards a mutual satisfactory conclusion.

A man who had been placed on probation for three years some months earlier, for a series of housebreakings in the Stratton Road area, and who I had spoken up for at the Quarter Sessions court, unfortunately learnt nothing from the experience as I again had to arrest him for a series of identical offences. This time he was sent down for a total of 21 months.

One of my regular offenders, a 17 year old, had to be arrested, once again, for breaking open a gas meter. He just could not stop regarding meters in other houses as cash boxes to be opened at will. This time, however, because of his repeated offending, he was sent for Borstal Training – usually a minimum of three years.

November 1958 found me helping PC Frank Bloyce with a fatal accident that had taken place in Shirley High Street. A 20 year old man, initially unidentified, had been struck by a car whilst crossing the road. The car had failed to stop but its number had been taken by a passerby. I attended the scene and took paint samples from a lamppost that had also been struck and arranged for photos to be taken by DC Ron Ledgerwood. One side of the road was only closed temporarily, with a uniformed officer performing traffic control, and cleared directly the photos were taken.

The car was also traced and I took paint samples from it to be compared forensically with those taken from the lamppost. They proved to be identical. The 25 year old driver was interviewed, admitted being the driver and was charged by PC Bloyce with manslaughter. He eventually appeared at Hampshire Assizes and was sent to prison for nine months.

The same month saw me taking a welcome break, a trip to Worthing to bring back a prisoner. It was a simple matter; he had been found there in possession of a Triumph motor cycle stolen from Southampton, and this offence had been, technically, booked out to me. I had, of course, done nothing about it, other than circulating the details, but it meant a day out.

I travelled there in a traffic car and returned to Southampton with the prisoner (no handcuffs needed). Before I charged him with the 'taking and driving away' (he denied any intention of keeping or selling the machine) I questioned him about other offences he might have committed.

My interrogation techniques had clearly very much improved by now as he admitted a number of breaking and entering offences, including a safe-breaking in an office. Unfortunately for him, his freely admitted confessions did him no favours as he was sent to prison for three years when he eventually pleaded guilty at the next Quarter Sessions.

My next important case, that December, proved the value of the station's 'message slips' system, recording all the daily occurrences, no matter how minor, that were read every day by all officers, including the CID. I was dealing with a serious assault and the message slips proved crucial to my investigation.

The circumstances were that one Saturday evening an Italian gentleman went to the Classic cinema and sat next to a young girl, with whom he had a conversation. He pulled his handkerchief from his pocket and a roll of £107 in bank notes fell out, which he replaced, but did not think she had noticed. They left the cinema together and at her suggestion they caught a bus to Shirley Library, where they got out.

He bought her some chips, which they eat together walking along, and, again at her suggestion, they went into the doorway of the Mafeking Laundry where they kissed. She then suggested they go to a secluded and dark alley in nearby Nightingale Road, which he happily did. Although his English was poor it was enough for him to think he was on to a good thing.

She then asked him for some money and when he refused struck him in the throat. He did not realise that, in fact, she had struck him with a penknife, narrowly missing his main artery and windpipe. She then ran away but he chased her, catching her and taking her to the Angus Café where he intended to summon help. During the struggle he realised that he was bleeding and that his blood had got onto her coat. Whilst he tried to force her into the café two youths came up and took her away along Shirley Road.

Staff in the café, seeing the struggle, dialled '999' and PC Cassell arrived on the scene soon afterwards. He was initially unable to get an account of what had happened, due to the man speaking in rapid Italian and broken English, but went with him to the RSH Hospital, where he was treated and detained. His wound was ½" long and 1" deep and had to be stitched.

I became involved the following day and went with PC Cassell to the hospital where we managed to get an account of the incident, together with a description of the girl. She was aged about 20, short blonde hair and dressed in a dark blue full length coat. We also went to the alley where we found a patch of dried blood. I was now dealing with a case of attempted robbery and grievous bodily harm. I took statements from the witnesses in the Angus café and made enquiries in the area without result. However, a week later, whilst checking through the message slips on the Monday, I saw that an 18 year old girl had been reported missing from her lodgings in Palm Road, Coxford, having left on Sunday a week ago. I thought this was something of a co-incidence, so visited Palm Road and questioned the landlady.

It then transpired that the girl had not returned home until 9.00am on the Sunday morning and was said to then be in a distressed state. She had also asked her landlady for petrol as she had some stains on her coat – a dark blue full length coat - everything fitted. I searched her room and found a large quantity of new condition gloves, clothing and jewellery, all still with labels, and formed the opinion they were the proceeds of shoplifting. I also found a number of documents with Bournemouth addresses in her room, so asked Bournemouth police to try to trace her and if so interview her about the property.

She was traced to her parent's home in Bournemouth and when interviewed admitted having stolen the items by shoplifting. She was taken to Bournemouth police station where I attended, with PW Norma Pledger, and questioned her. She admitted stealing the items but when I told her I was also making enquiries about an Italian who had been stabbed in Southampton she initially denied all knowledge, saying she didn't know any Italians and said "I don't know why you are questioning me"

I examined her coat and pointed out what appeared to be dried bloodstains on the front, adding that the girl concerned can be identified by the man and others who were in the Angus café. She then said, in a low voice "I am the girl".

She was returned to Southampton where she made a statement admitting everything and was charged by PC Cassell with attempted robbery and theft of the items found in her room. She later appeared at the Hampshire Assizes when she was placed on probation for three years with a condition of residence at Knowle Mental Hospital for 12 months.

Even when at home I found myself involved in incidents. One such was when a neighbour called at 7.00am to tell me that she had found Fred Harding, a neighbour who lived opposite me, in bed with his throat cut. Fred was something of a recluse and lived alone. The neighbour lived next door to him and acted as his housekeeper, so had the keys to the house.

When I entered I first went to the kitchen, where I saw a very large pool of blood on the floor, in front of the gas cooker, which had the oven door wide open with a cushion inside. All the taps were in the 'off' position and there was no smell of gas. I then went upstairs where I saw Fred, who knew me, in bed with a large gaping hole in his throat.

What astounded me was that he was conscious and smoking a cigarette, but smoke was coming from his throat. It appeared that he had cut open his windpipe. He told me that he had tried to gas himself, but it hadn't worked, so he had cut his wrists and his throat. He showed me several cuts on both wrists but they were not deep and not bleeding.

I asked the housekeeper to phone for an ambulance and tried some first aid. The ambulance soon arrived, at the same time as PS Ken Long and PC Bill Perrin, who also attempted to apply first aid to Fred. After he was taken to hospital, where he eventually recovered, I found a suicide note in the lounge.

What was most unusual was the extremely large sums of money scattered about the house wrapped in newspaper. It turned out that Fred, who had been an Echo salesman all his life, working the floating bridges, had packed up his loose change every day, wrapped in newspapers. He then left the packages on the floor of every room in the house, including the bedrooms, under the tables, on top of cupboards, in the outside toilet; in fact the bundles were piled up as far as the eye could see. As this appeared to have taken place over a number of years, many of the bundles had rotted, broken up by mice, and were generally in a chaotic state.

The house was secured and it was arranged for members of his bank to call, with a large van, and shovel up the bags of cash and take them to the bank for counting and placing in his account. I later understood that it amounted to several thousand pounds. He never returned home but I believe he recovered from the throat wound and died some time later.

My next case, although only a minor theft, well and truly established me as 'Lucky Jim' and was detected as a result of a massive stroke of luck. It started as a routine report. A man had left his Standard 9hp car on the forecourt of the Boundary Inn, Rownhams Lane, because it had broken down, but when he returned the following morning he found it jacked up on wall bricks with three wheels, jack, windscreen motor, dynamo and carburettor missing.

Boundary Inn, Rownhams Lane – now demolished
(Dave Goddard)

As I also had to visit nearby Aldermoor School which had been broken into, I decided to first have a look at the car in case there were some useful fingerprints. As I did so a nine year old boy came up and stood watching me examine the car. He said "Is that your car Mister?", so I told him who I was and that parts had been stolen from the car.

He then said "The man who took the wheels had a Standard 9 as well". I was surprised at this, and spent the next 10 minutes or so trying to get a description from him, when he said, casually, "Would you like his car number?" I was absolutely amazed at this. It turned out that his hobby was collecting car numbers of different makes and he had taken that of the thief. Had I gone to Aldermoor School first, or even not bothered to look at the car, I would have missed seeing the boy and the theft would have remained undetected.

As it was, I went with him to his home where he showed me his notebook with the car details. I returned to the station and phoned the local motor taxation at Clifford House to discover the owner. Today, of course, full information, including whether or not taxed and insured, is available to the police in a split second, but at this period the taxation clerk had to check his local paper records. If registered elsewhere he would phone the appropriate taxation authority, based on the vehicle plate lettering. Each district had its own allocation of plates, Southampton had OW and TR, followed by a number. If we needed this information outside office hours the headquarters station sergeant held the key to the taxation office and he would open up and check himself.

I went to the address given by the taxation office and saw the driver's wife. She informed me her husband was a railway guard at Redbridge Station. I asked her, casually, would she mind if I looked in her garage. Puzzled, she agreed, and, as anticipated, on the garage floor were three car wheels, dynamo, carburettor etc. It didn't take long to go to Redbridge Station and arrest him, obtaining a full admission. He was subsequently fined £10, more than a a week's wages.

My "Lucky Jim" name persisted one Sunday when Shirley High Street was absolutely deserted. PC Pat Rogers was the duty enquiry officer and was notorious for a conversation he had had with the Chief Constable.

Pat had been the night duty Information Room officer and had gone through an abnormally busy night shift. The Chief had booked an early morning call, which Pat had forgotten about, and when the Chief rang to complain at his early call being missed, Pat, who busy trying to write up the nights events, had replied something to the effect of "F… your early call, I've been choc-o-bloc all night and have got better things to do". To which the Chief replied "Do you know who you are talking to?" to which Pat replied "Yes, do you know who you are talking to?" When the Chief replied "No", Pat hung up the phone. It was for this reason that Pat had been removed from the Information Room and posted to Shirley as duty Enquiry Officer.

Back to this particular quiet Sunday. I went out for some fresh air, saying as I did so, "I shall be back in a minute Pat with a prisoner". It was a joke because Shirley appeared quite empty.

However, I strolled up Howards Grove and as I looked down the cul-de-sac at the rear of a block of shops I saw two young lads, 10 and 11 years old, pushing a small wheelbarrow from the back of the alley. I had a look and saw it contained a very large quantity of apples. Their explanation was they had found the rear door of Woolworths open and had helped themselves. But when I checked the premises I found a rear window smashed and completely removed, allowing the bolts to be opened in the rear door.

Of course, I was tickled pink to return to Pat Rogers with two diminutive prisoners. Before taking them home to their parents, to explain the position, as there had been similar forcible entries along that block of shops, I asked them about the break-ins and they readily admitted several of them.

The following day they came to Shirley police station, with their parents, to be reported for summons for the break-ins, but somehow I was not satisfied with the quick and ready admissions. I therefore went with them and their parents to the rear of the block of shops and asked them to point out how they broke in. They had no idea and indicated all the wrong places. I was satisfied they were not, in fact, responsible, and asked them why on earth they had owned up to things they hadn't done. I received the amazing reply "Because you were so nice to us we wanted to help you." Thankfully, they only received a Conditional Discharge when they appeared at the Juvenile Court.

The next incident involved one of the juveniles implicated in the "Dirty Gertie" indecency case. Then aged 17, now 20, he was arrested by me for a series of offences. He was part of a group of young men who were initially arrested for a simple case of theft, but who I tricked into admitting further more serious offences.

The circumstances were that new condition sheet lead was reported stolen from the site of the new Princess Anne Maternity Hospital, under construction in Tremona Road. The theft was booked out to me, so I immediately phoned Bill Taylor, the scrap metal merchant in Park Street, as he was a responsible and honest dealer. The stolen lead had a black strip painted along one edge, and Bill told me he had bought an identical quantity the previous day.

Bill knew the seller, another scrap metal dealer, who, when interviewed, said he, in turn, had bought it from two youths at an address in Coxford Road. This house was within 50 feet of the building site. I recovered the lead and it was identified as that stolen, so I went to the house and questioned the 19 year old youth living there. Faced with the evidence he readily admitted the theft and named another youth who was with him at the time.

I arrested the other youth, aged 18, separately, for the theft of the lead and they were each taken to Shirley police station and detained in separate rooms, guarded by uniformed PCs. The theft was straightforward, but there was something in their manner that disturbed me. I felt there was something they had not told me, so I let them wait apart while I went to the canteen, had a cup of tea and played a game of snooker. I then took a manila folder, filled it with a bundle of blank statements and crime reports, and went to the youth I felt was the most likely to confess something.

I indicated my folder and said "I have taken a statement from your friend – what was the first job you were involved in? To my amazement he looked at me and said "The Co-op at Totton, we got the safe from there". I showed no surprise, as though I already knew about this (I didn't) and said "How many jobs have you done?" and he replied "About ten I think". He then made a statement, involving breaking into a number of premises, naming two others, aged 16 and 18, who were also involved, one of them only for the lead theft. Now I was aware of what had taken place, it was a simple matter to arrest the others, including the now 20 year old involved with 'Dirty Gertie', and obtain full admissions.

When they appeared at Quarter Sessions for the breaking offences one of the 20 year olds was sent for Borstal Training, another placed on probation for three years and a third 20 year old fined £15. The fourth youth, who was only involved in the lead theft, was fined £5 at the magistrates' court. I felt no compunction at all at having tricked them with the manila folder; I was only after the truth, but I could not include this in my evidence.

Unbelievably, within a few months the 20 year old who had been fined £15 was arrested by DC Trevor Lobb and me attempting to sell George Handley an electric drill stolen from Green Lane School, broken into the previous night. Trevor charged him with the schoolbreaking and when he appeared at Quarter Sessions he was placed on Probation for three years.

By now I had built up a useful number of informants and contacts who readily gave me useful information. One was the proprietor of a café in Church Street and what he told me resulted in me having, irrationally, a conscience for many years to come. He told me that he thought it strange that a young boy would regularly come into his café on a Sunday morning, have a cup of tea and then be met by a man who would take him away in his car, returning about an hour later. He thought it strange. I therefore asked him to take a note of the car registration number the next time it happened and a week or so later he phoned to give me the car number.

I checked on the registered owner and found, on further checking, that he had a string of convictions for indecency with children. This meant that the next Sunday found me waiting in the café for the boy to turn up. When he arrived I asked him to come with me to Shirley police station, where it didn't take much effort for him to give me a statement explaining that the man took him to Stoney Cross aerodrome (an empty former wartime area) in the New Forest, where they indulged in mutual masturbation. The 15 year old boy was then taken home and the position explained to his parents.

I went to Warren Crescent and arrested the paedophile, taking him to Shirley police station where he readily admitted the indecent acts with the boy. He made a written statement and said he would plead guilty as he did not wish the boy to have to give evidence. As the offences had taken place in the Hampshire Constabulary area, I contacted Detective Superintendent Cyril "Tank" Holdaway, head of Hampshire CID and he asked me to bail the man to reappear at Shirley station later that week, when he would take him into custody.

Det.Supt. 'Tank' Holdaway. *(Hampshire Constabulary History Society)*

The following Tuesday the Superintendent sent for me and said "What did you say to the bloke you arrested for Hampshire on Sunday?" Puzzled, I told him I had said nothing unusual. I was then told that the man had been found that morning, in his car, on Stoney Cross aerodrome, dead, with a hose attached from the car exhaust.

Although I had no real reason to have his death on my conscience, and I could rationally justify everything I had done, I nevertheless regularly thought of the death. I looked back and thought that no complaint had been received, I had started everything myself out of a chance remark and was therefore really responsible. I knew that it was entirely the man's own action and that other children had been saved from a similar abuse, but it nevertheless weighed heavily on my mind for some years to come. If I had not followed up my hunch, he would still be alive.

I became involved in another incident whilst at home that July. I had been on duty until 7.15pm and later that evening was disturbed by a violent knocking on my front door. The caller was a bus driver who lived nearby and knew me. He told me that his conductor had been thrown down the stairs of his bus by a group of drunken youths and expected me to do something about it.

On going outside I saw a stationary double-decker bus with a small crowd alongside, shouting and arguing. Two youths, neighbours who knew me, were clearly drunk and on seeing me one of them shouted "You're not in uniform, you're off duty, there's nothing you can do, f...off." Another also told me the same, but when I caught hold of his arm, with the intention of taking him away from the crowd to reduce the situation, I was then struck on my shoulder. Two others then caught hold of me and struck me on the head and body. In the ensuing struggle we crashed through a neighbour's fence and I fell to the ground, where they started to kick me about the body (I had my arms around my head to protect my head from kicks). One of the youths shouted to my main attacker "He's had enough Danny, you'll kill him", and the kicking stopped. I managed to get to my feet and although somewhat dazed from the blows told the two main attackers they were under arrest for assaulting a police officer.

My wife, who had seen what was about to happen, had run down to the nearest telephone kiosk but a friend, John Paynter, ran past her and dialled '999' telling them the position. An attack on a police officer is always given the utmost priority, so Sgt Ken Long and PC Bill Thorne, with other officers, arrived within minutes.

I recall seeing the police car screech to a halt, the rear wheels rising slightly, with officers jumping out almost before the car had settled. I then caught hold of one of my attackers, but to my surprise the first person arrested was me. Because my shirt was torn and I was generally dishevelled, I was not initially recognised. But this was soon rectified and the two main protagonists were arrested, the others having dispersed as soon as the police arrived.

I was later found to have a bruised head, back and legs, with four fractured ribs so the two drunken youths, aged 17 and 20, were detained until they were sober. Bill Thorne had also been kicked in his stomach after arrival, so the youths were charged with two cases of assault on police, plus assaulting the bus conductor. I had no option but to report sick for two weeks.

When the youths appeared at the magistrates' court I spoke up for them, saying they would not have assaulted me had they not been drunk, adding they were basically reasonable lads, and they were fined £75 and £25 respectively. This was a large amount at the time. I had spoken up for them because they were neighbours and my family had to live with them – it was better to have them appreciative rather than resentful, and because had I not done so they would certainly have received a prison sentence. The courts took a very dim view of 'their' police officers being assaulted.

Sometimes a confession would come out of the blue, based on my dealing with offenders fairly and honestly. One such arose out of a simple case of theft. The police at Worthing informed me that they had found a man in possession of a motor cycle stolen from the Atherley Cinema car park, a theft that had been booked out to me. I enjoyed a pleasant trip to Worthing to collect the prisoner, a man I had dealt with several times before.

He was charged and because of his record kept in custody for a week to be then dealt with. However, just before he appeared before the court he saw me and said "I want to tell you about something I've got on my mind. I've done another job". He then admitted breaking into the Grosvenor Garage the previous March and stealing the safe, which he took away and forced open at home.

Unfortunately for him, when he eventually appeared at Quarter Session and pleaded guilty, he nevertheless was sentenced to three years imprisonment, because of his bad record and in spite of the fact that I spoke up for him in court, emphasising that he had freely admitted the safebreaking and there had been nothing to connect him with it prior to his admission.

Treating prisoners reasonably led to another unexpected outcome for me and I now break my self-imposed rule by giving the name of the offender – Victor Jackopson. The reason will become clear. One morning in July 1959 I received one of my usual calls from George Handley, telling me that a young man had tried to sell him a camera which he thought was stolen. He told the youth that he didn't buy cameras but his brother did and he would be in the shop later that afternoon. George kept the camera and arranged for the youth to return later.

I, of course, was present when the youth, Victor Jackopson, 18 years old, returned and, after some brief questioning, he admitted having stolen it after breaking into a house in Burgess Road. I then walked with him to Shirley police station – again, no handcuffs used - and we walked the length of Romsey Road and Shirley High Street chatting away normally. It turned out that Victor had been sleeping rough, so we gave him a hearty meal at the station and generally looked after him, no more than I usually did as a matter of course. He later admitted a further housebreaking and was charged accordingly. He had absconded from Hollybrook Homes and because he had no fixed address he was remanded in custody until he appeared at Quarter Sessions, when he was placed on Probation for three years.

Victor came to mind again several decades later, in July 1999, when I read in the local Daily Echo "Teddy Boy Finds Salvation in Jail". The article mentioned that the Rev. Victor Jackopson, a Baptist Minister, had written a book "From Prison to Pulpit" and when remanded in custody had turned to God and his Bible for help. He ran a charity "Hope Now" that assists orphans and street children in the Ukraine and South Africa. I contacted the Echo, and as a result my wife and I met up with Victor and his wife, sharing a meal with them at their home. This was duly reported in the Daily Echo.

(Southern Daily Echo)

Vic tracked by ex-jailer

By **Nina Kelly**

WHEN Vic Jackopson was arrested for burglary and sent to prison, little did he think that 40 years later he would be inviting the arresting officer home for lunch.

Following a Daily Echo article in July headlined Teddy Boy Finds Salvation in Jail, former Sergeant Jim Brown, now aged 67, wrote to Vic saying: "You are not the only prisoner of mine who has gone from strength to strength and kept out of future trouble. I have always maintained that everybody is entitled to make a mistake – it is the way you ensure the mistake is not repeated that makes all the difference."

As an amateur historian Jim has kept copies of his notebooks and even has the statement made by Vic on July 22, 1959. "It was a fair cop," Vic recalled, "I remember we walked down to Shirley police station where I was given bangers and mash and a cup of tea. It was kindness all round back in 1959. I'm fascinated that 40 years later Jim Brown should even remember who I was much less have the full details of my offence. We had a lovely time over lunch and the fact that we were both Christians meant that we had a lot in common. We exchanged books. He gave me the story of St Andrew's Methodist Church in Sholing and I gave him my book From Prison to Pulpit and Back Again."

It was alone in his solitary prison cell that Vic had turned in desperation to God and the Bible for help. A life-changing decision followed and on his release from prison Vic trained

to become a Baptist minister. This homeless ex-prisoner brought up in a children's home, now runs a charity, Hope Now, that reaches out to orphans, street children and prisoners in the Ukraine and South Africa.

"People always used to say to me that I would be in and out of prison all my life and they were right!" said Vic.

As a result of his prison ministry, nowadays on the right side of the law,

there are many who can similarly testify to experiences of faith that have helped turn their lives around.

In Ukraine where the re-offending rate for ex-prisoners is more than 80 per cent, Hope Now can point to the fact that out of 60 fledgling Christian prisoners that have been released in the past five years only one has re-offended.

"Imagine what that would save the government," concluded Vic.

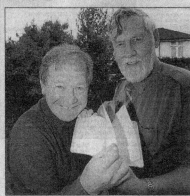

MEETING: Vic Jackopson and Jim Brown.

Victor gave me a copy of his book, in which he mentions me (promoting me to Inspector) and speaks kindly of his treatment. I, in turn, gave him a copy of one of my books, "The Story of St Andrew's Methodist Church, Sholing, Southampton". It was a most satisfactory outcome as far as I was concerned.

Police officers serving in the 21st century will find the following account somewhat unbelievable. It started when I received a phone call early that August morning, in a musical Welsh accent, from the police at Pembrokeshire. The station sergeant informed me that they had arrested a man who was wanted by me on warrant. The man had obtained a motor cycle by false pretences and had been arrested at Milford Haven in possession of the machine. The station sergeant said "It will need two of you, he's a big bugger".

I therefore phoned D/Supt Bob Masters to ask permission for another officer to go with me to Milford Haven. He had been promoted that June from Detective Inspector direct to Detective Superintendent, a considerable promotion indeed. He didn't take more than a second to respond with "No, you're not travelling overnight with the prisoner and you will be on the train with him all the time – there's no need for a second officer".

I therefore had to obtain sufficient cash from the General Office for the train journey, accommodation and meals, plus arrange for Bitterne police to let my wife know the position, as I would not be home until late the following day. (Home telephones were still a rarity). Milford Haven CID arranged bed and breakfast for me and met me at the station when I arrived at 11.25pm, exhausted, having travelled on a sweltering August day.

The following morning I went to the police station, to be met by the station sergeant who, on being told who I was, said "There's nobody with you. Have you seen him Man? Bloody hell, he's a big 'un." I then signed for the prisoner and entered his cell to explain I was taking him to Southampton. He was sitting on the cell bench, and when he stood up he towered over me. He was 6' 6½" and weighed 17½ stone. I took one look at him and thought "I'm in trouble".

I explained to him that I was sorry but I had no option but to handcuff him for the journey, and he replied "No problem, but I won't be any trouble, I just want to get it over with". I then tried to handcuff him before we left, but found that they were too small to encircle his wrist. I then said "I am going to Southampton and would like you to come with me. If at any point you decide you want to leave, just walk away and I will wait until you are well out of sight before I summon help".

I had absolutely no wish to argue with him. I am not a coward but it would have been impossible to detain him against his will; he could easily have destroyed me at any time he wished. As it was we had an uneventful journey to Southampton, the weather still unbearably hot, arriving at 8.00pm.

By the time I had charged him and seen him placed in a cell for court the following morning, it was 10.00pm – I had been away from home for almost 37 hours, with no extra payment or other compensation.

I submitted my expense form, showing I was just over my entitlement under Police Regulations, but meals on British Railways trains exceeded the entitlement and this was taken into account. My total expenses, including rail fares, all meals and overnight accommodation came to £9. 1s 3d, and this was 1/5d (7p) over the Police Regulations allowance.

What now follows is what 21st century police officers will find difficult to believe. Two days later I was ordered to report to D/Supt. Bob Masters and when I entered his office he angrily waved my expense form in my face, saying "What's this?", pointing to the meal receipt I had obtained on the train. He stabbed his finger at an entry of 3/2d (17p) for two pints of lager and demanded an explanation.

I explained the size of the prisoner, the weather conditions and the fact that I was alone, therefore needing to keep the prisoner happy, but he was incensed that I had treated both myself and the prisoner to what he considered an unnecessary expense. I therefore had to resubmit my expense form, minus the 3/2d (17p). After all that the prisoner was merely fined £30 – had it been worth it?

Sometimes I became involved in truly tragic incidents; one case was when I attended the scene of an explosion in Bramston Road, where an ambulance had been called. PC Tony Webb had attended and called for CID.

When I arrived I found that a 13 year old boy had been making home made 'bombs', using sodium chlorate mixed with the correct amount of sugar. He had flattened one end of a foot long copper tube with a hammer, drilled a hole in the centre to insert a fuse, and then packed it with the home-made explosive before flattening the other end. Whilst he was flattening the final end of a second 'bomb', placing it on a garden bench and steadying it with his left foot, it had exploded. I found part of his foot, still in his shoe, further up the garden, and the unfortunate lad was taken to the Royal South Hants hospital for treatment.

Under the circumstances no further action was taken against him. The 'bomb' was later exploded on waste ground near the docks by the Army bomb disposal squad.

Tony Webb and me holding the first unexploded home-made bomb, at the rear of Shirley Police Station. (My apology for us both smiling after such a tragedy, but it was some time after the event and the youth was recovering)

A tour of night duty in November gave me a surprise prisoner. I was in the Civic Centre Information Room at 4.30am when the burglar alarm of Lankester & Crook, Obelisk Road, Woolston, was actuated. There was a 4 minute delay before the alarm inside the premises was also actuated, so Bitterne police emergency car immediately attended.

At the same time I left the Civic Centre in the CID Hillman, driving at a very fast speed along the empty roads, going the wrong way round the Bullar Road roundabout and arriving in Obelisk Road just after the Bitterne car. The shop alarm had sounded as they arrived. We found a smashed window in the right hand front door of the double fronted premises, sufficient to gain entry, so it was decided to surround the building and await the arrival of the police dog and the keyholder.

Directly the dog arrived he, as tended to be their wont, marked the front door by cocking his leg, and when the keyholder arrived and opened the door the dog rushed inside and ran straight up the internal stairs. Most of the police officers followed, but

I made sure that one PC was left guarding the entrance whilst I strolled round, in the dark, to the left side of the building, shining my torch as I did so.

As I turned the corner a 23 year old man walked out from behind some shelving, saying, as he did so, the immortal words "It's a fair cop Guv". I arrested him without any trouble and he was subsequently charged with the forcible entry, but no way could I put his first words into my report. I amended it to his subsequent words, "Here I am, I might as well save you the trouble".

I did not charge him, that was passed over to one of the uniformed officers. I was far too busy on tours of night duty to do other than the initial action at the scene of an incident. I was responsible for the entire Borough during the night so had to attend many incidents during each tour of night duty.

The former premises of Lankester & Crook Ltd, *(Bitterne Local History Society)*

One aspect of CID work that occupied much of my time was preparing the antecedent history of prisoners, whether or not I was the officer in the case. Part of my function, when assisting uniformed officers dealing with criminal offences, was interviewing the prisoner and checking his criminal record to complete his or her detailed history for the information of the court.

Another type of crime that is time consuming is fraud, and early 1960 saw me dealing with several serious cases one after the other. I had dealt with many minor frauds, dud cheques and the like, as well as obtaining goods by false pretences (now said to be 'by deception'), but the next few were a bit different.

The first was a complicated series of offences involving a 37 year old accountant, 'Stanley'. He was the accountant for ten associate companies, formed into two groups at Andover and Gravesend and the Managing Director had called at Shirley police station to report he was suspicious of 'Stanley's' activities. He had discovered a cheque stub marked 'cancelled' and when he asked his bank for the return of the cheque found it was for £104 to a company in Romsey Road, Shirley.

The MD had called at the company premises and found the cheque related to a series of hire purchase agreements entered into with a finance company. Everything had been personally arranged by 'Stanley'. The finance company was one of an Andover group associate companies and when he checked with them they had no knowledge of any hire purchase transactions with the Romsey Road organisation. At my request the MD brought me a number of the various associate company ledgers and bank statements and I spent some considerable time checking them through. My desk was piled high with documents, but I still had to deal with normal break-ins, shoplifters etc.

As a result of steadily ploughing through the documents I found a number of discrepancies, with cheques drawn on one company shown as paid to another associate company but with no corresponding record in the accounts of the other company. I also discovered that 'Stanley' had purchased a Triumph car from Anglesea Motors in Shirley Road, paying for it with a cheque for £312. 7s 6d, drawn on the account of an associate company. The cheque book stub and corresponding ledger entry made by 'Stanley' showed this amount as falsely having been paid to yet another associate company. This appeared to be a straightforward case of larceny as servant, as it was 'Stanley's' employer who had lost the £312. 7s 6d, not the motor dealer. I contacted Gravesend and Andover police, as although there were distinct offences committed in Shirley, others took place in their police districts. It was agreed that as I had all the evidence I would deal with the case, including offences committed in their areas.

I then interviewed 'Stanley' at length, showing him all the documentary evidence, plus statements I had obtained from witnesses involved in his transactions. He readily agreed to assist me in compiling the facts involving offences he had committed and when I submitted my case papers I included the fact that his assistance in preparing the case against him was invaluable. Although I was no accountant, I had common sense and was able to follow the various paper trails. I was also friendly with him throughout the investigation in order to get his full co-operation.

He was eventually charged with various offences of falsification of accounts, including those committed in Andover and Gravesend, larceny as servant and obtaining by false pretences. His reply to the charges, as recorded by me, was "I would just like to thank you for the way you've treated me and apologise most sincerely for all the work I've given you."

When he eventually appeared at court, after a series of adjournments at the request of the defence, his counsel made legal submissions and the charges of larceny as servant were dismissed. The defence quoted case law establishing that buying articles by means of an unauthorised cheque on his employer's account did not constitute theft from the employer but was obtaining by false pretences.

I was annoyed at this legal loophole as the prosecuting solicitor had agreed with my view that it was the employer who had lost the amounts involved, not the seller of the article, so this was my first case overturned on a legal point. However, 'Stanley' had no option but to plead guilty to the charges of falsification of accounts and was sentenced to two periods of six months, consecutive, making 12 months in all. I was more than satisfied with the outcome of my lengthy and time-consuming paperwork.

One of the reasons a detective is assigned to a uniformed officer, when dealing with criminal offenders, is to ensure that the legal points are clearly proven and the correct charges made. A detective's work is also overseen and his evidence checked by a higher rank, for the same reason, so I was not alone in believing the correct charges had been brought against 'Stanley'.

It is also very important that the chain of evidence is properly established, with continuity in the handling of property. If all the points of law necessary to prove a case are not covered, or there is a gap in the handing over of property from one person to another, then the case can collapse in court.

My next lengthy fraud investigation started very simply. Norman Tucker, a second hand dealer trading as the Swop Shop, in Shirley Road, told me he had bought a transistor radio from a young boy and thought it might be stolen. It was in new condition and worth much more than the £8 he offered. The boy had signed the Swop Shop receipt book, giving a name and address in Malmesbury Road, Shirley.

I went to that address and saw the occupier, who I shall call 'Lizzie'. She denied all knowledge of any lad selling a transistor radio but agreed she had several children, including a young boy. I spoke to her son and although he denied selling any radio I was suspicious and felt he was not telling the truth.

I therefore obtained the Swop Shop receipt book, returned to Malmesbury Road and asked 'Lizzie's' son to write his signature, comparing it with that in the receipt book. They were identical. 'Lizzie' then admitted that she had asked her son to sell the radio and that she had obtained it on hire purchase. I made an appointment to see her later that week, but when I returned to the house and saw her husband found she had left the house the day after I saw her, taking her four children with her. I saw a massive pile of correspondence on the floor of the front room and on looking through found they all related to items obtained on hire purchase or bought from mail order firms, addressed in different names but all with the same or similar Malmesbury Road addresses.

I took them back to the station and as I checked through realised they related to all manner of items bought on hire purchase but with outstanding repayments. I listed a very large number of vacuum cleaners, radios, record players, tape recorders, refrigerators, oil and electric heaters, typewriters, carpets, washing machines, electric shavers, Goblin Teasmaid sets and spin dryers, totalling several thousand pounds.

It became very apparent that 'Lizzie' had an organised system of obtaining articles on hire purchase and selling them for a 100% profit. It was doomed to eventual failure as although she had used various false names the majority showed her correct address. I searched the house more thoroughly, finding more letters as well as fresh letters arriving almost daily, building up an unanswerable case of fraud, but involving a mountain of paperwork.

I managed to trace her brother, after discovering he was responsible for some of the purchases and subsequent sales, and he made full admissions of various offences, based on the paperwork I had recovered. 'Lizzie' was circulated as wanted and eventually arrested by DS St John, Hampshire Constabulary, and I interviewed her at Fratton police station.

She made a full and frank admission of thefts as bailee and was taken to police headquarters where she made a detailed statement, under caution, admitting everything. I charged her and her brother with four offences of theft and 'Lizzie' with three further offences of obtaining credit by fraud. 'Lizzie' had 71 further offences taken into consideration and her brother 37 further offences TIC. Property to a total value of £2,808 was involved with 'Lizzie' and £1,598 with her brother. Considerable sums for that time.

'Lizzie' and her brother later appeared at Southampton magistrates' court, where they pleaded guilty and asked for the other offences to be taken into consideration. 'Lizzie' was sentenced to three periods of four months, consecutive, and four lots of two months, concurrent, making her total sentence one of 12 months. Her brother received similar sentences, also amounting to 12 months in all.

However, before they appeared in Court I found myself on another murder squad.

12. MURDER IN MAYFIELD PARK – 1960

At 5.00am on the morning of Sunday 21 February 1960 I was woken by the doorbell. The uniformed colleague told me "You are to report to Bitterne Station at six o'clock – a girl has been found murdered in Mayfield Park and you're on the squad".

The parade room at Bitterne Police Station was packed when I arrived for the briefing from DI Eric Coleman. He explained that the previous afternoon several children were playing in Mayfield Park, Weston, when one of them, nine year old Iris Margaret Dawkins, slipped and fell into a stream at around 4.00pm. Because she was wet and covered in mud she went home to change, leaving her 13 year old brother Malcolm behind.

DI Eric Coleman (subsequently Superintendent)

When Malcolm arrived home and found his sister had not returned his parents became concerned. Bitterne Police were informed and a search of the area carried out. Her body was found at 11.00pm, laying face down in a boggy area, and a subsequent post-mortem revealed that she had been stabbed no less than 37 times, some of them after her death.

The squad was given her description – dressed in a woollen pale blue jumper, dark blue jeans, black plimsolls and a white hat – and we were individually detailed to make door to door enquiries in the Weston Estate adjoining Mayfield Park

I was initially allocated Barnfield Road, Close and Way, adjacent to Mayfield Park football pitch.

Iris Dawkins *(Daily Sketch)*

We were instructed to list the occupants of each house, to ask if any of them were in the park the previous day, if so did they see anybody in the bushes, if so obtain a description, did they know of anybody having a knife, anybody in the area have a mental history, had anybody suddenly left home?

All these and other answers soon filled a large section of my notebook. I was wearing my battered old grey duffle coat and this seemed to attract the attention of the press, who were in evidence everywhere, national as well local newsmen.

Some photographers followed me and a number of my photos subsequently appeared in the national press. I was, of course, only one of the many Detective Constables on the squad.

Door-to-door enquiries in Barnfield Road. *(Daily Sketch)*

None of the squad went off duty until late that evening, and the following days were fully occupied by not only door to door questioning over a wider area but following up various leads and enquiries that were booked out to us individually. (More than 3,500 individuals were interviewed in the course of the investigation.)

Written reports had to be submitted, to be collated, indexed and cross-referenced to co-ordinate items of interest. Conferences also took place each afternoon and evening, updating us on the progress of the investigation and suspects that had come up.

On Saturday, 27 February, a reconstruction took place in Mayfield Park, involving as many as possible, especially children, who had been in Mayfield Park on the afternoon of the murder a week earlier.

I was allocated to the Mayfield football pitch, now packed with children and sightseers. The press were again out in full force and my duffle coat appeared to be a great attraction for them.

DAILY HERALD Feb. 22 1960 3

Did you see girl's killer?

THREE children found themselves caught up in a murder hunt—a girl in tartan slacks . . . a small boy with two toy guns . . . a serious-faced girl in the back seat of a police car.

They had answered a loudspeaker appeal by police seeking the killer of nine-year-old Iris Dawkins, found dead with more than a dozen stab wounds in a Southampton park on Saturday.

The children were asked to describe everything they saw as they played in the park.

They were also asked if they saw any-

CHILDREN QUIZZED IN MURDER HUNT

one near the wood where Iris was found . . . someone who might be the killer.

Detectives questioned more than 60 children in the park where Iris was found lying face down a quarter of a mile from her home.

She is thought to have been murdered while scores of people were watching Soccer games on a recreation ground 100 yards away.

Houdini man dies in chains

THE body of a 29-year-old London man, dressed in a skin-diving suit and gas mask and chained to the bed, was found in his Toronto flat yesterday.

Police say the man, Peter Corfield, a draughtsman, had died while practising a Houdini escape act.

PADLOCKED

Last night his father, Mr Thomas Corfield, of Valley-road, Streatham, said: "Peter took up escapism as a hobby three years ago. He used to try various ways

of escape from different gadgets."

Toronto police say that Peter had been dead for five days. Heavy chains over his rubber suit padlocked him tightly to a steel bed. An Army gas mask, with eye-pieces taped, covered his head. A post-mortem examination showed he had died from asphyxiation.

Peter, who was single, left a structural draughtsman's job

three years ago to work in Canada.

Said his father: "He was boyish in many ways but had a very mature mind and was a first-class draughtsman."

Missing teacher —Yard to help

Scotland Yard last night was asked to trace 23-year-old Lillian McCarthy, a teacher, who has been missing from a Bloomsbury, London, Y.W.C.A. hostel since February 4.

THE HUNT IN THE PARK

Police ask children in the park "Did you see Iris?" She was playing here with other children just before she was murdered.

Top: *(Daily Herald)*

Left: *(Daily Sketch)*

Right: On Mayfield Park football pitch.

(Daily Sketch)

A break through came on Monday 29 February when a 10 year old boy stated he had seen Iris whilst she was heading home. He was taken, with his father, to Bitterne Police Station for more detailed questioning, where he said he had a knife with him and whilst playing 'chase' with Iris they had both fallen.

He was holding his knife "and it might have gone into her". He also said "When she fell over I fell on top of her and I think the knife went into her shoulder, just a little bit. She was lying down and her eyes were open and she was breathing all right, I thought she was playing".

The boy was allowed to leave Bitterne Station and reports were submitted to the Director of Public Prosecutions. The boy later withdrew his previous statements, saying he hadn't, in fact, seen Iris and did not have a knife. However, following a reply from the DPP, the boy, who was only called "Jeffrey" because of his age, was charged with the murder.

He appeared before Mr Justice Pilcher at Winchester, on 12 July 1960, and on the second day the Judge ruled that there was insufficient evidence and it was unsafe for the trial to continue. He instructed the jury to return a 'not guilty' verdict and 'Jeffrey' was released.

One aspect that the reader may find comical, arising out of this tragedy, is that before the murder squad was closed down, with the murder considered solved, the about to be appointed Chief Constable, Mr Alfred Cullen, first addressed us. He checked that the parade room was secure, and in a lowered conspiratorial tone said "I do not want what I am about to say to go beyond this room and discussed elsewhere." We wondered what on earth was coming.

He continued "I am proud of the work you have done and am aware that many of you have used your own vehicles on this lengthy enquiry." (There was only one CID car in the Force, used by senior officers only, and we had all worked nine continuous days of 12 to 14 hour tours of duty without a break, so we anticipated something special coming up, although he was regarded as 'careful' with expenditure.)

He then said, "I have therefore decided that each of you will receive a special payment of ten shillings (50p) towards your petrol expenses, but I repeat, I do not want others to know of this as it is a confidential payment". Petrol was five shillings a gallon at this time.

Chief Constable Alf Cullen

The murder was considered as closed, until eight years later when DC Dennis Luty, a member of the Vice Squad detained a man in Mayfield Park with a knife. He initially admitted he was waiting to rob somebody of their wallet, but then said he was responsible for the murder of Iris Dawkins in Mayfield Park eight years earlier.

At the time of the murder he was 13 years of age and living in nearby Lawrence Grove, Weston, leading off Archery Grove. He made a written statement detailing how the killing had taken place. Everything he said fitted exactly what was known at the time, including an accurate description of the stab wounds.

One fact that had never been published, and not even told to the murder team but restricted to a handful of senior officers, was that Iris had been stabbed twice in the throat. He also gave a very accurate description of the actual murder scene, another fact that had not been released to the press, and took officers to within a few yards of where Iris' body had been found.

He later appeared at Hampshire Assizes, Winchester, and after adjourning for two and a half hours, the jury returned a guilty verdict and the man was sentenced to be detained during Her Majesty's Pleasure.

Dennis Luty justifiably rose through the ranks, reaching the high rank of Detective Superintendent with the internal investigation division (known in the force as the 'rubber heel squad', investigating the wrong doings of police officers) but sadly, died in December 2006.

I have seen the official police photographs of the murder scene, with the poor girl's body lying on the muddy ground, as well as the mortuary photos showing all the terrible stab wounds in detail. I found it very upsetting, even though I was hardened to such scenes, as I had two very young daughters and could identify with the parents.

(For a more detailed account of the murder, see my book "Southampton Murder Victims".)

After the murder investigation I returned to normal duties, a round of house and shop breakings, minor thefts, shoplifters, but an increase in the fraud cases involving selling goods the subject of a hire-purchase agreement where the goods remain the property of the original owner.

There had been some changes in the Force structure by this time. Charles Box had retired 1 April, 1960, replaced, as previously stated, by Alf Cullen. Det/Supt. Bob Masters was made Chief Superintendent (the first one in the Force) as well as being appointed Deputy Chief Constable, and Ch/Insp. Wilf Weeks was promoted to Det/Supt.

One case at this time stands out in my memory. It started when a 29 year old free-lance car salesman, who I shall call 'Richard', approached a finance company in Shirley Road and asked to be directly financed in the sale of motor vehicles. 'Richard' had a very good background, a public schoolboy, a former private tutor in the household of the British Ambassador to Rome, Sir Victor Mallett, followed by being an assistant master at a Preparatory School.

The finance company agreed to finance him and he was given hire purchase agreement forms to be completed in respect of his customers. 'Richard', over the next three weeks, submitted completed agreements alleging the sale and delivery of eight top quality vehicles to various customers. He was paid the outstanding balance in respect of these vehicles, amounting to £2,600 but when repayments were not received by the finance company they made enquiries and discovered the sales were bogus.

The finance company secretary called at Shirley police station to report the position and I made enquiries to confirm that the alleged sales were made to non-existent customers. Further enquiries showed that the vehicles actually existed and 'Richard' had purchased them, on his blank HP Agreements, from various garages. In every case he placed a deposit on the vehicle, so as to obtain the registration book from the seller and also insured them with various insurance companies, using the false names and addresses shown on the HP Agreements. It transpired that he did this so that the finance company's suspicions would not be aroused should they decide to check with the taxation authority. He had therefore perpetrated a carefully organised fraud which was, in the short term, cleverly planned to avoid detection.

I then discovered that 'Richard' was in possession of a yacht in the Christchurch area and intended sailing to the Channel Islands. The information came from a man who was, I felt, partially involved in the fraud, but I decided to use him as a prosecution witness. This move proved invaluable as I was able to obtain a warrant for 'Richard''s arrest and travel to Weymouth with DC Ian Sharrocks, with the informant, who was able to point out 'Richard' outside Weymouth railway station, where he had arranged to meet him.

It was therefore simple to detain him, travelling back to Southampton where he was later charged with six offences of obtaining money from the finance company by false pretences.

When the case first came to the magistrates court, when 'Richard' appeared on remand, I once more learnt how important it was to keep accurate records of everything, including the proper itemising of property. His solicitor, Alan Woodford approached me, in the presence of the Court Officer, Insp. Ted Booth, and alleged that when I arrested 'Richard' at Weymouth he had a map of Weymouth in his possession, marked with an X and some writing. It was alleged that I had told 'Richard' "You can't have this" and tore it up in front of him. Mr Woodford said he required this map as an exhibit, obviously intending to use this as a means of attacking my integrity and to show I had behaved improperly.

This was a gross untruth and I was delighted to get the prisoner's property from the Station Sergeant and recover the map, handing it to Mr Woodford. After the remand Mr Woodford apologised to me for making the allegation, also instructing his client to do the same, which he did.

The case involved a mass of documents, copies of the agreements, statements from witnesses etc., but I ensured that all the legal requirements were fully complied with, with no possible loopholes. I had learnt something from my earlier experiences.

The defence tried delaying tactics, with the committal proceedings adjourned several times, but when 'Richard' at last appeared before the Recorder at the Quarter Sessions, to my annoyance the case was put back to the next Quarter Sessions. All the time 'Richard' was on bail, but when he finally appeared to be dealt with he was found guilty and sentenced to a total of 21 months imprisonment. Honour was satisfied.

The time sequence of events may be of interest to serving police officers. 'Richard' was arrested on 4 June and my extensive enquiries were completed, with case papers and large number of exhibits, submitted in time for the committal on 29 June. He then appeared at Southampton Quarter Sessions on 26 July and dealt with. It was only because of a defence request that the trial, lasting three days, was adjourned to 26 September. I believe that as long as a year now regularly takes place between committal and trial.

My duty with Shirley CID came to an end on 2 October 1960, when I attended the Metropolitan Detective Training School at Hendon. I was also simultaneously transferred to Headquarters CID, this to commence on my return from Hendon.

13. NSY DETECTIVE TRAINING SCHOOL – 1960

I was delighted to be sent to such a prestigious establishment, the school in Hendon where all the famous New Scotland Yard detectives had been trained. All the instructors were experienced detectives and my course tutor was the well-known DI 'Jock' Forbes, a former member of the renowned Flying Squad. During the after hours drinking sessions he regaled us with stories of how the Squad had trapped London villains, stories that cannot possibly be repeated.

It was here that I discovered something unique; the public house behind the NSY building sold, not just the normal crisps and sandwiches, but cooked sausage and mash. This was the first time I had ever known of cooked food being sold in a public house, something my parents, who had run a number of Southampton public houses, had never thought of.

The training was intensive, with points of law gone into in great detail. Some of the outside lecturers were outstanding in their field, including such personalities as Sir Theobald Mathew, KBE, MC, the Director of Public Prosecutions. We also attended post mortems carried out at St Thomas' Hospital by the distinguished pathologist Keith Simpson, who explained the finer points of determining cause of death.

One amusing incident springs to mind. The law of evidence was being discussed and it was emphasised that a confession extracted by means of force is inadmissible, so violence of any sort towards a suspect, no matter how slight, should never be used. A visiting overseas student, looking puzzled, put his hand up and when asked for his question said "If you don't first hit them, they don't say nothin". He was corrected in no uncertain terms.

A visit to the Black Museum, restricted to police officers, was also fascinating. Exhibits from notorious murders that we had all read about, blood stained weapons and gruesome photos, brought home what detective work was all about.

On my return from the ten week course, now a fully qualified and experienced detective, I collected my personal belongings from Shirley and took them to police headquarters CID, where I was allocated my own desk.

The students and instructors, 10 December 1960, with Sir Theobald Mathew sitting fifth from left and DI 'Jock' Forbes third from right. I am standing in front row, third from right.

14. HEADQUARTERS C.I.D. – 1961

I was delighted to be back in the large CID office in the Civic Centre, with my own personal desk and was warmly greeted by the other officers, as although it was in no way a form of promotion, it was nevertheless recognition that I was now in the centre of things. This office was also directly responsible for dock matters, in conjunction with the British Transport Docks Board police, so stowaways came under its remit and I had many of those to deal with.

However, my first duty was to report to the Army Camp, Winchester, weapons range, to become authorised to handle police .32 and .38 calibre revolvers. Six of us at a time were trained by DC Ken Holmes, an experienced weapons instructor. As I had spent my National Service with the 60th Rifles I was very familiar with firearms, of all types, so found it straightforward. However, DC Norman Roberts frightened us all with his habit of closing both eyes, holding the revolver with both his arms fully outstretched and waving them about wildly as he did so. Poor Norman had never handled a weapon before and we feared for our lives at times.

On the odd occasion, when a firearm needed to be carried for a specific duty, we drew a Webley Scott .32 semi-automatic pistol from two of the six revolvers held in the Police Lost Property Department safe in the Civic Centre. I suspect that these pistols were in fact weapons surrendered by members of the public who had given them up during arms amnesties, because there were no spare magazines, no holsters and the guns and their ammunition were kept in old cardboard boxes. The Deputy or Chief Constable's permission had to be obtained before any officer could be issued with either of the two Webley Scott pistols.

It wasn't long before I was issued with a revolver to carry out my first of many Bank of England armed escorts. Uniformed officers attending in marked police cars were issued with larger .38 weapons but I carried one of the Webley Scott .32 semi-automatics. DI Bert Adams issued me with a revolver and ammunition, and told me that the weapon had to be concealed in one pocket and the magazine of six rounds carried in another pocket. I retorted "Did that mean that if we were held up by an armed gang I was to shout out 'please wait, play fair, give me time to load'?" He told me that these were his instructions but what I did was up to me. I therefore loaded the revolver and placed the safety catch on. It would thus be simple to make it ready for action.

The procedure was that we met the bullion train at Southampton Central Station, stood by whilst large wooden boxes of banknotes were loaded into a lorry and when completed climbed in the back with the boxes and travelled with them to the Bank of England in the High Street. The large black metal side gates in the High Street were opened, something one just never normally saw happen, and we entered inside and waited whilst the boxes were manhandled down a chute at the rear of the bank, sliding down directly to the vault inside. It was always a fascinating experience.

Life continued much as it had at Shirley, but with many more shoplifters, forcible entries and stowaways to deal with. I also dealt with a case of bigamy for the first time – a novel experience and a very simple and straightforward matter to write up. The man was committed to the Hampshire Assizes on 3 March and appeared on 9 March, when he was conditionally discharged for 12 months. Such a rapid court appearance could never take place today.

I also found it interesting to discover that I had to deal with thefts on board ships, as they did not come under the jurisdiction of the BTDB police. In every case I was supplied with a first class meal, so looked forward to such reports.

To confirm that my nickname of 'Luck Jim' still held, I was on late turn, driving the CID Hillman, accompanied by DC Ian Sharrocks, and as we drove along Commercial Road at 11.25pm we noticed three men standing alongside a motor scooter. None of them seemed to be dressed for riding it, so I stopped the car and walked back to check them. As I did so one of them, with a pillion passenger, rode towards me on the scooter.

I called out for them to stop, but they drove past me towards Totton. We gave chase in the car and managed to force them to stop in Millbrook Road.

We questioned them and when Ian asked one of the men for the number of the machine he replied "You can read it for yourself". This immediately resulted in both men being detained and taken to PHQ, where they eventually admitted having taken it from near the Gaumont Theatre. They were both soldiers based at Marchwood and intended to return there on the machine. Both were charged with taking and driving away without consent and were dealt with at court the following morning. The driver was fined £20 and his passenger £10, both being disqualified for 12 months. A good little routine 'stop job'.

I had a good number of such lucky 'stop jobs', especially when driving the unmarked CID Hillman, as those checked did not realise I was a police officer until they were stopped. I seemed to have a 'nose' for suspicious individuals and to recognise when I was being lied to.

I later suffered an embarrassing incident. The receptionist at the Sailor's Home in Oxford Street reported that one of the residents had climbed over the counter and stolen cash from the till. When I attended, with DC Tony Bushrod, she gave me the man's description and said he had gone into the nearby Grapes public house.

When we entered the Grapes I saw a man answering the description, told him who I was and asked him to come outside. He, aggressively, told me where to go, and it took a considerable struggle to take him outside and forcibly get him into the CID car and taken to PHQ. On arrival I was told that the Sailor's Home receptionist had phoned to say she had seen the struggle outside and that we had the wrong man.

I apologised to him, telling him it was his own fault because if he had come outside when asked it would have been resolved. He made no complaint at all, and when we took him back to Oxford Street we were amazed to discover that the thief was still inside the Grapes. We arrested the right man this time, but again after a struggle.

The Grapes public house (Dave Goddard)

What I felt to be one of the 'perks' of the job, travelling to other parts of the country to collect prisoners, fell to me several times. Travelling to Goole, West Riding, to collect one of my prisoners arrested there, was enjoyable because I was well and truly entertained by the local CID officers.

But this was more than equalled when I had to fly to Dublin to collect one of my wanted persons. The local Garda CID encouraged me to try some real Irish Guinness, having explained that bottled Guinness is a single X strength, the draught Guinness supplied to England double XX but that in Ireland, and only exported to the United States, treble XXX. They also told me that if the froth at the top of the glass vanishes, the glass will be filled again for free. I had no option but to try a pint, finding it so delicious that I had a second pint, together with a double Irish whiskey. The local CID officers then carried me back to my hotel, semi-conscious, and I truly fell in love with Ireland, but had to fly back to Southampton the following morning with my prisoner and a terrible hangover.

This case showed a difference in sentencing policy to today and was a simple case of theft of cash from an unattended jacket. On our return to Southampton he was charged with the theft of £110 and when dealt with at the magistrates' court remanded in custody to Quarter Sessions for sentence because of his long record.

He was eligible for Preventive Detention and I had to serve the appropriate PD Forms on him. His record meant he was now liable for a sentence of between five and 14 years, even though the offence charged was relatively minor. In the event he received a sentence of three years for the simple theft. Preventive Detention, with its long sentences, followed a conviction of Corrective Training, where one would receive a sentence of between two and four years.

My stubbornness, when it came to following up on a hunch, showed itself when the manager of Austin Reed, Tailors, Above Bar, came into the CID office one Saturday morning to report a suspicious customer. He said that a man had entered the shop that morning to purchase a suit. He gave his name as Heppel, staying at the Royal Hotel, and as the suit needed some alterations was to return that afternoon to pay for and collect it. The manager had phoned the Royal Hotel to check on something and was told they had no resident of that name. The manager then realised that the man answered the description of someone described in one of the organisation's internal notices as wanted for 'bouncing' cheques in one of their branches,

I checked the Police Gazette, based on the manager's internal notice, and found it referred to a man wanted for false pretences, giving his name and full description. I then waited in the shop for some time that afternoon, until the man came in to collect his suit. I stood behind him and watched him write a cheque as payment. This was important as there was only a power of arrest for false pretences when found committing.

However, I then realised that he did not match the description of the wanted man at all, so there was only the matter of not staying at the Royal Hotel to be cleared up. I therefore waited until he left the shop and stopped him on the pavement, telling him who I was and that he answered the description of a wanted man. Although this was untrue I somehow felt there was something not quite right about him.

I asked him his name and address, and he told me 'Heppel', staying at the Royal Hotel. I asked him, very politely, if he would mind coming to PHQ with me so I could verify his identity, and he replied that although it was inconvenient, as he had friends waiting for him at the hotel, he didn't mind as long as it would not take too long.

When we arrived at the CID office I asked how long he had stayed at the Royal Hotel and he said he hadn't yet booked in, but was about to. At my request he showed me a letter addressed to him, with a London address, together with a cheque book in the name of Heppel. I then telephoned NSY and they confirmed there was no record of the cheque book being stolen. At this stage I had no genuine reason to detain him further, but had a hunch that everything was not what it seemed. I therefore politely asked if I could search him, calling him Sir, but he angrily refused, saying he now wished to leave the station. I asked him to please be patient for a little longer, continuing to call him Sir, then saw the duty DI and asked permission to phone the London bank shown on the cheque. I had to ask permission for this because such a call was expensive. Permission was refused.

I then, without permission, phoned the bank anyway, and by a tremendous stroke of luck caught a bank clerk in, although banks then closed all day Saturdays. When I gave him the cheque book number he excitedly said "Is he still with you? We have been chasing up these cheques for two weeks. It was stolen in the post", giving me the London address on the envelope the detained man had shown me. I took further details from the bank clerk and then returned to the man and said, no longer calling him Sir or in a gentle polite voice "I'm not asking, I'm telling, turn your pockets out. I'm going to search you, you're nicked."

He looked me straight in the eye and calmly removed his wrist watch, saying "You'll want this, it came from a shop in the smoke," (slang name for London). He gave me other articles he had obtained by passing cheques from the book and explained he had been staying in a guest house when a letter arrived, containing the chequebook, for another resident, and he had opened it. He was later handed over to the Metropolitan police and dealt with there. I was very pleased with myself. It turned out that a police-woman had dealt with the reported theft but had failed to enter the details in the stolen property index.

An interesting theft came my way; a car with no identification plates. A 1961 Ford Consul de Luxe, two tone blue, newly manufactured by the Ford Motor Company at their Dagenham plant, was delivered to the Percy Hendy Ford Dealers in Dorset Street. It was unregistered and only identifiable by the manufacturer's unique numbers stamped on the chassis, radiator and engine.

When the assistant manager went to collect it for display in their showrooms, it could not be found and when a search of all their premises failed to locate it the theft was reported to the police. Two weeks later PC Bob Noyce, Traffic Dept., saw an identical model, bearing the registration number 107UCR, parked in the car park at the junction of Ordnance Road and Bellevue Terrace. Bob checked with motor taxation and discovered that this number had not yet been allocated, so the case was passed to CID.

I commenced discreet observations on the vehicle at 11.00am and maintained them until 2.02pm, when I saw a man go to the car, appear to be on the point of unlocking it, change his mind and enter a house in Ordnance Road. I continued the observations and was joined by DS Jim Glass. The man, who I shall call 'David', returned at 2.45pm, unlocked and opened the car boot to place something inside, then unlocked the car front door, then closed it and walked away.

We stopped him, told him who we were and asked him if he owned the car. He said he certainly did, having bought it from a dealer three weeks before Easter. This was several weeks before the vehicle was actually made. He was therefore arrested and taken to PHQ, where he refused to answer any further questions, telling me "I'm not saying anything. All you are doing is writing this down and acting like a schoolboy". This did not endear him to me.

The car displayed a current excise licence, altered to conform to the false number, and it was found to have been stolen from a car parked in Ordnance Road, where

'David' lived. We also found that some of the identifying plates on the car had been altered, with a figure 1 altered to 4; otherwise it conformed to the numbers allocated to the stolen Ford. However, another plate on the radiator was unaltered and this showed the full correct numbers.

The Ford Consul outside the CID office, and the stamped engine number
(Hampshire Constabulary History Society)

'David' was extremely uncooperative and sarcastic. At one point, when asked how much he had allegedly paid the dealer for the car, said "£750 in cash, but I've eaten the receipt". When I told him I was going to charge him with stealing the vehicle he replied "I demand you produce evidence to prove ownership of the car." He continued to insist he had bought the car and when further questioned merely replied "You told me I'm not obliged to say anything".

I had no doubt whatsoever that he had not only stolen it from the showroom (he was also in possession of the ignition key) but had stolen and forged the excise licence. To play safe I charged him with both stealing the car, value £760, and the alternative charge of receiving it knowing it to be stolen, as well as the theft of the excise licence.

'David' had a long list of convictions and was eligible for Preventive Detention, but when I tried to serve the PD forms on him he refused to admit the convictions. I had to obtain written and fingerprint proof, a time consuming business. He was proving difficult throughout, but it served no useful purpose. When he eventually appeared at Quarter Sessions, after a three day trial, he was found guilty of receiving the stolen car and of stealing the excise licence.

I was therefore right to have considered the alternative charge, as he was sentenced to five years and one year's imprisonment, consecutive, making six years in all.

It was a regular practice to carry out a midnight road block, with traffic cars and uniformed officers, on the main roads out of Southampton. Vehicles would be searched, in an effort to discover stolen property, especially if there was an increase in breaking offences. I was involved in such a check one night, at the Chilworth Crossroads, because there had been a number of cases of safebreakings.

This particular night I walked along the row of waiting vehicles, looking at the drivers as I did so, and saw the occupants of one, a man and wife, dressed in evening clothes. I saw that the headlights were on full, and asked the driver to please use his sidelights. He then turned the lights off altogether, then back on and the ignition off, and then turned on the windscreen wipers. I pointed this out to him and told him this was a police check and would he mind telling me where he came from? He then mumbled something and I could only make out the words 'party' and 'hotel', so I asked him to please get out of the car.

To my amazement he got out, caught hold of the side of the car and cart-wheeled along its entire length before falling to the ground – hopelessly drunk. PC Roy Harvey was nearby so I passed the case onto him, a very clear case of drunk in charge, but no breathalyser yet invented, so it was the opinion of the police officer and police surgeon that counted.

30 May 1961 saw me taking part in a Careers Exhibition at Southampton Guildhall. The Borough police had a stand and I was chosen to represent the CID. It gave me a break from enquiries, but I had a backlog to catch up on when I returned to the office.

From left to right are: PC George Cordery and his dog, PS Fred Wallace, Cadet Keith White, myself and Insp. George Mansell.

In June I dealt with an interesting fraud case. An electrical retailer, 'Doug' in Dean Road, Bitterne, entered into an agreement with a finance company to be financed in respect of the sale of electrical goods on hire purchase and credit terms. The arrangement was that 'Doug' would be paid by cheque for the total value of goods sold each week, and he would collect the weekly repayments from the customers and repay the finance company each month.

During the ensuing three months 'Doug' submitted various hire purchase and credit agreements, for which he was paid, but after the first month failed to pay any money obtained from customers' repayments. The finance company reported the matter when they discovered that 'Doug' had just been made bankrupt with debts of nearly £3,000, so they were now suspicious.

I made enquiries into the matter and by examining a mass of documents and checking on those concerned, discovered that not only had 'Doug' failed to repay money he had collected from customers, many of the agreements were fictitious. He had therefore committed offences of obtaining money by false pretences from the finance company, as well as fraudulent conversion of money collected on their behalf.

My enquiries were quite extensive, including taking statements from customers, the finance company and obtaining a statement of affairs from the Official Receiver. I obtained a warrant for his arrest on a specimen charge and when I carried it out 'Doug' was co-operative when questioned and readily admitted the offences. I charged him with six offences and he had a further 20 offences taken into consideration. When he eventually appeared at court he was fined a total of £75, something that didn't make sense to me in view of his financial position.

A change in the law came into effect on 3 August 1961 when a new Suicide Act made it no longer a criminal offence to attempt to commit suicide – something I felt was long overdue.

One of my off-duty relaxations was sea fishing and one late evening I spent it fishing from the end of the Jetty in Weston Shore. It was a good spot for bass and flounders, and on this particular evening I was joined by DS Norman McDonald. We were quite successful and carried on until the early hours.

At around 1.45am I lost some bottom tackle when it became caught up, so returned to my car on the shoreline to get some replacement. As I approached my car, parked in complete darkness, I saw a small group of children who, on seeing me, ran away. I instinctively gave chase, but they were too fast for me, so I continued the chase in my car, noticing packets of sweets strewn along the road as I did so. I found two of the children in Swift Road and told them who I was, taking them back in my car to Weston Shore, where I was joined by DS McDonald. I then found some packets of sweets on the floor of my car, where one of the children had sat.

The two were taken to Bitterne police station, where I discovered that a group of eight boys and girls, aged between 12 and 14, had been reported missing from their home that evening. It didn't take long to discover that the confectionary kiosk on Weston Shore had been broken open, with a large quantity of sweets stolen. My fishing expedition concluded with me spending the rest of the day tracing and interviewing a total of eight children, in the presence of their parents, and reporting them for summons for the thefts. I was saddened that because of their previous record, six of them were sent to an Approved School and two placed on Probation for two years. DS McDonald was most concerned that I made it very clear in my report what we two were doing on Weston Shore, in the darkness, in the early hours.

I was again 'Lucky Jim' when I was called to the scene of an unprovoked attack one August afternoon. Two men, after having a meal in the Empire Restaurant, Oxford Street, had, without warning, badly assaulted a man on the pavement outside. They ran off and an ambulance and police were called. The PC attending called for CID and by the time I attended the injured man had been taken to hospital. Once I knew the position I asked the manager if I could take the waitress in the CID car to look for the men responsible, and he agreed.

We then toured the area whilst I discussed the assault with the witness. From her description it seemed possible that the two men were seamen, so after touring the lower town area we entered the docks. I saw that the RMS Queen Mary was berthed there and asked the waitress if she had ever been on such a large ship. She hadn't, so I took her on board, showing the master at arms my warrant card. Such a thing would be impossible today because of the high security measures in force.

I'm afraid I didn't bother to ask permission of any ship's officer, but took the witness for a tour of the ship, admiring the wonderful fittings. We then entered the forecastle crew quarters, a labyrinth of alleyways and cabins, and whilst walking down a corridor a man, stripped to the waist and with a towel around his neck, walked out of a cabin in front of us. The witness exclaimed "That's one of them" and I immediately detained the crewman, who readily admitted having been involved in the assault.

RMS Queen Mary

It was a million to one chance that we came across the man. I didn't really know that he was a seaman and in any event could have searched the ship for a week without seeing him. Had we walked down the corridor a matter of minutes earlier or later we would not have come across him. I certainly justified being called lucky, and when the case came to court his defending counsel did not believe that it was pure chance that we had come across him; he maintained that I had received some information.

The circumstances were the prisoner, aged 20, said that when he was 10 years old he had been indecently assaulted by the injured man, and when he and his friend came across him they decided to punish him. Unfortunately, the man suffered a severe eye injury and without urgent treatment could have lost the sight in one eye.

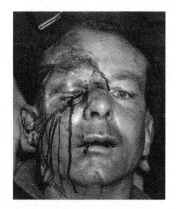

The injured victim, with me supporting his head whilst the official police photo was taken *(Hampshire Constabulary History Society)*

The prisoner made a voluntary statement about the assault, declining to say who his friend was. I removed his clothing, blood stained, from his cabin, before charging him with grievous bodily harm with intent, a serious charge. When he pleaded guilty at the Winchester Assize court he was conditionally discharged for 12 months and I was quite satisfied with that result.

August 1961 saw me on duty at the County Ground for the Hampshire v Australia cricket match, looking for pickpockets. I had an enjoyable day, on duty from 10.00am until 7.40pm, but didn't have a clue what I was supposed to be looking for. I had no training or expertise in this area but suppose it satisfied the Chief Constable's requirements.

A change in my financial circumstances came about on 1 September 1961 when a decision was made that from that date officer's pay would be monthly, i.e. one twelfth of annual salary. It would be paid in cash until the last pay day in March, 1962, from when it would be paid by cheque. This was to allow time for officers to open bank accounts, something that few of us, including me, had. I opened one with the Midland Bank but it was some time before we managed to get back, financially, on an even keel. Salaries were paid directly into our accounts in July 1962.

One case that I have regretted for many decades started one evening when DS Geoff Hayes, DC Ian Sharrocks and I toured the lower town in the CID car. We had visited a couple of public houses, purely to see if any informants were there, of course, and then bought some pies in the St Mary Street pie shop. We sat in the car outside St Mary's Church, in Chapel Road, eating our pies, close to the underground public toilets in front of us. We then saw a very well-known local TV presenter enter the toilets, leave after a short time, then return, then leave again, and then once more enter the toilets.

Having had two pints I needed to go to the toilet, and when I went down to the urinals stood at the first stall to urinate. I saw the TV presenter, standing at another stall, look at me and I smiled at him in recognition, but to my surprise he then walked over to me, with his penis in his hand and stood alongside me. I was still urinating and as I finished he suddenly put out his left hand and caught hold of my penis. I immediately drew away and indicated he should follow me up the stairs, where I told him I was a police officer and took him across to the CID car, where I told DS Hayes what had happened.

The unfortunate man then said "Do you know who I am? This will mean the finish of my career". DS Hayes told him he would be taken to PHQ to discuss the matter and the poor man said "What have I done, my God, what have I done? This means the finish of me. I implore you, I beg you, you don't know what this means to me, my life, my career, all I've worked for. I've had so much worry this past week and don't know what came over me; I've never done this sort of thing before."

DS Hayes felt he had no option but to report the man for summons, for indecent assault, but the TV Presenter was never heard of again. He left Southern TV suddenly and it was rumoured he had gone to Australia. I have always deeply regretted taking the action I did, but homosexuality was then considered to be a very serious offence and could not be overlooked. Times have now changed, of course.

I not only became involved in numerous thefts and other offences on board ships, but because the docks were part of Southampton, and thus under our ultimate jurisdiction,

I also sometimes had to deal with thefts within the dock complex. One such theft occupied me full time, with long working days, and became a major incident.

It started with a report in November 1961 from the docks CID of a large scale theft from the International Cold Store at 108 Berth, where foodstuffs were stored on behalf of various wholesalers. The British American Tobacco Company, Millbrook, had a large quantity of export market Senior Service and Rough Rider brands of cigarettes stored there under refrigeration. The brands were exclusively sold overseas and therefore not available in this country.

The reason for storing the cigarettes under refrigeration was that it was suspected that the tobacco might contain the egg of a tobacco weevil. The tobacco company knew that exposure to low temperature destroyed the egg and it was decided to carry out an experiment to see if the cigarettes could still be sold.

Because of the valuable nature of these goods the cartons, each containing 12,000 cigarettes, were stored in chambers 4 and 8 of the Cold Store, which were padlocked when not being worked as a special security measure. All Cold Store keys were handed in to the docks police at the end of the working day, normally 10.00pm and collected by the early duty engine room staff at 8.00am the following day.

When the cigarettes had completed their refrigeration storage they were returned to BAT, when two cartons of Rough Rider cigarettes were found short. A week later, when the Senior Service cigarettes were returned, it was discovered that the consignment was 15 cartons short. All the cases could be identified by the code numbers marked on the side of the fiberite cases and on each carton of 200. The 139,000 cigarettes had a manufacturing value of £1,391, but their street value was considerably more. These losses were reported to the BTDB police with the preliminary investigation carried out by DS Jack Welfare and DC Jack Diaper.

The International Cold Store at 108 Berth, Herbert Walker Avenue *(Jeff Pain)*

They discovered that an electrician, who I shall call 'Eddy', frequently collected the Cold Store keys from the police at 12 Gate, including those of chambers 4 and 8, an hour or more before he was due to start work at 8.00am, in some cases arriving as early as 6.00am. He needed access to chamber 4 and 8 because it was his responsibility to check the temperatures there, but these early arrival times were not necessary.

The facts were reported by docks police to DI Bert Adams, who decided that I would take over the investigation, as the officer in the case, in conjunction with DS Welfare and DC Diaper.

This was not a problem as I had worked with these officers before and knew them to be extremely efficient and easy to work with. We worked as a team, regardless of rank or position, with only the end result in mind.

DI Bert Adams – later D/Supt Regional Crime Squad

It is essential to prove theft and DS Welfare and DC Diaper obtained the necessary documentation and took statements to legally establish that the missing cartons, with their identifying serial numbers, had been deposited in the Cold Store but were missing when the two chambers were emptied. I would have had considerable difficulty in carrying this out myself but the docks officers had the expertise and experience for doing this.

Further enquiries at the Cold Store revealed that 'Eddy' was the only person who would be on his own in the Cold Store with access to the chambers containing the cigarettes. His early arrivals were not authorised or needed and checking the key book at the 12 Gate police point showed he had arrived for work early long before the cigarettes had been stored there. We suspected he was responsible for stealing the cigarettes and because he had always made early visits, this could be because he also stole meat and chicken stored there. There was a steady and continual unexplained loss of these items at the Cold Store.

We interviewed 'Eddy' at some length at his home, but he denied all knowledge of the missing cigarettes and accounted for his early visits by saying he was conscientious and always checked the lifts as they were continually breaking down. His home, garden and car were searched but nothing incriminating was found so we realised there was nothing substantial against him to warrant further questioning.

However, I later received information from an informant that a man living in Sholing Road, 'Frank', was in possession of cartons of cigarettes, and DS Welfare and I went there early one morning and questioned him. DC Diaper and DC John Baker remained at the front and back of the house to prevent property being removed.

'Frank' at first denied possessing a large quantity of cigarettes, but when told we intended searching the house, saying if he objected we would remain there whilst one of us obtained a warrant, he admitted having cigarettes in his bedroom. We then recovered 7,800 Rough Rider cigarettes and 100 export Senior Service. 'Frank' declined to say where he had obtained the cigarettes, saying he wished to first see his solicitor, and he was taken to Bitterne police station.

As a result of further information we visited another man in Dukes Road, where, after some similar questioning, he admitted having received 2,000 Export Senior Service and 850 Rough Rider cigarettes from 'Frank'.

He had sold or otherwise disposed of some but we found 850 Rough Rider cigarettes in the house, so he was also arrested and taken to Bitterne police station. 'Frank' had, by then, seen his solicitor, Bernard Chill, and now said he wished to make a statement. In this he admitted having bought 74,000 cigarettes from 'Eddy', the Cold Store electrician, and gave us the names and addresses of others he knew had also bought some from 'Eddy'. We then knew that we had a lengthy enquiry as quite a number had to be seen with, hopefully, more cigarettes recovered.

One factor that greatly helped our investigation was that we told suspects we were anxious to recover as many cigarettes as possible, because they 'had a bug' and we wanted to avoid them being smoked. Because BAT did not want any undue publicity about the tobacco weevil, it was not mentioned in witnesses' statements, or in our evidence, and was therefore not publicised in court.

'Eddy' was arrested and taken to police headquarters and detained so that he would be unaware of the others we knew we would be visiting. He declined to answer any questions until he had seen his solicitor, William Ackroyd. He was searched and two padlock keys were found in his pockets. He said they belonged to the Cold Store Engineers' department, but when we later checked this it was found to be untrue.

'Eddy' was then detained whilst we visited a number of premises, interviewing the householders and recovering a large number of Rough Rider and Senior Service cigarettes. After initial denials, admissions were made of the cigarettes having been purchased from 'Frank'. 'Eddy' was charged with the theft of the 74,000 cigarettes we knew he had sold to 'Frank', and when he appeared at court was remanded in custody for seven days, whilst we continued to trace and interview others we believed had purchased some of the stolen cigarettes.

However, before being transferred to Winchester prison 'Eddy' said he was prepared to assist in the recovery of further cigarettes and was taken to a lock up garage in Cleveland Road, Bitterne Park. One of the padlock keys found in his possession fitted one of the garages, in which we found 63,400 cigarettes. The carton serial numbers established they were stolen from the Cold Store.

It then came to light that I had slipped up badly. When I first arrested 'Eddy' he was placed in the small interview room at the back of the CID office for three or four minutes whilst I contacted his solicitor.

I had neglected to first search him and he later told us that whilst in the interview room he had torn up the rent book for the garage and placed the pieces in the waste bin. A search of the room revealed the pieces were still there and I pieced them together with cellotape and it became a part of the evidence. Had I searched him thoroughly before leaving him we would have traced the garage and recovered the 63,400 cigarettes much earlier. This was a lesson well learnt and I never made the same mistake again. Our subsequent enquiries proved to be a time consuming and complicated affair, as some individuals who had bought from either 'Eddy' or 'Frank' had, in turn, sold some to others at a profit. We thus had a chain of transfers to follow in our attempts to recover cigarettes.

To simplify the position, during the week that 'Eddy' remained in custody we visited the addresses of 15 men and women in Bitterne, Totton and Christchurch (We obtained permission from the police in the areas outside Southampton beforehand.) After many denials, and following successful searches, a total of 92,100 cigarettes were recovered and nine individuals charged with receiving stolen property, with others used as witnesses. 'Eddy' was charged with both stealing and receiving the 139,000 cigarettes from the Cold Store and granted bail by the magistrates. We had also discovered that he had sold joints of ham, stolen from the Cold Store, so he was also charged with that theft.

I completed a very detailed report, outlining the progress of the various enquiries, with lists of the different witnesses needed for the charges against each defendant, as well as a chart showing the distribution of cigarettes after the initial sale by 'Eddy'. However, the complications then increased. Nine of the accused were committed for trial at the next Quarter Sessions, some indicating they would plead guilty, others not so, but 'Eddy' failed to appear part way through the committal and a warrant was issued for his arrest. I then discovered that he had sold a Humber Hawk car whilst it was still on hire purchase, committing a further offence of larceny as bailee.

When I checked his home address in Blackthorn Road I discovered that 36 year old 'Eddy' had left Southampton with a 17 year old girl who had been reported as missing from her home. The girl returned a week later, in a distressed state, saying that 'Eddy' had raped her in the Maplton Hotel in London. She made a statement saying that although she originally went away with 'Eddy' willingly, when in the hotel he placed elastoplast over her mouth, threatened her with a knife, removed her clothing and forcibly raped her. The police surgeon examined the girl and said he thought her hymen had been torn very recently.

West End Central police were informed and arrested 'Eddy' at the London hotel, and I travelled there to collect him. I found a roll of elastoplast and a knife in his possession, and took the bloodstained hotel sheets that had been seized by the Metropolitan police. I returned with 'Eddy' to Southampton, charged him with the theft of the Humber Hawk and questioned him extensively concerning the girl's allegations. He denied any forcible rape, saying that she gave her consent. I therefore submitted a report concerning this alleged offence, asking for a direction on a possible charge of abduction of an unmarried girl under the age of 18 years.

The trial of all the accused in connection with the cigarettes took place at the February 1962 Quarter Sessions, resulting in 'Eddy' receiving a sentence of five years. In view of this it was decided to take no further action in respect of the abduction or alleged rape as the abduction only carried a maximum of two years and the rape was difficult to prove. Of the others convicted of receiving, 'Frank' received eight months, two others receiving six months, one three months and four others fines of £100, £30, £30, and £10 respectively. One woman was found not guilty.

There was a sequel to the case when I had the pleasure of a trip to Stafford to prove the conviction of one of the defendants who had been sentenced to six months for receiving cigarettes. He was in breach of a Conditional Discharge at Stafford Quarter Sessions and I had to attend, together with a Certificate of Conviction for the Southampton offence signed by the Town Clerk. The man received a further six months, but concurrent.

I later attended a sad case of an accidental death on board RMS Queen Elizabeth. The ship was berthed at the Ocean Terminal and the deceased had been employed by Harland and Wolff the previous day but had failed to 'clock off' at the end of his shift and it was assumed he had returned home. However, the following day, as he had not, in fact, returned home, a search was made of the ship and his body found in the ship's bilge, where he had been working.

RMS Queen Elizabeth berthed at the OceanTerminal *(Bert Moody)*

A metal floor plate had been removed during work carried out when the ship was last in port and had not been replaced. It appeared the deceased had slipped into the resultant cavity when alone in that area, and fell about six feet into a mixture of oil and water. I was present when his oil soaked body was removed from the bilge and when it was searched at the mortuary not only was his tally (a numbered metal disk allocated to individual workmen) found, a large number of others were also found belonging to workmates in his section. I was satisfied that his death was accidental, but the Harland and Wolff manager was most unhappy to discover that most of the gang had left the ship early, leaving the deceased to hand in their tallies when he was the last to leave. At the inquest a verdict of misadventure was brought in.

I seemed to have a large number of ship enquiries booked out to me, thefts, forcible entries, stowaways etc. and I became very familiar with the shipping fraternity. Among the ships I visited during 1962 alone, in addition to *RMS Queen Elizabeth* was *RMS*

Queen Mary (three times, a suicide, sudden death and statement for another force); *RMS Saxonia* (stowaway); *SS Oriana* (theft); *RMS Edinburgh Castle* (theft by crew member); *RMS Pretoria Castle* (forcible entry to stores); *SS Northern Star* (arrest of stewardess for Met police); *RMS Capetown Castle* (forcible entry to store) and *SS Himalaya* (theft).

I was then appointed Deputy Coroner's Officer, a privileged position, as I relieved DS John Creighton, when he was on holiday or sick leave. John had become Coroner's Officer following the retirement of DS John Jefferis. I was taught many new procedures and my ship visits became even more frequent, starting with the *SS Mauretania* and continuing with too many to mention, certainly several each month. It involved mainly passengers but also crew members who had died during the voyage and kept in the ship's hospital until it berthed at Southampton. A special procedure had to be followed with shipboard deaths, to include a copy of the ship's log and statements from the master or first officer.

One shipboard death nearly cost me my job. Docks police were called early one morning to a Russian fishing trawler, the *Enesei* as they wanted an ambulance. When the police arrived they were told it was no longer needed and the crew refused to allow the police on board. It then transpired that the ship's 29 year old First Officer had been shot through the heart with the ship's small calibre rifle and had left a suicide note. They stated they were awaiting the arrival of Russian embassy officials from London.

I went to the ship with DI Bert Adams and explained that I was the Coroner's Officer and as such had authority over any body in the port, whether or not on board a foreign ship. They then allowed us on board, where we saw the very young captain, who spoke excellent English. He explained that the suicide note stated the deceased had received a letter from his wife saying she had left him, taking with her their small son. Whilst we were waiting the arrival of the embassy officials all the crew who passed us, without exception, had serious faces and appeared not to speak English. We were made to feel most unwelcome.

Once the officials arrived, in a large black limousine, all dressed in long black overcoats and black homburg hats, I explained that if I was allowed to view the body and carry out satisfactory enquiries, I would contact HM Coroner and see if he would give permission for the body to remain on board and return to Russia. They were pleased with this and when DI Adams and I saw the body, with a small hole in the heart region of his chest, and examined the rifle, we were satisfied there were no suspicious circumstances.

We then found that all the crew spoke excellent English, the captain opened a bottle of Vodka, brought out some black bread, white butter, loads of caviar, and we then toasted the Queen, Winston Churchill, Stalin and as many personalities as the captain could think of. There were smiles all round and each time the captain managed to fill each glass right up to the very brim, with the contents downed at one gulp. By the time we finished the toasts DI Adams and I were not fit for anything, most especially the CID car I had driven down in, parked at the ship's gangway. We had no option but to ask the docks police to collect us from the ship and take us to their office until we could be driven back to the Civic Centre. We were 100% guilty of being drunk in charge of a motor vehicle.

I also had to attend many post mortems and became very familiar indeed with the public mortuary. All deaths during the course or immediately following an operation in hospital were also personally dealt with by the Coroner's Officer, who required a copy of the anaesthetist's report as well as a record of the operation.

I found I got on very well indeed with HM Coroner, Mr Douglas Harefield, who was satisfied with the inquests that I arranged, organising witnesses, their expenses etc. and generally acting as the clerk of the court. I found this an interesting departure from my normal duties, but my paperwork still awaited me when I returned to the CID office.

I came close to a misconduct report one night whilst driving the CID Hillman Estate over Northam Bridge far too fast. As I approached the traffic lights they started to turn red and I was forced to step hard on the brakes. To my dismay the car skidded and spun around, hitting an illuminated bollard in the process, knocking it over. I had to report the incident as the bollard had to be repaired, but before I submitted the accident report a colleague pointed out to me that the tread on the front tyres were far below the required standard.

Vehicle maintenance was the responsibility of the traffic department and when this was brought to their attention I was told that an accident report was unnecessary, they would handle it. The vehicle was taken off the road, the tyres replaced, and I heard no more about it. I think I was rather lucky as I know that as the road was empty of traffic I was travelling far too fast and the accident should have been avoided.

I later dealt with a somewhat unusual offence, working with a gas board official. An anonymous letter had been received that a house in Radcliffe Road was bypassing the normal gas supply and the gas board needed to check on it. The 35 year old occupier allowed us to enter and on walking down the passage from the front door I pulled aside a small curtain and saw an amazing and somewhat frightening sight.

A piece of bicycle inner tube joined the inlet and outlet gas pipe, completely bypassing the meter. Another pipe, consisting of alternate rubber tubing and lead pipe led to a gas fire that was continuously burning in the living room. There was an improvised hot water system in the kitchen with a gas ring under the boiler, again continuously burning on a low setting. There was no Health & Safety legislation at this time and the fire risks, with burning fires that could not be extinguished, fed by rubber tubing that was perishable, was frightening. I had no option but to arrest the occupier and charge him with theft of gas, value unknown, and offences under the Gas Act by preventing a meter from registering.

By this time, August 1962, I had a very heavy case load, a large number of crimes to be investigated and written up, whether detected or not, case papers to be completed for prisoners I was dealing with, and constantly being taken up with Coroner's Officer duties. I had worked many allocated rest days without the opportunity of taking them off at a later date, so one day, when on late turn (9.00am to 1.00pm, back at 8.00pm until midnight) I decided to spend the complete afternoon clearing a load of paperwork. I had worked until late the previous day and was tired, but the backlog of reports concerned me and I wanted to clear the decks. I had also dealt with several thefts during the morning

I therefore had my lunch at headquarters, worked right through the afternoon and early evening, breaking off for a meal, and reported on officially at 8.00pm. Just before midnight, I was on the point of asking DS Bill Pritchard if I could get away, when a '999' call was received that a girl had been stabbed in a car in Chantry Road and had been taken to hospital. Bill and I went to the RSH Hospital and, when medical staff said it was in order, questioned the girl, who had two puncture wounds in her left breast.

She told us that her boy friend, 'Carl', had just been discharged from a 12 month prison sentence and she had told him she was pregnant. 'Carl' was not too bright but he managed to work out that he could not be responsible, and became extremely angry. Later that evening they were in a car, driven by a friend, travelling along Chantry Road, when she told him she no longer wanted to be with him. He then struck her in the chest and when the friend dragged him away he ran off. The girl then found blood on her chest and realised she had been stabbed.

Bill and I returned to PHQ and I circulated 'Carl' as wanted for grievous bodily harm, a serious S18 offence. By this time it was 3.00am, so we reported off duty and drove home, with Bill following a short distance behind me. He lived in the Chessel area and I lived in Sholing. As I drove up Lances Hill, who was walking down, on the opposite side of the road? 'Carl'. I had dealt with him before so stopped, got out of the car and walked across to him. He recognised me, and started running, throwing something in a front garden as he did so.

I caught up with him and as I was concerned he might have a knife, told him to raise his hands as I was going to search him. We were then joined by DS Pritchard. I found two bottles of medical drugs in 'Carl's jacket pocket, but when I tried to search his trouser pockets he tried to prevent me, saying "You can't do this, you haven't got a search warrant."

He then started to struggle, but DS Bill Pritchard helped restrain him and I continued searching, finding a cloth bank bag containing £22.10s in loose change in a trouser pocket. I asked him where it came from and he admitted having broken into the chemist shop in Bitterne, near the top of Lances Hill. I also found a large quantity of loose tablets and he said he had broken in for the tablets and had taken some.

I cautioned him and he replied "I suppose she told you I tried to kill her. It's true, I really did Mr Brown. If I can't have her nobody can." I asked him what he had done with the knife and he told me it wasn't a knife he'd used, it was a pair of scissors and he'd thrown them away when he saw me. We were then joined by officers from Bitterne, including Insp. Bill Rafferty, who arranged a search of the front gardens along Lances Hill. It didn't take long for them to recover a pair, 6" long

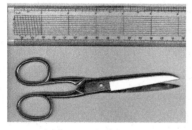

The scissors used by 'Carl' to stab the girl

We all then returned to headquarters where he insisted he wanted to make a statement, but wanted to write it himself. I therefore wrote out the formal caution, which he signed, and out the formal caution, which he signed, and he then wrote, and wrote, and continued to write, a rambling statement in which he repeated that he wanted to murder the girl, with a lengthy explanation of the reasons. At 10.30am I told him that had to break off writing as I needed to charge him and bring him before the court for a remand.

I then charged him with breaking and entering the Bitterne chemist shop and he appeared before the magistrates. He was remanded in custody and we returned to the CID office where he continued to write his statement, completing it at 11.50am. By this time I was pretty exhausted, but called at the chemist shop on my way home to have the bank bag and tablets identified and take a statement from the chemist. On returning home at 2.00pm I went straight to bed, getting up in time to return to complete my 8.00pm to midnight tour of duty.

I felt quite satisfied; after all I had cleared up a serious assault and detected a break-in before it had even been discovered. So when I arrived and was told that D/Supt Wilf Weekes wanted to see me, I expected some form of congratulations. Instead I received a telling off. He angrily pointed out that I had circulated 'Carl' as 'wanted' before reporting off duty at 3.00am, so his description etc. had been included in the daily crime bulletin distributed to all divisions and other forces. He felt it embarrassing to have this circulated when all the time the man was in custody. He said "I know you were busy, but you should have cancelled the circulation once you had arrested him. These things are important."

Without thinking I blurted out "But surely that doesn't matter Sir, nobody else was really looking for him", and I received another blast for being cheeky. Not a single word of congratulations. I thought of how I had worked without a break for 32 hours, returning to complete my tour of duty that evening, without a word of thanks. Although I loved the work I also thought, for the first time, "What am I doing? Why am I sacrificing my home life?"

I saw so little of my wife and daughters, and when at home was often irritable, wanting only peace and quiet. I began to wonder whether the long hours were worth it and that perhaps I should reconsider my position in the Force. Of course, I soon got over it, but the seed was planted.

A week later, when 'Carl' appeared on remand I charged him with assaulting the girl with intent to cause grievous bodily harm, but when the time came for the committal the prosecuting counsel had an additional charge of attempted murder made against 'Carl'. When he appeared at the Hampshire Assizes three months later he was found not guilty of attempted murder but guilty of the GBH. 'Carl' received two years Corrective Training for the GBH, two years concurrent for the shopbreaking and three months concurrent for a breach of his probation order.

Life returned to normal and the same day that 'Carl' was committed to the Assize was the start of yet another fraud case. This time it was a 32 year old female cashier employed by a firm of credit drapers in Ogle Road. 'Violet' was responsible for the cash received into the branch from customers and for banking it daily, maintaining all the appropriate records. 'Violet' was also responsible for the employees' wages, making up the weekly pay envelopes with the cash she had in hand. She also, of course, prepared the wage sheets, including the purchase of National Insurance stamps, which she would fix onto the employees' cards.

The company Head Office became concerned when they discovered that some GPO receipts for the purchase of Insurance stamps had not been received, and their concern increased when a visit from a Ministry Inspector revealed that six National Insurance cards were missing and 'Violet' was unable to properly account for it. The facts were therefore reported to PHQ and I was booked out to investigate. When I questioned her, accompanied by PW Jane Gurman, she initially denied having misappropriated any cash, but when told that I intended going through the books "with a fine toothed comb" she admitted having taken cash on a regular basis. It was a straightforward case but involved a good deal of complicated paperwork.

I charged her with larceny as servant and falsification of accounts, to which she later pleaded guilty and was placed on probation.

I was surprised in January 1963 to read in Daily Orders that the police pillars in 'B' Shirley Division were to be discontinued. Instead points would be made at designated telephone kiosks during the day, so the station could ring them if they wished to pass on a message. The night shift had to ring in at their nominated four points during the night, by dialling 192 and quoting an official credit card number. This was extended to other divisions by February

Pillar 10 at the junction of Medina Road/Winchester Road, before its removal (*Southampton Archive Services*)

My duties as Coroner's Officer increased when John was sick for a while, and I had a large number of inquests to arrange. They all went smoothly and I was now very confident in dealing with all the legal aspects of an inquest. One incident I look back on with some amusement. The Registrar reported that a death certificate had been requested, with the death certified by a hospital doctor as due to barbiturate poisoning. This, of course, was not a natural death and should have been reported. It was, in fact, a suicide. HM Coroner was told and he instructed me to get the doctor in and "read the riot act", so I phoned the RSH Hospital and said to the doctor's secretary "Will you please tell Dr ** to report to my office at 10.00am tomorrow morning?".

She was horrified at my audacity; doctors are not dictated to like that. She wanted me to arrange a visit for me to see him at the hospital. I told her that it was not a request; it was an instruction on behalf of HM Coroner. When the poor doctor arrived the next morning, dressed in what was obviously his best suit, I saw that he was quite young and looked worried. I felt sorry for him so put him at his ease and merely explained the law on a doctor's authority to issue certificates. He left looking rather relieved.

On one of my night duty tours, whilst touring the town area in the CID car with dog handler PC Eric Fielder and his dog Wendy, I heard on the radio that the occupier of a flat over a café in Canute Road heard noises in the shop below and believed they had been broken into. We made our way to the scene, passing a man in Oxford Street carrying a sack, and I dropped Eric off at the café where the uniformed unit had already arrived. I went back to check the man with the sack, stopped him, told him who I was and asked what was in the sack? He replied "Potatoes Sor", in a thick Irish accent.

I looked inside, saw it contained over 2,200 cigarettes in packets and said "Get in the car, you're nicked". He said "Why?" and I replied "Because they are not potatoes." He looked in the sack and said, in a very surprised voice "So they're not Sor." He was, of course, responsible for the break in and was duly dealt with.

'Lucky Jim' came to the fore again in May 1963. There had been a number of thefts of representatives' vehicles containing samples along the south coast, including Southampton, and it was decided that observations should be carried out in Queensway, outside the large Edwin Jones store. The thefts usually took place, for some strange reason, on a Thursday, so PW Sybil Hart had her private car fitted with a police radio and we kept observations together for several successive Thursdays, from 11.00am to 3.00pm, without success.

But at 12.25pm the next Thursday we took note of an obvious 'Rep', in a two tone cream and blue Ford Zodiac, parked outside the front entrance of the store. We were parked on the opposite side of the road. He locked the vehicle, which appeared full of clothing, and went inside. Although the pavement was crowded with shoppers, I happened to take note of two men walking past the Zodiac, slowing down and glancing inside it as they did so. I said to Sybil "I reckon they're going to have a go" and we both watched them carefully. There was a pre-arranged code word to say over the police radio, letting all police vehicles know that the operation was being carried out, but we had no reason to say it at this stage. Traffic department cars and motor cycles were available in the nearby area, but well away from the store.

Edwin Jones store, now Debenhams, in Queensway

The photo was taken from the spot where we were parked and the centre entrance to the store, outside which the representative had parked his Zodiac, is adjacent to the second car from the left.

We saw the two men retrace their steps along Queensway and on drawing level with the front passenger door of the Zodiac one of them suddenly bent down, as though he had dropped something, placing his hand on the car door handle as he did so. He then looked through the car window at the dashboard for several seconds whilst the other man stood nearby. We saw them then continue along Queensway, where they were joined by a third man, with whom they had a brief conversation, on the corner of East Street.

The first two men then walked slowly back along Queensway, past the car without looking at it, but the third man, following some distance behind, stopped at the car and looked at the dashboard for some considerable time. He then continued along the pavement, joined the other two and they went away. I decided that a theft was imminent and gave a warning to the other vehicles, telling all units to be in position.

Sure enough, about ten minutes later, all three men returned along Queensway, the first two continuing past the car whilst the third man went directly to the Zodiac, unlocked the driver's door with a key and sat in the driver's seat. I immediately gave the code word over the air and Sybil started the engine of our car. The stolen Zodiac was then driven slowly along Queensway, turning left into East Street, with the other two men following on foot. Sybil Hart followed the stolen car, at a discreet distance, whilst I gave a description of the three men and details of the stolen car over the air.

The Zodiac then turned into Lime Street, where it stopped and was joined by the other two men, who got into another Zodiac parked there. Both vehicles then drove off, followed by us, with me giving details of the second Zodiac and the direction the two cars were taking.

A police traffic car, driven by PC Norman Edmonds, then approached the two cars in St Mary Street, travelling in the opposite direction. The traffic car turned round in the middle of the street and a chase started, with Sybil's car and other police vehicles involved, coming from all directions. The driver of the stolen Zodiac stopped outside Kingsland Square and got out and ran away, closely followed by Sybil and me, but was chased and detained by Inspector Vic White.

The driver of the other Zodiac was caught and arrested by PC Norman Edmonds when the car was forced off the road by him near the Civic Centre, but the passenger ran off and vanished in a crowd of people. That was the last time he was seen and a search of the area proved fruitless. The two men were taken to the CID office at PHQ, where I questioned them separately.

It was soon discovered that the second Zodiac was a stolen vehicle bearing false plates. Both men admitted the theft of the first Zodiac and its contents from outside Edwin Jones store and made voluntary statements detailing their involvement.

They were charged with the theft and remanded in custody for a week, during which time a photo of the third missing man, a known associate of the two in custody, was received from New Scotland Yard. It was placed with a number of others and positively identified by me, Sybil Hart and Norman Edmonds but enquiries by the Metropolitan Police failed to locate him so he was circulated as wanted.

It was revealed that the men had easily obtained the ignition key number for the Zodiac outside Edwin Jones as it was stamped on the ignition keyhole. They then obtained a duplicate from Halfords in the High Street. Such woeful vehicle security is out of the question today.

I interviewed them a week later, when they appeared on remand, and further charged them with driving the cars whilst uninsured, unlicensed and with dangerous driving. They admitted possession of the second stolen Zodiac with false plates but denied stealing it, so were charged with receiving. They also admitted identical thefts from Bournemouth, Birmingham, Leicester and London and these were placed on TIC forms. I charged one of them with the theft of a similar car in Brighton, as he was the only one involved in that particular offence.

Both appeared at the magistrates' court a week later and received sentences of six months, were disqualified for two years and committed to Quarter Sessions for sentence on the charges of theft.

They appeared before the Recorder, Ewan Montague, the following month when one was sent to prison for four years and the other for 30 months. We knew that they were members of a notorious London gang, believed to be the Richardson Brothers, and part of a nationwide series of thefts, but extensive enquiries still failed to trace the missing third man.

It was a very satisfactory conclusion and an absolute delight to actually witness the theft taking place in front of us, followed by the excitement of the chase.

Life was not all work and crime however. We were able to enjoy annual dinners at such places as the police club in Hulse Road and the Dolphin Hotel in the High Street. The following photos were taken at such events and thoroughly enjoyed by everybody.

A CID dinner at the police club in Hulse Road

**Another dinner, this time at the Dolphin Hotel, where we were entertained by
Frankie Vaughan and the King Brothers**

**Frankie entertaining
us, with one of the King
Brothers**

It was around this time that a story was circulated about one of the traffic officers. It was said that he had been the observer in a traffic car when it chased a stolen open back van. During the chase, with speeds reaching well over 80mph, the van passenger had thrown various objects out of the window, into the path of the pursuing patrol car, with several near disastrous results.

The worst moment came when he reached out of the window into the back of the van and dragged out a complete spare wheel, which he threw into the road directly in front of the police car. The observer later said it was a hair-raising moment.

The van was chased along the main Winchester road, where the driver lost control and left the road, travelling down a steep bank before colliding with a tree at the bottom. It is alleged that the observer ran down to the damaged van, dragged out the passenger who had been throwing things and first asked if he was injured.

On being told that the man was all right he then said "You've heard about police brutality? Well its f………. true" and thumped him hard in his jaw. We all found this account perfectly acceptable as the observer and driver had been put at considerable risk of life and limb, without real cause. We were also told that the man never complained, accepting that it was a justifiable punishment. I think times have now changed.

My next case is one that I often recount when talking about my police experiences. I dealt with an afternoon break-in in a terraced house in Campbell Street, occupied by an Indian couple. The front door had been forced by bodily pressure and a large amount of gold stolen. I discovered that it was common for Indians to keep a quantity of Indian gold in their home, as well as wearing it as ornaments.

I made the usual door to door enquiries and found that two black men and a woman, all thought to be Nigerians, had called at the adjoining houses during the day, saying they were looking for lodgings with Indians. I took note of their descriptions, not as suspects but merely as a possibility.

When I returned to the CID office and circulated details of the break-in, I noticed that DC Ian Sharocks was also circulating a forcible front door entry to a house in Denzil Avenue, not too far from Campbell Street. In his case three Nigerians, two men and a woman, were actually seen at the door of the attacked premises, so they were clearly responsible.

I returned to see Mr Singh, resplendent with his long beard and white turban, his wife with her Indian clothing and mark on her forehead, and told them of the three Nigerians now thought to be responsible. I asked him to let his fellow Indians know of them seeking lodgings with Indians, suggesting that if they called they should let them in and contact the police immediately.

What I love telling people, trying to imitate an Indian accent, is what Mr Singh then said to me. "You know Mr Brown, we have been here for over twenty years and we had no trouble until all these bloody foreigners come." Unfortunately, we never did trace those responsible, but had a good laugh at Mr Singh's sentiments.

DS Jim Glass was something of a character and I always enjoyed accompanying him on enquiries, but I was rather shaken one day when he asked me to go with him to the Criterion pub in St Mary's Road as he intended to give someone a 'good hiding' and needed me to cover for him. I had no idea of the background, but Jim had a serious problem with one of the two notorious O'Connell brothers and was going to settle matters once and for all.

He told me to wait outside, went into the Criterion and came out with the two brothers. I stood by in the road, next to one of the brothers whilst Jim and the other brother took off their jackets and set too on the pavement. It was a hard fist fight, with no quarter given, and my function was to ensure the other brother didn't interfere, which he didn't. Both men fought to a standstill and at the end shook hands and agreed the problem, whatever it was, was resolved, with respect shown on both sides.

The question of a complaint against police just didn't arise; it was a dispute between two men regardless of their position or background. I wonder if the same thing could happen today?

I then became, for the first time, the subject of a complaint. I had been on Late Turn keeping observations on offices in Brunswick Place from the darkness of St Andrews Park. A number had been broken into and it was a regular routine to keep watch during the late evening.

Whilst doing this I was approached by a prostitute, walking in the parks, who offered her services. Apart from the fact that she was extremely ugly and dirty, I have always had a fear of catching a venereal disease and in any event was happily married. It was very therefore easy to point out that she had approached a police officer and was in danger of being arrested.

As I had better things to do than arrest a prostitute, I merely warned her about her soliciting in the parks and noted her name and details, discovering she had just arrived from London and was trying Southampton for the first time. When next on duty I passed her details onto DS Graham Swain, who was then on Vice, and thought no more about it.

However, some weeks later I was instructed to report to Supt. Eric Coleman at Portswood Police Station. He first asked me if I had checked a prostitute in Andrews Park and when I agreed it was me he asked for my pocket book. Having confirmed my entry of her details he then told me she had complained that I had, in fact, made use of her sexual services whilst in the parks.

I was taken aback at this and told Eric that this was absolutely incorrect but I had no explanation for her making such a statement. Eric clearly believed me and said that she had been arrested for soliciting in the parks and when she told the vice squad officer it was the first time she had been there, she was informed of my report some weeks earlier. She then made the accusation about me.

I was not suspended from duty, although suspension was normal in such cases and I had fully expected it. Eric informed me that the investigation would be taken over by the now Assistant Chief Constable, Bob Masters.

I was extremely relieved a few days later when Bob Masters phoned me to say he had interviewed the woman at length, and she now admitted she had invented the story in revenge for me telling the Vice Squad about her. Bob Masters became my friend for life.

Some people just never listen when offered an escape from a criminal conviction, and the landlady of a public house in the town centre was one of them. I had received information from one of my prostitute informants of a quantity of rings being sold by a man who I knew to have convictions, and I traced several of those named by her and recovered a quantity of good quality rings. They were identified as having come from an antique shop broken into in Fareham, when 80 rings were stolen.

In each case, all I was after was (a) recovery of the property and (b) enough evidence to convict the offender. To this end I told this to each person I interviewed, stressing that I did not wish to pursue a case of receiving stolen property, merely evidence that they bought them (innocently) from the thief.

I obtained enough evidence for the police at Fareham to arrest the thief, who told them he had sold a quantity to the landlady of the Southampton public house. When I saw her, however, she denied all knowledge of having bought rings from a customer, although I knew for certain that she had. She proved very difficult to speak to, initially demanding to see my warrant card, which I showed her but refused to let her take it from me when she attempted to. Although she had a clear view of it she still insisted that she wanted to phone police headquarters to check on me, returning satisfied but clearly very unco-operative.

I told her that the man concerned was in custody and showed her his photograph. Although she eventually admitted that she had seen him she continued to deny being given any rings, so I told her she would be taken to PHQ whilst I contacted Fareham police for more detailed information. Her reply was "I want to see the Chief Constable. You're accusing me of having stolen rings. I'll sue you for that." None of this endeared her to me. The rings were all said to still have the price tags on them when she was given them.

I was given a detailed account of how she had been given the rings by the thief, who only received a £5 deposit, including the fact that she showed him a letter in her handbag she had from her solicitor regarding her receiving cash from the sale of a house, thus demonstrating that she could pay the balance owed. I searched her handbag and found the letter mentioned by the thief, but she still denied everything. It was clear to me that she had obtained the rings for only £5, had sold them on for a large profit and consequently could not return them.

She ended up being charged with receiving 82 rings, knowing them to be stolen and elected to go for trial at the forthcoming Quarter Sessions. However, to my surprise, when she appeared she pleaded guilty and got away with a £60 fine plus £15 costs. I felt this was wrong because she clearly had received the benefit of a considerable sum by disposing of the rings, obtained for a mere £5, and the fine did not reflect this. I had by now become accustomed to the injustices of the court system, not unjust to the accused but to the victim.

My working life was that of a very full workload, break-ins and prisoners galore, with several periods as Coroner's Officer when DS John Creighton was on holiday or sick leave, and I found that the paperwork was piling up on me. I also still very much resented the episodes where I had to pay back a miserly sum for buying a prisoner a drink during a lengthy overnight escort and where I received a telling off for not cancelling a wanted person who I had arrested during a 36 hour tour of duty. I really felt that my senior officers did not value their subordinates and, probably because I was also constantly tired, felt depressed.

This culminated in a decision that I had never heard of before; a detective requesting a return to uniform duties. I still have a copy of my written request, dated 20 October, 1963, in which I stressed that I had not passed my promotion examination to sergeant and whilst I was engrossed with CID duties was unable to carry out any study towards it.

I had absolutely no interest in the road traffic law in general, Vehicle Construction & Use Regulations in particular, of the liquor licensing and gaming laws or any legislation that did not involve criminal activity, and consequently had virtually no knowledge of them.

I had been a dedicated detective for over six years, and although I realised that I might be jeopardising my career prospects by asking to leave the CID, I also felt that my home life had suffered terribly as a result of my long hours and heavy workload.

I had two very young daughters, who I loved dearly, but had little time or energy to spare to be with them during their formative years. I felt that a return to uniform duty would enable me to regain my peace of mind and lead a normal family life.

My wish was quickly granted and I returned to walking the beat on 10 November, posted back to Shirley Division, the furthest point from my home, not Bitterne where I lived or Portswood where I had never served. I thought my superiors could have been a little more considerate.

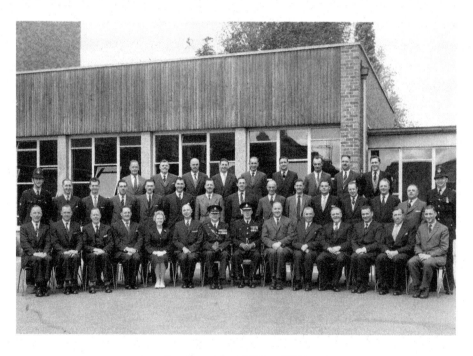

Southampton CID c. 1962

Rear Row: DC's Norman Roberts, Jock Adamson, Bob Shergold, Alan Dewey, John Webber, John McCullagh, John Baker, Trevor Lobb and John Porter.

Centre row: PC Ken Saunders, DC's Ron Ledgerwood, Ray Weston, Ian Sharrocks, Bryan Davies, Peter Bascombe, Bert House, Ken Holmes, 'Paddy' Phillips, Jim Brown, 'Spud' Murphy, John Parris, 'Polly' Perkins, Archie Davies, PC Gordon Cruickshank

Front row: DS Arthur Offer, DS Fred Williams, DS Terry White, DS John Crieghton, DPW Glad Hobbs, DI Bert Adams, Dep.CC Bob Masters, CC Alf Cullen, D/Supt Wilf Weeks, DI 'Paddy' O'Sullivan, DS Jim Glass, DS Norman McDonald, DS Bill Pritchard, DS Geoff Hayes.

15. BACK ON THE BEAT AGAIN – 1963

"I've 35 days in the book, Skipper". Shirley Clerk Sergeant Bill Domone looked at me horrified. "Piss off", he replied, "You should have taken them before you left". (Although CID officers fully accepted the long unpaid hours of overtime, we all scrupulously maintained a note of the rest days worked and took them off as and when we could. In my case I had accumulated a total of 35 weekly leave days worked and had no intention of losing them.)

"That's all right Skipper", I replied, "The money paid in lieu will come in handy". I was then the recipient of a very grim look from PS Bill Domone, a moment's thoughtful silence, then "All right, you bugger, you win." I grinned as I walked out of his office. At last I had won something.

My first tour of duty, on nights, resulted in two prisoners within two hours. I had been given Team Car duty and we had a call at 1.25am of a West African man disturbed whilst trying to enter the front door of a café in Millbrook Road by means of a duplicate key. I found the man answering the description in nearby Waterloo Road but he denied having been near the café. I searched him and found a bunch of keys on a ring and a separate loose key. He told me the loose key had been given him by his friend, a lorry driver who was sleeping in his cab further down the road. The two were friends and had stayed together in lodgings in Birmingham.

When I questioned the lorry driver he denied giving the key, saying he had only given him a lift from Birmingham and didn't know him. I arrested them both as I found the loose key fitted the café door and the lorry driver had stayed there in the past.

At Shirley police station the lorry driver then admitted having kept a spare key from when he had stayed at the café earlier in the year and the West African admitted his intention of breaking in during the early hours, together with the lorry driver, to see what they could find. My interviewing technique, fine tuned as a detective, still stood me well. I charged them both with attempted burglary and when they appeared at Quarter Sessions in December the West African pleaded guilty and was sentenced to three months, but the lorry driver was acquitted.

I quickly found that working the beat was a relaxing and gentle way of working, compared with the hectic and stressful duty of a working detective. I had ample time to look in shop windows as I walked along, very confident indeed of being able to deal with whatever came my way. It was also great that PS Bill Domone, true to his word, regularly gave me 8 hours time off, sometimes either side of a rostered leave day, giving me three consecutive days to relax at home. Life was good.

I found I was still 'Lucky Jim' as routine checks on people turned up trumps. One was a man seen cycling late at night on a machine that appeared too small for him. When questioned he admitting being a Sapper from Marchwood riding a cycle he had taken from a nearby garden. He was fined £5. I also stopped a car and, on questioning, discovering the driver was disqualified (he received six months imprisonment)

On 30 December 1963 I had to give evidence at Quarter Sessions in the trial of the passenger in the stolen Rep's car taken from outside Debenhams the previous May. What happened upsets me to this day. He was the only one of the gang to escape at the time, but had been identified by several of us in a photo identification parade. He had a long list of previous convictions, many for serious theft and one for armed robbery. The Metropolitan police found he had left home with his whereabouts unknown, and he was circulated as wanted.

He was seen in November by a member of the Flying Squad, chased through the streets and caught when trying to climb a wall at the end of a cul-de-sac. His excuse for running away was that he thought he was being attacked, even though he admitted he recognised the police officer. As I had by then returned to uniform duty, DS Graham Swain dealt with him but the man denied all knowledge of the thefts and Graham was unable to get an admission. However, Graham also failed to arrange an identification parade before charging the man, so the first time I saw the accused was when I was in the witness box.

When I came to give my evidence I felt confident in the witness box, stating categorically that I could identify the man in the dock as one of those I had seen involved in the theft, but defence counsel made great play of the fact that I had not seen the men responsible since the previous May, seven months ago, and even then only seen them for a matter of minutes.

I looked at the prosecuting counsel appealingly, as I knew I could say that I had, in fact, identified the accused by photograph only two days after the offence, but saying that would reveal that he had a previous conviction. I was sorely tempted to do so, when repeatedly asked how I could be certain of the accused's identity, but I decided that in all fairness and to avoid a retrial, to not mention the photo identification. I did go as far as saying I had not seen the accused <u>in the flesh</u>, emphasising the words to imply I may have seen him in another way, but that was as far as I could go. The prosecuting barrister did not re-examine me, allowing me to explain how I was so certain of the prisoner's identity, so I had to assume that the truth would have been too dangerous and liable to force a retrial.

I remained in court at the conclusion of the prosecution case and heard a defence witness, a reporter from a national tabloid newspaper, give evidence of being at a party in a London club on the day in question. He said he took a photograph of the accused during the party at a time when it was impossible for him to have been in Southampton during the theft, and produced a copy. It is absolutely certain that the man was lying but his evidence could not be disproved. As a direct result of this fabricated evidence the man was found not guilty, and when this was done I saw a member of the jury look directly at me and laugh. This puzzled me at the time but I was distracted as this was one of the rare occasions that a prisoner in a case of mine had been found not guilty.

It was not until some weeks later, when I looked back on the event, that I recalled that before the trial started, when members of the jury were waiting outside in the foyer to be called, I realised that the tabloid reporter was talking to some of them outside the court entrance. At that time I assumed that all those waiting were prospective jury members. There is no doubt in my mind, to this day, that the reporter was an associate of the London criminal gang and had given false evidence, as well as prejudicing the jury beforehand, but there was no way I could prove it. The injustice still upsets me.

Beat work continued to be relaxing, serving summonses, dealing with traffic accidents, minor traffic and other offences and the occasional prisoner, such as finding a deserter from HMS Mercury, and arresting a youth riding a stolen motor cycle in a copse at Lordswood. Both these cases arose when I had a 'Phase A' Probationer attached to me for a while, PC Mike Cobb. Mike was initially interested in reporting people for such things as having the wrong size lettering on a motor cycle rear plate, but I persuaded him that crime was far more important; such minor matters were best left to the traffic department. We checked persons seen at night and my questioning revealed a Navy deserter. I took Mike with me, going into empty properties, anywhere where we might find somebody up to no good.

It was while walking through the copse at Lordswood that we were nearly knocked down by a youth riding a motor cycle. It didn't take long to discover the machine was stolen and Mike was delighted to be involved with a prisoner. Mike turned out to be a first rate copper and later became an outstanding detective.

I then took the promotion examination for Sergeant and later found I had passed. A small victory and justification for returning to uniform duty.

My next case of interest started when I was taking one of PS Bill Domone's eight hours time off at home. A man living some distance away, in Acasia Road, somehow knew I was a police officer and where I lived and called with seven obscene photographs that had been given to his 14 year old daughter. He knew the man, "Alf", as he lived opposite and when I checked this with Archie Davies the following day I discovered "Alf" had convictions for larceny. I was therefore surprised when "Alf" also called at my home later that day, wanting to explain how the obscene photographs had come about.

He said he had more and they had been given to him at work. The girl had been given them in mistake for some holiday photos. I cautioned him and told him I had yet to complete my enquiries and arranged to see him at Woolston police station later that evening. I then interviewed the 14 year old girl as I had discovered she had told the man about me being given the photos and where I lived.

I questioned her, in the presence of her mother, and took a statement in which she stated the man had first indecently assaulted her when she was only 10 years old, by placing his hands in her knickers and touching her private parts. He had also persuaded her to masturbate him.

This had gone on for several years and the girl had thought she was equally wrong in taking part and had therefore not told anybody. Her statement also described how he had sometimes pretended intercourse by laying on top of her, both undressed, until he ejaculated.

When I questioned "Alf" at the station he admitted the offences over a period of time, and under further intensive questioning said that other young girls had also been similarly treated. I arranged to see him again when I had completed further enquiries to trace the other girls involved.

It did not take me long to trace the two girls he mentioned, but on questioning them other girls came to light and I ended up arranging for statements to be taken by policewoman Gladys Hobbs from a total of six girls, ages ranging from 10 to 13 years, living in nearby Blackthorn Road and Merryoak Road.

They all involved indecent assault and inducing them to masturbate him, but when I read the statements I saw that the girls had been more than willing participants.

Many of them, over a period of years, had regularly called at his house on their own, sometimes with another girl or, several times, with two other girls, when the indecency took place. One had declined his invitation to perform oral sex on him, but another allowed him to perform oral sex on her.

All of them, although five of them were still only 11 years old, believed they were equally guilty and had therefore never made a complaint. The fact that he often gave them 6d, a shilling, chocolates or gramophone records was also a factor.

I later saw him again at Woolston police station, questioned him about the various offences, all of which he admitted, and charged him with 10 specimen cases of indecent assault and gross indecency. The girls were all examined by Dr Yetman, the police surgeon, and found to still be virgins.

"Alf" appeared before the magistrates that May, pleaded guilty and was sentenced to six months. An unjust result, I felt; he had seriously affected a number of innocent children and should have been more severely punished.

By this time I was one of the most senior and experienced officers on the section and was accordingly given tours of manning the enquiry office and being the emergency driver for periods. This gave me even more experience of dealing directly with people collapsing, traffic accidents, sudden deaths, break-ins, and other emergencies.

Probably because I was regarded as so senior on the section, I was approached by a new probationer on the section with a personal problem. He told me, in strict confidence, that he was going to resign because, "I have put a PW in the pudding club and she wants me to marry her". I knew the policewoman concerned and was suspicious that she was more than likely not pregnant but merely wanted to get out of her spinsterhood. I therefore told the PC, who I believed would do well in the Force, that he should not resign but wait for several months before doing anything drastic. I was right, she wasn't pregnant, they didn't get married and the probationer eventually rose to a far higher rank than me.

One traffic accident, taking place in Redbridge Road, still amuses me. When I arrived a man was lying on the pavement, semi-conscious, with a minor leg injury. An Austin 7 Coupe, 1938 model, was nearby and I asked the driver what had happened. His reply is still in my pocket book, "He fell out of the door just after we came round the corner. The door is OK so long as you don't lean against it." The vehicle was in a terrible condition and when I reported him under the Construction & Use Regulations his reply was "This won't mean the car will have to come off the road will it?"

The Daily Order of 10 March 1964 recorded the fact that there was now ONE light-weight fibre-glass protective shield for use in dealing with armed or besieged criminals, kept by the station sergeant at police headquarters. In a test, a 12-bore shot gun fired at point blank range had failed to pierce it.

I then found myself in trouble. It was a very hot and sunny Friday 24 April 1964 and I was seeing the children across the road at the Atherly Girls School, Hill Lane. Southampton had just been awarded City status, so I was no longer a County Borough officer but a City officer. Our uniform would soon change, with a different helmet denoting out City status. The official dress code was to wear Gannex raincoats, but a Daily Order had just been published stating that summer uniform would come into effect the ensuing Monday. The Chief Constable alone decided when the weather was suitable, not individual officers; this ensured we were uniformly dressed.

However, I had decided I could not wait until Monday so had left my Gannex off and because it was so hot wore my summer uniform, i.e. shirt sleeve order. I was met at the school by a very angry Insp. Joe Skelton who tore me off a strip for failing to wait until Monday. He reported me under the discipline code to the divisional super-intendent, Supt. Bill Hayter, who I had to see when I returned to the station. Bill had a job to keep a straight face but impressed on me that I must follow orders and not do my own thing. I agreed and apologised, so that was the end of my first discipline offence.

I next dealt with a serious accident that took place at Millbrook Roundabout. When I arrived I saw a damaged bicycle in the road with the rider lying alongside. When I examined him I could see that he was clearly dead and enquiries revealed that the car concerned, a 1956 black Vauxhall Velox, number unknown, had failed to stop, so I had a fatal 'hit and run' to deal with. Unlike modern times, when a team of specialist accident investigators deal with all fatal accidents, I was left alone to take measure-ments at the scene, take witness statements etc, and deal with the matter in my normal routine way. I had to liaise with the Coroner's Officer, DS John Creighton, to have the body identified and be present at the post-mortem, and make enquiries with the local vehicle taxation office to try to trace the vehicle concerned. Although I spent some time in the taxation office trying to identify similar vehicles in the Southampton area, nothing came of it and the matter remained unresolved. I continued to make enquir-ies for several months but at the inquest the following July the verdict was "Run down while pedal cycling in circumstances unknown". Not one of my success stories.

One unexpected side effect of my enquiries was that I questioned an 18 year old man, living in Argyle Road, whose car fitted the description. I could not connect him with the fatal hit and run but said to him "You appear to be rather worried. Have you got something on your mind?" He replied "I suppose I have really", to which I said "Would you care to tell me about it?" Further questioning resulted in him being charged with various thefts from unattended vehicles and me recovering property from his house – all because he initially fitted the bill for a fatal but although cleared of any involvement I felt he was still worried. My intuition still worked well.

My tours of duty as relief emergency driver became more frequent, with me attending an ever increasing number of traffic accidents and emergency ambulance calls. I found I was able to deal with all manner of injuries, with my first aid training coming to the fore. One especially upset me, although I took the correct action, when a three year old boy had a piece of plastic tubing stuck down his throat, resulting in severe laceration and bleeding. I had no problem dealing with injured adults but dealing with injured children, especially several cot deaths, was particularly upsetting.

Another example, in Wimpson Lane, was a six year old boy running into the road after a ball and being hit by a van. He was quite badly injured, but recovered in hospital, and my initial first aid proved helpful.

One helpful aspect of being emergency driver was that when carrying out night duty Team Policing there was always another officer to be the officer in the case and complete the paperwork. Such incidents as seeing a Lambretta scooter driven along Millbrook Road in the early hours, with the young rider appearing unfamiliar with it. It didn't take much questioning to discover it was a case of Taking Without Consent, but PC Ken Martin, my observer, took over and dealt with it, relieving me of any further involvement or paperwork.

It was during this period that I became a Branch Board member, the equivalent of a trade union shop steward, although the police are not allowed to join a union or to take strike action; to do so was an arrestable offence. I had to see the Chief Constable, Alf Cullen, to be told my limitations but also the fact that I had access to him at any time if I needed to resolve an issue. It also meant I was allowed to spend a full day at official Branch Board meetings with other members, to discuss force matters. I found this aspect very interesting, especially as the draconian supervision by senior officers was gradually lessening.

An unusual suicide then came my way. A 65 year old man was in All Saints Ward, General Hospital, waiting for an operation, but was found dead in the ward bathroom at 7.55am by the Ward Sister. What was unusual was the fact that a loaded and cocked .32 Webley & Scott automatic, with two bullets in the magazine and one up the spout, was found in the bath alongside him, and he had a bullet wound in his right temple. Nobody had heard the shot and nobody suspected he had brought the weapon in with him. No explanation, other than that he was frightened of the operation, was forthcoming.

A spell of CID duty followed, when Shirley division was short of detectives due to sick leave. I was quite happy to be given this duty, which lasted several weeks, as I enjoyed the freedom of movement and the cases I dealt with, without becoming too deluged with cases. Many of them were routine shoplifters.

One incident was a first for me. A number of thefts had taken place in the ladies cloakroom of the Fine Fare store in Shirley High Street, so a trap was set using an invisible chemical dye. A handbag was treated and left in the cloakroom. When cash was found missing I was called and interviewed the staff, without testing for the dye, something I had never used before. When the staff were told that a secret dye had been used, it didn't take long for a 16 year old girl to admit being responsible.

I again had a regular supply of prisoners from George Handley, the second-hand dealer in Romsey Road, with individuals trying to sell him stolen property, and plenty of shoplifters from the local shops and stores.

'Observations' were a regular and boring occurrence, keeping watch on premises when the area was subject to a series of break-ins, invariably with nothing happening whilst trying to remain unseen. One instance did pay off. A patrolling PC found a motor cycle on waste ground at the rear of the Bricklayers Arms, Wimpson Lane, bearing an excise licence for a different machine that had been reported stolen. The cycle's false number plates were home made using white adhesive tape and it was decorated with red and white chequered tape. I kept observations for over an hour, and saw an 18 year old youth go to the machine and turn the petrol on. I arrested him as he caught hold of the handlebars but he denied having stolen it, insisting he was collecting it for a friend whose name and address he did not know. When he was taken to Shirley police station and searched I found he had a roll of red and white chequered tape and a roll of white adhesive tape. The youth then admitted having stolen the machine, also the fact that he was already disqualified.

He was charged with the theft and driving whilst disqualified and kept in custody over the week-end, to appear in court on the Monday. His troubles were not over, however, as I saw him in his cell just prior to his court appearance and cautioned him. He immediately slumped back on the seat, saying "Oh no, not something else." I then told him I had made enquiries at the address where he had been lodging and discovered he had had sexual intercourse with the 14 year old girl living there. His reply was "Oh God, this means going to Sessions". He admitted knowing her age and was further charged accordingly, but was merely fined when he eventually appeared at court.

My good friend Bob Masters retired in June, 1964, and was replaced as Assistant Chief Constable by John Wilkins, a former Superintendent in Bristol City.

When I returned to normal beat work I was frequently given emergency driver duties, with a consequent high level of incidents to deal with, but found I could cope with this quite easily as I also had periods of beat work, giving me ample time to complete my reports. I also took part in August in the Civil Service Procession, marching to St Marys Church, led by the Chief Constable. It took me back to my army days, when marching with the 60th Rifles was much faster.

I experienced my first frightening crowd control that October when I was part of the team controlling the large number of teenage girls outside the Gaumont Theatre, Commercial road, when the Rolling Stones pop group appeared there. Bulky men, dockers, even violent drunks, presented no real problem, but trying to control and keep back a crowd of shrieking, screaming teenagers, hell bent on getting to their idols, was a truly frightening experience, one I didn't want to repeat.

I was also given periods of plainclothes observations, to help the divisional CID, and one event in particular involved me helping out a murder squad. A 60 year old Southampton taxi driver, George Newberry, was found battered to death in Ampfield, on 22 October 1964, and although the murder was dealt with by Hampshire Constabulary, his taxi was found abandoned not far from his Southampton home in Northumberland Road. A joint murder squad with members from both Forces was therefore set up and although I was a uniformed PC I was detailed to spend several weeks in plain clothes making door to door enquiries and completing a lengthy murder questionnaire.

The murder was eventually detected when a savings bank withdrawal form, getting cash from Woolston post office with George Newberry's stolen bank book, was retrieved. Basil Ballard managed to bring to light a good thumb print on the form, an unusual thumb print with a twinned loop, and this matched that of a man convicted of store-breaking. A good detection, bearing in mind the withdrawal form had passed through several hands before reaching Basil.

A completely new police organisation was set up on 30 October 1964 when the formation of No.6 Regional Crime Squad took place. My good friend Ken Holmes, newly promoted to D/Sgt, with DC Ian Sharrocks and DI Arthur Offer were transferred to this new system. The principle was that serious crimes were to be investigated across Police Force borders, but in close co-operation with the forces concerned. It proved a great success, following a number of serious organised gangs being broken up, and was increased in strength over the years.

It was during this period that I lost the use of my beloved two-tone blue Vauxhall Cresta, with its front bench seat and steering column gear change. I was driving along Palmerston Road, returning from giving evidence in the civil County Court, when a car drove from Pound Tree Road, across the halt sign without stopping, and collided heavily with my nearside. I was forced across the road, into the wall of the Eagle public house, where I suddenly stopped and shot forward in my seat, hitting my knees on the dashboard (long before the days of seat belts).

I suffered a severe pain, believing my knees were broken, when the other driver rushed across, forced open my smashed nearside door and called out "Can I help you Officer? I am a first aider". My reply is unprintable, suffice it to say I told him, in no uncertain terms, that I was a first aider myself and was not going to have a first aider anywhere near me to touch what I wrongly suspected to be a broken leg. The car was a write off but I suffered no more than severe bruising. At least it was a traffic accident I did not have to deal with.

George Handley gave me a nice little fraud case to deal with, starting when a woman tried to sell him a new condition pushchair for a fraction of its price. My enquiries resulted in a series of false pretences where property was obtained by the woman and her husband by cheques, even though the account was overdrawn, and then selling the goods for cash. I had many enquiries to make, sorting out their bank account and cheque stubs, obtaining statements and recovering property, ending up with a long list on an 'other offence form'

To my surprise, in late November 1964 I was instructed to report to the traffic department in Hulse Road to receive lectures over two days and then become qualified as an authorised vehicle examiner. I had no idea why I had become so qualified, but it became clear the next month when I had to again report to Hulse Road, this time to be measured for motor cycle uniform clothing. Southampton police were to have a new system on 1 April of divisional motor cyclists, working 8.00am-4.00pm; 4.00pm-midnight shifts, patrolling continuously within each division. This would give an immediate response to 999 calls, as well as the divisional emergency driver, giving a two-fold response to such calls. I had been selected for this new duty, the first of other 'firsts' to come

In the meantime I continued to have many periods as relief emergency driver as well as spells of plain clothes observations and other plainclothes duties. I dealt with a large number of domestic disturbances, with the man striking his partner, but when she then refused to make a statement no action could be taken against him. I found this very frustrating at times, especially when the female partner was badly injured but still did not want any action taken.

As all ambulance and fire calls were attended to by the emergency driver, no matter how trivial, my experiences were continually broadened, with good personal contacts made with ambulance and fire crews, all working to the same end.

To my great surprise, I was detailed at act as Coroner's officer again, only for a week, in the absence of DS John Creighton on sick leave. It was pleasant to get back into that routine for a few days and I felt pleased to know that I was still regarded highly enough to take on this important duty.

As duty emergency driver I took part in February in what was called a "Hue and Cry Plus". A wage snatch had taken place that morning in St Marys Road when £2,000 was taken by six masked men, armed with coshes, escaping in a Ford Zephy. As part of the laid down procedure I searched the area roads leading off The Avenue, but the car was found abandoned in Northam Street. It had been a long time since I was last so excited. Amazingly, this incident was followed the next month with another Hue and Cry when three men, armed with a gun, iron bar and axe, tied up the postmaster of Redbridge Post office and left, with the contents of the safe, in a light blue new condition Anglia. The vehicle was not traced and nothing came of the search, but again an exciting time for a while.

Another incident involving a small child was upsetting. A 15 month old baby was badly scalded on the neck and back when she was placed in a bowl of hot water by her mother and my first aid could only consist of placing the child in a bowl of cold water, to her great distress, until the ambulance arrived. The mother, living in one of the poorer parts of Aldermoor estate, was clearly incapable of proper baby care and the social services were informed.

An interesting incident occurred when I attended to a complaint of indecent assault on a seven year old girl. New tower blocks were under construction in Windermere Avenue and a workman on site, wearing a green hat and dressed in white overalls, was responsible. When I arrived on the scene most of the workmen had left the site, but one, dressed in green trousers and fawn mac, but no hat, was in the process of leaving. I spoke to him, asking if any of the workmen wore white overalls, and he said that one did but he had left the site.

A corporation bus then arrived and he said "I must go now, here's my bus" and ran off to catch it. I then realised that his trousers were clean, even though he admitted being a workman on the site, also that he was nervous and a bit agitated when I had spoken to him. I therefore followed the bus, stopping it in London Road, boarded it and asked the man to come with me, which he did (I didn't give him any option.) He entered my car, where I asked him if he wore overalls and if so were they white? I also asked him if he wore a cap. He admitted wearing white overalls and having a green beret. I pointed out that at no time had he asked me why I was making enquiries and then told him about the assault on the seven year old. He said he had been working on the 21st floor all afternoon so it couldn't have been him, so I then pointed out I had not mentioned where the offence took place. I added that when I first saw him he had failed to tell me he wore white overalls, explaining that I would be arranging an identity parade. He then admitted being responsible and made a written statement, under caution, but was only fined when he appeared at court.

Whilst on one of my final tours of night duty, I was told to attend a complaint of a noisy party in a side road leading off Winchester Road. On arriving at the bungalow I could hear the noise of shouting and laughing long before I arrived at the front door, which I had to bang very loudly before someone answered. When they did, to my surprise and caught unawares, my helmet was taken from my head by a young lady, a glass of drink placed in my hand, and I found myself the centre of attention in a more than merry group I immediately recognised from Southern Television. Well known reporters such as Julian Pettifer were celebrating some event and they were impossible to stop.

Realising the experience was, in fact, more than agreeable, I radioed the station and spoke to the duty sergeant, Joe Casson, explaining the situation. He arrived within minutes, with the emergency driver, and they both joined in the party with me, remaining for some time. No doubt the neighbour who complained assumed the police were attempting to deal with the matter, and Joe did manage to get them to reduce the noise level, but the party continued unabated, to the enjoyment of us all.

My final case as a beat officer, one that I found very difficult to handle, came during my last tour of night duty. A complaint had been made by the General Hospital that food was regularly missing from the main kitchen and the night staff were thought to be responsible. I therefore kept observations outside the main entrance at 5.15am, prior to the night staff leaving, and at 5.30am saw two of them leave, each carrying a holdall and bucket type bag. I stopped them asked if they had foodstuffs in their bags, and both agreed they had. What I then found difficult to handle was that they both pleaded with me to let them go, one of them saying "Oh my God, my four babies, you don't know what this means to me". The other then took out her purse and offered me £20 to forget all about it. Both women became extremely agitated, one of them saying "My babies, I'll go to prison, I'm going to be sick", whilst retching violently.

I was on my own, dealing with two distressed women, who were getting worse by the minute. I was unable to stop one of them taking something out of her bag and placing it behind a wall, so I took possession of both bags and recovered a 6lb tin of oranges from behind the wall. Both became hysterical, crying out, with one of them saying "What's going to happen to my babies, my husband leaves for work at eight o' clock and there will be nobody to look after them".

I managed to persuade both of them to get into the police car and took them to Shirley police station, whereupon one of them immediately fainted. I began to wish I had never become involved. Both were questioned, once they recovered somewhat, admitting the theft of quite a considerable amount of foodstuffs. They were bailed to appear at Shirley later that night, when, after making further enquiries at the hospital, I reported them for offences of larceny as servant. Both were still distressed and one of them became sick again. Not my day. When the women appeared before the magistrates several weeks later they were only fined £5 and £3 respectively, but their good character, and their jobs, were both lost.

I was delighted when my duties changed dramatically on 1 April 1965, when I took over my first shift as one of the two Shirley divisional motor cyclists.

16. DIVISIONAL MOTOR CYCLIST – 1965

The first change for me was my uniform trousers, tailor-made, with the lower section of the legs tightly bound to make room for my high fur-lined zipped boots. I also had a heavy-duty jacket, leather gauntlets with a white plastic top and a black crash helmet and goggles.

There was, however, little to distinguish my machine from other motor cycles, no distinctive coloured police markings, only the word 'POLICE' in blue, marked on the back and on the distinctive front white fairing. But I had a fitted radio, with aerial, and a police siren, so vehicles could be left in no doubt as to my identity. My machine, Reg. No. 11CTR, was a 750cc Triumph and I loved it from the minute I collected it from the garage in Hulse Road. I immediately felt the power and difference from riding my own former 350cc machine.

PC Jim Brown entering the old Shirley Police Station for his meal break

This was, in many ways, the happiest period of my police service. Being in the open air throughout my eight-hour shift, one of the first to attend emergency calls within the division, aware from my radio as to what was happening throughout the city, and the sheer pleasure of being able to ride at whatever speed I chose, was a joy.

I was soon brought down to earth on my first day, when my first duties were covering the Oakley Road/Tebourba Way school crossing, one of the mundane duties that, although a responsible one, was boring and irksome.

My normal routine was to first cycle to Hulse Road to collect my machine, check it and ensure the tank was full, then report for duty at Shirley police station. Other than being given specific tasks, such as a school crossing, I was then free to roam the division, going wherever I wished but answering any emergency calls. At the end of the 4pm-midnight shift I had to ensure the machine was hosed down and cleaned for my colleague taking over the following morning. We all did this, faithfully, and nobody was ever left to collect a dirty maching at the beginning of the day.

I was normally the first on the scene, but once I had taken the immediate action, given first aid, etc., I would normally also be joined by either the divisional emergency driver or beat officer, who would take over, leaving me free to roam and be available for another call. I thus avoided a lot of the routine paperwork, other than sometimes having to submit a short report about my initial action, such as arresting somebody, obtaining details of witnesses etc.

Sometimes I had to deal with the matter myself, such as a sudden death where an elderly couple were found dead in bed together, with the gas tap not fully turned off.

Another instance was an 11 year-old lad who caught his arm in a power wringer whilst playing with it alone. I had to call the fire brigade to get his arm, which was found to be fractured, released, and then accompany the ambulance to the Royal South Hants hospital.

I reported my first ever 'speeder', a 19 year old idiot who overtook me at night on a wet Shirley Road at around 60mph. I followed him, during which time he overtook vehicles waiting to turn at junctions, with a high risk of a collision if they had actually turned and at a speed never less than 55mph in a 30mph zone. It was not just a question of speeding, it was dangerous driving, and he was stopped and reported as such. He was the first of many drivers exceeding the speed limit, but if the excess speed was not too great, and the road conditions were favourable, the majority were merely cautioned and their documents checked. It was always a question of whether the speed was actually dangerous to other road users, depending on the weather and road conditions.

My police club snooker opponent, PC Norman Chalk, traffic department, got his own back for my cheeky 70mph dash down Middle Road when I was a detective. I returned to the Hulse Road garage just before midnight, with enough time to hose the machine down, but then could not find my pedal cycle. After some time hunting for it I looked up, and there it was, hanging from the ceiling. It took me some time to find the ladder that Norman had used, but when I next saw him I acknowledged that we were now even.

I suffered a shock, literally, when I drove onto the forecourt of the closed Blue Star garage in Millbrook Road during rain and placed my feet on the ground. There had been an electrical short on one of the forecourt signs, unbeknown to me, until I became grounded. It was not a severe shock, but enough to unsettle me for a while.

One evening call enabled me to help save a life. A 65 year-old man, a night watchman, was reported to have deliberately struck himself on the head with a heavy mason's hammer in an unusual attempt to commit suicide. When I arrived at the scene he was in the act of trying to hang himself with a cord from a door handle and had to be restrained. He had tied the cord around his neck, then tight to the door handle before slumping down in a sitting position. Fortunately I was joined by PS Ken Carter, traffic department, who helped me restrain the unfortunate man and render first aid.

Ken Carter, then a Chief Inspector, in 1976 when Southampton Football Club beat Manchester United 1-0 in the FA Cup Final (*Hampshire Constabulary History Society*)

Looking through my notebook for this period I am struck by the very large number of motorists I cautioned for speeding, all presenting no danger whatsoever in spite of exceeding the limit. I suppose that as a motorist I have sympathy for decent individuals being penalised for what can amount to a technical offence under circumstances where no danger to others was present. Real 'speeders', those greatly exceeding the speed limit under wet or heavy traffic conditions, overtaking or cornering recklessly, deserve punishing and I did not hesitate to prosecute under such circumstances.

I soon found that I was still 'Lucky Jim'. Early one June evening I was stationary astride my machine at Millbrook Roundabout, when I heard on my radio that a two door saloon had been stolen from Ringwood during the previous 10 minutes. I took note of its number and, to my surprise, 15 minutes later I saw it travel around the roundabout towards Tebourba Way.

I immediately radioed the information to the control room and followed the car, at a discreet distance, along Tebourba Way until it stopped at traffic lights at the junction with Oakley Road. I saw the car contained two men and that the driver's window was open. I therefore quickly drove alongside, reached in and removed the ignition key, barking at them "You're nicked. Climb over and get in the back seat."

They looked at my grim face and did so, without a murmur. I then told them the car had been reported stolen, cautioned them and one said "We didn't know it was stolen" and the other "We bought it off a chap at Ringwood. I thought it was a bit fishy". Other police vehicles soon arrived and they were taken to Shirley police station, where they readily admitted the theft and held to await an escort from Hants County officers.

I experienced one of the most dangerous pursuits of my life in September, a chase that was inexplicable until many years later. It started innocently enough, late one evening whilst I was travelling along The Avenue. I was travelling north and had just overtaken and acknowledged PC 140 Peter Brown, traffic department, on his motor cycle, travelling south.

I reached Bassett Crossroads, where the traffic lights were showing red, and as I waited I saw a red MG Midget sports car turn into the Avenue from Burgess Road in front of me at around 40-45mph. It passed me and continued down The Avenue, accelerating to what I estimated to be around 70mph. I gave chase and when I reached the car saw that it had slowed down to 30mph as it was then immediately behind Peter Brown, travelling at that speed, in his clearly marked traffic motor cycle.

I pulled alongside the sports car and indicated to the driver to pull in to the side of the road and stop. The driver pulled into the side of the road, slowed down, then suddenly changed into a low gear, turned out his lights and accelerated, passing Peter Brown and turning sharply left into Westwood Road. Both Peter and I gave chase, with the car reaching 55mph, and I managed to draw level as we were both approaching a parked car on our nearside, my intention being to 'box him in' and force him to brake. However, although the driver was clearly aware of me alongside he veered out towards me, forcing me to swerve and drop back. The vehicle lights were still out.

The chase continued for some time, around various roads, all at a fast speed, and once I managed to pass him, and position myself directly in front of him, decelerating as I did so. But instead of slowing down he swung violently to his offside and overtook me. There was no question but he must have been aware that I was a police motor cyclist as my marked rear plate was clearly visible.

At one stage the car drove into The Avenue again, this time entering between two cars travelling south, forcing the second car to brake violently to avoid a serious collision. The sports car continued along The Avenue, travelling to its offside, and when I again drew level I was forced to drop back suddenly as the car veered across my path as we approached a car travelling towards us. I came very close to a head-on collision with the approaching car because of the sports car forcing me across the road. Peter Brown, behind me, was giving a running commentary to the control room, so that other police vehicles could assist.

All three of us travelled north along The Avenue at 70mph and as we reached two lines of traffic travelling north ahead of us the sports car overtook them going to his extreme offside and forcing an oncoming car to brake violently to avoid a head-on collision. We all then went through the Basset Crossroads traffic lights at red, although there was heavy traffic in all directions at the time, causing them to swerve and brake in all directions.

The chase continued into Glen Eyre road, where the sports car lights came on for a short while before being turned off again as it turned into Elmsleigh Gardens. We then saw it collide with the offside rear of a parked car, coming to a halt some distance away with a burst front nearside tyre.

When we reached the car Peter Brown reached through the open window and seized the driver's arm, which I promptly handcuffed. The driver was then 'assisted' from the car as other police vehicles arrived at the scene and we searched the sports car, thinking from the way the driver had attempted to escape, that it must contain valuable stolen property. Nothing came to light but I did notice a blanket spread out in the boot with a pile of loose change scattered over it.

I cautioned the driver and asked "Why have you taken such fantastic risks to avoid being stopped and why didn't you pull in when I first told you to in The Avenue"? His unexpected reply was "I didn't see what you wanted to stop me for". When again asked why he had suddenly pulled away when first stopped, his explanation was "I thought you were picking on me". I searched him, finding nothing suspicious, and the duty Inspector, Harry Jackson, then arrived, instructing me to remove the handcuffs and merely report the driver for driving at a speed and manner dangerous. I was stopped from further questioning the driver to discover his true reason for trying to get away and had to carry out my orders.

It was not until many years later, when I reflected on the chase, that I thought of the driver possibly being involved in the sale of controlled drugs, hence the loose change on the blanket in the boot. At the time there was no drug problem, as far as I was concerned, and at no time in my police service did I have any real personal involvement in dangerous drugs. I now think that the driver was probably selling cannabis, but we were not allowed to make a more thorough search of the car or question the driver, so I will never really know. What I do know is that I was put at serious risk several times during the hectic chase.

My first aid training came in useful when I was called to an accident in Millbrook Goods Yard. A 30-year old man had caught his left hand between two train buffers whilst the engine was still moving, severing two fingers and badly damaging a third. I was able to reduce the bleeding until the arrival of the ambulance and felt satisfied I had been of some help.

My spell of duty as one of the first divisional motor cyclists came to an end in October when, to my great surprise, I was told I was being transferred to the traffic department as one of their motor cyclists.

The seven months I had spent in Shirley division had not only been enjoyable for the freedom of riding a motor cycle for a complete shift, but for the large number of incidents I had attended. Traffic accidents galore, domestic troubles, sudden deaths, speeding offences, every day had given me something interesting to deal with, me more often than not being the first one at the scene.

I had never been enthusiastic about traffic offences, being concerned mainly with individuals who committed deliberate criminal offences, and I had thought this was generally known by my superiors. I was therefore somewhat puzzled by this new attachment, but felt reassured when told "It's only temporary. We'll see how you turn out".

17. TRAFFIC MOTOR CYCLIST – 1965

My first Sunday morning, reporting for duty at Hulse Road on 17 October, started well, or so I thought. I was joined by PC Tony Webb, an experienced traffic officer, who instructed me on the handling of my new motor cycle, a Triumph Saint 1,000cc machine. It was immensely powerful, compared to my Shirley division machine, and I looked forward to seeing just what it could do. It was not long before I found out.

My tour of duty had started at 7am and at 8.10am Tony and I had travelled together to Chilworth Road, by which time I had just got used to handling the Triumph. I decided to open the machine up a bit, to see how it handled at speed, but unfortunately I overdid it. Travelling fast around a sharp left-hand bend on an unfamiliar motor cycle is not to be recommended. To my dismay I ran out of road, veering across to my offside as I rounded the bend, fortunately with no traffic coming towards me. I dropped into a deep ditch, and as I slowed down, whilst travelling along it, felt a sense of relief that I had avoided serious trouble. My relief was short-lived as I encountered a large drain pipe blocking the ditch, hitting it violently, forcing both machine and rider into the air at a considerable distance.

When I landed on the ground I felt sick, both at the thought of what I had done as well as the physical pain I had in my left shoulder and wrist. As I lay there, Tony came across, satisfied himself that I was not seriously injured, and called the traffic department for assistance. Whilst we waited I saw a number of Chilworth motorists, probably on their way to church, stop on seeing a police officer lying on the ground next to a damaged motor cycle. Tony spoke to them and they then all carried on.

I later asked Tony what he had told them and he replied "Just told them it was a civil defence exercise and there was nothing to worry about." The fact was we had left the force area and were trespassing on County territory. None of us wanted Hampshire officers involved; we didn't know them well enough to be sure of what action they would take. I was taken to the General Hospital by traffic Sgt John Talbot and found to have yet another broken wrist. The machine was badly damaged. It had only just returned from the workshops, following damage when an abnormal load fell on the rider and machine. The machine's call sign? 13.

I soon discovered the esprit de corps that existed within the traffic department. Tony Webb made a statement in which he said that I had accelerated to chase a car whose number plate was similar to one reported stolen, and Sgt John Talbot submitted a report confirming that black ice on the road (there wasn't) had caused me to lose control. John became my friend for life.

Unlike CID, when I reported sick for half a day with a broken wrist, this time I was off for seven weeks, following which I took a week annual leave, reporting back for traffic duty in late December. My first week back was spent as an observer in traffic cars, with such PCs as Den Barrett, Bill Perrin, Les Newman and my old friend Norman Chalk.

It was while I was out one evening with Normal Chalk in his Wolseley that I had my first taste of advanced driving. We were travelling along South Front, towards Queensway and Norman said "Have you ever been in a controlled skid?" I hadn't, so as the road was virtually empty at the time he accelerated towards the roundabout and as we reached it managed to make it skid. Under perfect control, we skidded round the roundabout, at all times facing the same direction, until he reached Hanover Buildings, which we entered as though we had merely turned right from South Front. I was deeply impressed but knew I would only be able to carry out such a manoeuvre myself if I attended the advanced police training course at Maidstone. To go there would mean I was accepted full time as a traffic officer, and I was unsure about that. As it turned out, so were my superiors.

I was then entrusted back with my Triumph call sign 13, which had now been fully repaired. I worked two shifts, 7.00am to 3.00pm, and 3.00pm to 11.00pm. One of the plus factors of being on the traffic department was that I was able to return home for my meal breaks. The town was divided into five spheres and each day I was detailed by the duty sergeant to patrol a sphere, sometimes two coupled. All I had to do was to travel around the area, rarely attending 999 calls, just monitoring traffic and 'showing the flag'. I attended some traffic accidents, but was normally quickly relieved by the divisional motor cyclist or emergency driver, so I had a peaceful and enjoyable life. The day was usually uneventful, but sometimes broken by such things as a 'Bank Patrol', when I followed the bullion van, accompanied by armed officers in traffic cars or, as I had done, in the back of the bank's van.

'Lucky Jim' came to the fore again one evening in Bursledon Road when I chased and stopped a car that I had seen driven towards me at a fast speed. The occupants were two men aged 18 and 19 and when I spoke to them I instinctively felt suspicious for some unknown reason.

I asked the driver for his driving licence, but he didn't have it with him, so I asked him for the vehicle's registered number. When he gave me a totally incorrect number I asked him to get out of the car to look at the number plate. He then said he had only bought the car two weeks earlier, but when asked couldn't remember the seller's name. I then noted the name and address of both driver and passenger and asked the passenger if he was a friend of the driver. Both men answered simultaneously, one saying "I've known him a couple of days" and the other "I picked him up hitch-hiking." That was enough for me,

I radioed for back-up and both were taken to Bitterne police station where they were searched. I found documents on them with different names and addresses to those they had given and after some further questioning they admitted having stolen the car from a bowling alley in Portsmouth. They also admitted that a bunch of ignition keys I had found on the passenger had been stolen from different cars they had taken in that area. Both men were then handed over to an escort from Pompey.

I also had duties of escorting abnormal loads, but mindful of the fact that my machine had been damaged when a load once fell, I ensured I always kept well in front of it, with lights flashing and signalling approaching traffic to keep clear.

My notebooks for this period rarely mention speeding offences, but one was worthy of reporting. A car, seen in Bursledon Road at 60mph, late at night in wet conditions, ignored the fact that as I followed him my flashing blue light was illuminating the interior of the car. The driver had also overtaken four cars dangerously so I had no sympathy whatsoever. A few minutes later I found I was escorting an ambulance to the RSH hospital following a serious accident in Northam Road, another task that fell to me several times. This, so soon after the speeding offence, confirmed that I had been justified in reporting him.

One incident I attended was initially very worrying. A child, aged 3½ had fallen 20 feet onto concrete from a bedroom window in Hinkler Road and had suffered stomach and head injuries. However, it turned out these were not serious and he made a full recovery.

By this time I had ceased to cycle to Hulse Road to collect my machine. I had now replaced my car, and this gave me an added little personal pleasure. It was my habit to return home to Sholing by way of Northam Road, travelling over Northam Bridge en route. The bridge was notorious for 'speeders' and the regularly badly damaged front walls of the houses on the Bitterne Road side of the bridge bore testimony to this.

When I travelled over Northam Bridge at the end of my shift I would often look in my rear mirror and see somebody approaching me at a fast speed. This especially happened late at night, after I had completed my 3-11pm tour of duty. When this happened I would maintain a fixed just under 30mph speed, keeping to the centre of the road, forcing the fast approaching car to reduce speed. I then suffered flashing lights, sometimes horns sounded, as the frustrated driver tried in vain to overtake me, with me changing my position to prevent him passing. I had it off to a fine art to allow him to approach me on my nearside, and then force him across the road onto the forecourt of the filling station just before Bullar Road, and stop directly in front of him.

I would regularly see the other driver get out of his vehicle, ready to do battle (the early 'road rage' offenders?) but then see me walk towards them, my uniform silver buttons the first to be noticed, then my trousers and high boots. They could then see that not only was I a police officer, I was a dreaded traffic officer, and they immediately calmed down. I always only cautioned them, but I am sure they thought twice before driving over the bridge the same way again.

My temporary attachment to the traffic department came to an end, not unexpectedly, in March, when Supt. Bill Hayter, a former traffic officer now in charge of Shirley division, sent for me to ask if I would consider becoming his division's first CID Enquiry Officer. The Force had decided that in addition to that function being carried out at headquarters, both Bitterne and Shirley would have the same assistance for their CID staff.

I jumped at the opportunity and accordingly 1 March 1966 saw me back into the CID way of life, but without the excessive workload.

18. SHIRLEY C.I.D. OFFICE – 1966

My wife was delighted to learn that my hours were now a permanent 9.00am to 5.00pm, with Sundays off and a half day Saturday. My duties, as they had been when I carried out the same function at Headquarters CID, were to deal with telephone enquiries, take statements from callers and generally assist the detectives in any way possible.

DS "Mac' John McCullagh, who was in charge of Shirley CID, was delighted that I had joined his team and we immediately recalled when we had both been the only two DCs in the PHQ CID office when the uniformed enquiry officer received a phone call. From the conversation it was obvious a shoplifter had been detained at the Edwin Jones store and DS Fred Williams was standing at the counter reading through the routine message slips, with his back to us.

I looked at Mac, he looked at me, and we tiptoed across to the door leading to the cell passage, quietly opened it and ran along it as fast as we could. We could hear Fred bellowing from the office, but we continued until we reached the safety of the main corridor and then to the canteen. We were both far too busy to deal with a routine shoplifter and thought it was about time that Fred got his hands dirty. It didn't do us much good as he soon found us and angrily booked Mac out to the job.

I quickly found that Mac had other ideas about the nature of my duties at Shirley. I had taken a statement from a caller reporting the loss of his post office savings book from his lodgings, and we knew that a fellow lodger, Reggie, was a thief I had dealt with several times. Mac decided that as I knew him I should deal with the theft.

I therefore went to the lodgings in Newlands Avenue, questioned Reggie, searched his room and found the missing savings book. He had made several withdrawals and had no option but to admit everything and was thus arrested and charged. Because of his past record the magistrates sent him to Quarter Sessions for sentence and he received a 15 month sentence. I thought it an unusual sort of office job.

The Force underwent a dramatic change on Monday 1 August, 1966, with the introduction of an integrated personal radio system, the first of its kind in any Police Force in the country. Sufficient dual-frequency sets were available for all patrolling officers who, for the first time, were able to communicate immediately with both the main Information Room and their own divisional station, where sub-controls were located.

Every beat was allocated a call sign and all vehicles could be contacted throughout the town.

The following month another innovation came into being, our first Woman Inspector, Mrs J. Hopkins, who had transferred from the Met.

My alleged office duty, with Mac in charge, had meant, in fact, that I became a part-time detective, although still a uniformed PC, and I was regularly asked to assist with the interrogation of prisoners who uniformed officers had detained at Shirley. Mac thought I was particularly good at obtaining confessions and used me accordingly. I quite enjoyed this aspect of my work, although once I had got them to admit everything they were handed over to the officer in the case for him to obtain the voluntary statement of admission, disregarding anything I had been told. I therefore did not need to even submit a report or make a note in my pocketbook as the officer in the case then asked the right questions so his evidence could be used.

I was more than happy with this as it reduced my paperwork and court appearances, but at the same time allowed me to become involved in real police work. Mac also regularly told me to report in plainclothes to assist with observations to help with various incidents of break-ins, indecency etc.

One example of this occurred that December when Mac detailed me to work a late shift and maintain observations in the Portland Street area, with DC 'Robbie' Roberts, because of a number of recent break-ins.

At 11.20pm we saw four men pushing an Austin Mini Van along Portland terrace with the driver at the wheel. The van drew into the kerb and stopped and the men walked away. It transpired that the battery was flat and they were helping to start it, without success.

We went to the van and saw the driver slumped over the wheel, so asked if he was alright. I had the response "Do you want a punch on the nose?" We could then see he was drunk, so pulled him out of the vehicle, when he staggered and became very abusive, asking me if I would like my face smashed in and shouting obscenities. We arrested him, took him to the nearby headquarters where the station sergeant questioned him, confirming he was well under the influence, and called Dr Yetman, the police surgeon, to examine him. The man was asked if he wanted his own doctor called, getting the reply "He's in Weymouth. By the time he gets here I'll be sober."

The man refused to give a urine sample when asked, saying he'd had 10 whiskies as he was celebrating his 21st birthday. After Dr Yetman certified him as being under the influence and incapable of driving, and when the man had become sober, I charged him with being drunk in charge of a motor vehicle. In reply to the charge he stated he was not guilty so he was bailed to appear at court, for a remand, the following morning. Because of his attitude, and the fact that at 2.00am I assisted in a search of the Vincents Walk area where a man had been disturbed, I had no opportunity of obtaining the man's antecedent history or completing the case papers before I went off duty at 3.00am

As a good indication of my superior's attitude in this period, the following may be of interest to current serving officers: I was woken at 9.15am the following morning and told that PS Des Barnes wished to know whether it was possible for the case papers to be completed for this case before the court sat as a guilty plea was now anticipated.

I sent a reply that it was not possible, giving my reasons, but a further visit was made by an officer saying that Inspector Harry Langrish (the court officer prosecuting that day) had instructed me to report at once and prepare a digest of the Form 22 (offence report) so that the case could be dealt with that morning. I did as instructed, angry at his complete and utter lack of consideration, the convenience of court officers being considered more important than my welfare. I was also annoyed that consideration was being given to the accused, who had been difficult but now wished the case dealt with quickly.

I spent considerable time in the Shirley CID office over the next few months, interviewing complainants, taking statements, helping with crime reports and dealing with phone enquiries, I also became involved in several enquiries, mostly of a minor nature.

A practical joke on newly appointed DC Trevor Witt worked well when he joined the division. We waited until we were all in the canteen having lunch and arranged for station reserve officer PC Frank Browne to call through the hatch "Break-in reported at 390 Shirley Road." None of us moved and Trevor said to Mac, eagerly, "I'll go Skipper". This would have been his first case and directly he left we all rushed to the typing pool front office and watched him drive the CID car into Shirley Road and turn right. A short while later the car returned, driving slowly past the station, then a few minutes later returned and entered the forecourt. We saw him look at the number that could just be seen on the front door - '390'.

My office work changed dramatically when Southampton and Portsmouth City Forces amalgamated with the Hampshire Constabulary on 1 April 1967. I found I became yet another first for Shirley, now part of the newly created 'E' division, enlarged to the west to include Totton and district. I was no longer PC 150 Southampton City police; I became, to my great surprise, DC 1430, Scenes of Crime, E division, Hampshire Constabulary. I was a detective once again.It had been decided that in addition to the existing SoC team based at what was now Southampton Central 'F' division, Bitterne and Shirley police stations would have their own individual SoC officer and I had been selected (but not really asked.) as the first one for Shirley. This was my third 'first' newly created position at the station, but I was getting used to being asked to take on a new rôle.

19. SCENES OF CRIME – 1967

The new Force had got off the ground early. Well prior to the actual amalgamation date of 1 April 1967, I had been approached and asked how I felt about being a Scenes of Crime Officer. I was happy about another change of direction, so found myself, before I knew it, attending a two-week Scenes of Crime course in London with the Metropolitan Police.

It was a fascinating experience; detailed lectures on various forensic subjects from senior Scotland Yard officers and scientists; how to set anthracene traps to invisibly mark objects; attending post-mortems carried out at Guy's Hospital by the renowned pathologist Dr Keith Simpson; instructions on the correct collection, labelling and retention of exhibits and, amusingly, how to take impressions with Plaster of Paris. I say amusingly because that particular lecture started with a view of a life-size Plaster of Paris erect penis, made, I was told, by a previous Southampton officer on the course. It was, of course, a well-known practical joker on the F Central division team, sadly now deceased.

The course was more than worthwhile and I learnt a lot, making me feel confident that I could carry out an efficient examination of any scene, murder or otherwise. I often wonder how much more efficient we would have been if the marvel of DNA had been discovered at this time. The nearest we came to it was the knowledge that a person's blood group could be broken down into sub-groups, reducing the possibility of a match from one in several million to one in several thousand. It did not prove that a blood trace came from an individual but could be good circumstantial evidence. It could also be ascertained from saliva, providing he or she was a 'secretor'.

I started my new situation as a Scenes of Crime officer on 17 April by instructing PC Keith Burton, my replacement, on his duties in the CID office, warning him that he would find himself being allocated specific CID duties. He was more than happy about this as that was the career he wanted – he did more than make the grade and later became an excellent detective.

The first difference I felt, following the amalgamation, was the fact that I was issued with a large expense book, in which I had to detail all meals incurred away from the station, travelling expenses etc. This was far removed from my City experience, but I realised that the new Shirley E division extended far to the west and I had to travel to what had been County areas as a SoC officer. In the City days, if I travelled to the Civic Centre from Shirley for any reason, then any meal I took in the canteen was at my own expense. Now, however, Force policy meant I was travelling to a different division, from E to F Central, so was therefore entitled to be paid for both mileage and my meal. What a dramatic contrast for us all.

Before I fully took up my new duties I was seen by DS Ken Crossland, the officer in overall charge of the South Western area of the Force. He gave me an explanation of my general responsibilities and the methods used by the SoC Section, as well as supplying me with a wide range of materials and equipment.

By this time I owned an estate car, and this held my fingerprint and other forensic material. This was necessary as I not only had to attend areas well outside the old Shirley division; I now took my turn to be on a week's 24-hour call for the entire New Forest area, travelling to areas as far away as Hythe, Lymington, Lyndhurst, Brocken-hurst, Christchurch etc. I enjoyed such trips, especially as I was being well paid for them with generous expenses.

One such call-out, however, annoyed me. My bedside phone rang at 5.00am request-ing my urgent presence at Lyndhurst police station where a car had to be examined. I dressed, bleary eyed, and drove to Lyndhurst as fast as possible. On entering the station I saw the desk duty constable and asked for details. "Was the car involved in a murder? A rape? A robbery?" The reply was "No, it was taken from outside a pub last night and has just been found abandoned in the Forest". I looked stony faced at the officer, "You mean I have been called out, on a 30 mile round trip, just to check a Taking Without Consent? You idiot, it can easily wait until your own SoC Officer arrives later this morning, I'm doing nothing." I then left the station thinking I had just met a 'carrot-cruncher', a term we City officers applied to some former County officers post-amalgamation. When on 24-hour call normal day duty still applied and my sleep had been disturbed without good reason. I was most unhappy.

The knowledge I had obtained on the NSY course and my years as a working detec-tive, when I had carried out my own scenes of crime examinations, stood me in good stead, and I gradually built up considerable experience, sometimes with trial and error. My notebooks were almost immediately filled with details of crime scenes I visited, using my own recording system, with my exhibits in sealed and signed containers and envelopes. I also took saliva and blood samples in incidents of violence and rape (semen can also reveal a man's blood group), as well as a number of elimination fingerprints from bodies in the public mortuary.

I attended all manner of scenes, with the interesting duty of taking exhibits to the Aldermaston Forensic Laboratory for examination. It was a fascinating establishment, top security but with easy and immediate access for me, after showing my warrant card at the entrance. I found I was a regular visitor and became well know to the security staff.

Fingerprints found at the scene had to be photographed by new Force photographers, as well as the former City ones; elimination prints taken from individuals with legitimate access; exhibits prepared for court, properly labelled and presented. Overall I soon became quite an expert in taking fingerprints, plaster casts of tyre impressions, and finding and recovering relevant forensic material at the scene. I soon found that I was in great demand throughout my working day, attending the scene of every crime in the enlarged E division.

One great difference was that I initially had to be called out from home by a visit from an officer from Bitterne police station when needed, and it was soon realised that this was inefficient. The Force therefore, at no expense to me, installed a telephone in my home, with an extension in the bedroom (regrettably, regularly used at night when I was on call). Domestic telephones were not common at this time and I was one of the very few in my road to have one. Of course, I had to record all my personal calls and pay for them accordingly.

I quickly found my way around Hampshire (well before the advent of SatNavs) and although some addresses in the New Forest area were difficult to find at night, I always got there in the end. It was irksome when some properties had no number, merely a name, often set back from the road and extremely difficult to locate at night.

I was still a Police Federation Branch Board member, and this gave me a break in May when I attended a week-long Annual Federation Conference at Scarborough, expenses paid by the Federation.

At the end of May I paid my first visit to the Hampshire Constabulary Headquarters in Winchester. I had by now sat and passed the promotion exam for sergeant, having had much more time and opportunity to study, and was summoned to appear before a Promotion Board. I felt that I acquitted myself well, giving an account of the differing duties I had performed during my service and showing my good breadth of experience in so many different areas. From the tone of questioning the senior officers, none of whom were known to me, seemed more than satisfied and I awaited the outcome.

I did not have long to wait. I was instructed to report to Hulse Road on 24 July for a week-long Pre-Promotion Course, meaning I would now be promoted for certain, some time in the future. The course was interesting, full of how to look after your team and to command respect. I did not think that many of my senior officers had ever been on such a course.

Over the ensuing months I attended a very large variety of crime scenes, many of them well outside Southampton, but I had by now become accustomed to being a County rather than a City officer. They soon became routine, with marks found at the scene being identified with convicted individuals, having to attend court to give evidence of finding and handling the exhibits, it all soon became second nature to me. The vast majority of cases were minor and routine, but some are worthy of a mention. Such as 2½ lbs of nitro-glycerine, Nobel 808 high explosive, found in a stream off Brockenford Lane, Totton. It was starting to sweat, making it liable to explode if knocked, so it was carefully packed by an Army Major from the bomb disposal squad and, to my horror, arrangements made for me to take it to Woolwich Arsenal for disposal.

The Major assured me it was safe to travel, but couldn't guarantee my safety if I was involved in a major traffic accident. Needless to say, the following morning I collected the parcel from the rear of Totton police station and drove carefully to Woolwich Arsenal, in my own car, with the high explosive in my boot, worried whenever I saw a vehicle close behind me. My notebook records me claiming seven shillings and three pence for my lunch in London, but doesn't record the several pounds I lost in weight.

In October I attended a lecture on Dangerous Drugs, my very first knowledge of the subject and a problem that was only just starting to rear its ugly head. However, I never became involved in a drug enquiry; that was left to the small specialist squad that had been set up.

I had an unusual scene to visit. A terrace of houses in Millbrook Road had a communal attic roof, running the entire length of the terrace, and following a complaint from one resident I had to check this attic, confirming that small holes had been made in the ceilings of the bedrooms and bathrooms. It was my 'unpleasant' duty to look through these holes to confirm their location and look for clues. I found no real clue as to the identity of the perpetrator, but did, by accident, come across one portly lady sitting on the loo. Luckily for me she did not notice anything unusual so I was spared from having to defend myself.

Rustling was not an offence we ever came across in the City, but I was called out to one case at Wilvesley Plain in the New Forest, where two heifers were found slaughtered, having been shot in the head and skinned. I took samples of blood and hairs, wondering if they would ever prove a match with a human. Of course, a suspect could possibly have been found with traces on their clothing, so it was not really a futile exercise.

I had been the SoC officer for several buggery offences, involving young boys, and also a number of rapes on women, but one rape in particular filled me with extreme anger, one where I found it difficult to remain objective. On New Year's Day a young girl had foolishly accepted a life home in a car driven by a man described as 'a tall, well built Jamaican'. He had stopped the car in a country lane outside Southampton and subjected her to a forcible rape. Not only was she a virgin, it subsequently turned out he had also given her a venereal disease. Fortunately, after getting away from him she took note of his car registration number so he could be traced. The driver was arrested by DC Ken Holmes the following day and I was present when his prisoner, 'Michael', a Jamaican, arrived in the station.

He was obnoxious from the outset. As Ken searched him, in front of me, 'Michael' immediately alleged "Where is my money? You have taken £20." He was obviously trying to make false allegations in an attempt to unsettle us. Ken calmly carried on, ignoring 'Michael', who continued to mouth obscenities and say he was only being picked on because of his colour. Neither Ken nor I rose to the bait and Ken took special care not to do anything that could be misconstrued as being violent or racist.

However, Ken left and returned with a mug of warm coffee for his prisoner, and I left to get a drink for myself. When I returned a few minutes later I saw that Ken's shirt and jacket were soaking wet. He explained that after 'Michael' had sipped the coffee, he threw the mug directly at Ken and then seized him by the throat screaming "You are a racist pig. It's only because I am black you have arrested me". 'Michael' was very strong, but Ken is also very well built and banged 'Michael's head on the CID office wall to make him let go, which he eventually did. Ken told me he then said to him, " I don't care if you are black, yellow or f...... green, you are not going to assault me or anyone else and get away with it." Ken later told me he was convinced that 'Michael' would kill a police officer some time in the future.

'Michael' refused to answer any questions and the following day was taken to Shirley police station where I examined his car for forensic material. We had to wait for the arrival of his solicitor before I could start and I took samples, and 'Michael's clothing, in his presence. I later removed one of the car seats as it contained traces of what I believed to be blood. This was later confirmed, the same group as that of the girl but different to 'Michael's, by the Aldermaston Laboratory. Fibres from the girl's clothing were also found on 'Michael's clothing. All this corroborated her story.

I was giving evidence at his committal at Winchester magistrates' court later that month when 'Michael' decided he'd had enough. He shouted and screamed, said he was leaving, managed to evade the escorting prison officer and jumped out of the dock. I ran out of the witness box and with the prison officer, we both fell on him to restrain him. The magistrates left the bench, frightened, and I spoke to 'Michael' in a calm and steady voice, saying "Come on 'Michael', don't be silly", in a reassuring tone. Unseen by anybody, except the prison officer, I was pulling his little finger back as far as I could, as we handcuffed him, whilst he continued to scream. The committal was then adjourned to February. When I saw him briefly, before he appeared in court, he told me, in no uncertain terms and with great feeling "I am going to f........ kill you when I get out". I am certain that he meant it; he was that sort of person.

There was a sequel. He was convicted at the Hampshire Assizes that April, after pleading not guilty and forcing the unfortunate girl to give evidence of her harrowing experience. When 'Michael' was sentenced to 8 years in prison he shouted obscenities at the Judge, who merely nodded his head and said to the escorting prison officers "Take him down", whereupon 'Michael' suddenly vanished from sight, his shouting gradually dying away. It appears that he had somehow fallen down the several steps leading to the corridor below, no doubt due to his effort to continue shouting at the judge. I was later informed that he died some years later in prison, so I was spared the thought of a reprisal.

I had an amusing brush with a traffic warden when called out early one morning to a break-in at a newsagents and tobacconists in Ringwood. I arrived in the early hours but could not park my car at the rear of the premises as I could see fresh tyre tracks there, ready for me to take Plaster of Paris Impressions. I had no option but to park in the front of the building, on double yellow lines, to take in my fingerprint and other equipment.

An hour or so later I was busy dusting a rear door for prints when a member of staff told me that a traffic warden was writing down details from my car. I said "Please explain that it is a CID police car, exempt from the regulations, and that I will move it as soon as I can. If it is causing a real problem I will move it further down, I am but examining a crime scene". She returned to say "he wants to see you".

I then saw the 'jobs worth', further explained the position, but he continued to say I was committing an offence. I then explained that if he gave me a ticket it would be refused by the station so he was wasting his time. I later returned to find a ticket on the car, which was, of course, torn up by the officer in charge at the station, saying "He's an idiot. We are trying to get him moved".

One case gave me great satisfaction. A stolen car, used in an armed robbery at Brighton, was found abandoned on the forecourt of private flats at the junction of Shirley Road and Roberts Road.

I examined the car and found it had been wiped clean of fingerprints and false number plates had been made using self-adhesive white plastic numbers, of the sort found in any hardware shop. I saw that one letter had just started to peel away at the corner, so I bought a large piece of clear plastic, carefully removed each number and letter with a pair of tweezers and mounted them on the clear plastic. I had worked out it would be impossible to peel off the protective wrapping wearing gloves, and, sure enough, many of the letters and numerals showed a fragment of fingerprint on one of the corners.

I had them all photographed and spent an hour in the Shirley police canteen with a pair of scissors, cutting off the fragments and gluing them together as though they were a jigsaw puzzle, eventually ending up with large portions of a thumb and fore-finger print. These were also photographed, checked and confirmed to be those of a convicted criminal. It was enough to secure a conviction and I was smug about the outcome.

A final case, among the several hundred I dealt with as a SoC officer, was when I was called out from home in the early hours to attend a break-in at an antique shop in Lyndhurst. It had come about when four London criminals were stopped by a patrol car whilst driving north on the motorway in the early hours. When the car boot was routinely examined it was found to contain a large quantity of antique silverware and pottery. The men said they had found the articles by the side of the road and were looking for a police station to hand them in. For some inexplicable reason they were not believed, but taken to Basingstoke police station and all stations asked to check the antique shops in their area, hence finding the one at Lyndhurst.

When I examined the attacked premises I found that an exterior door and two inner doors had been forced open with a jemmy or similar instrument, with wood and paint chippings scattered everywhere. The shop was over 100 years old and appeared to have been painted and repainted many times, the paintwork becoming very thick with brittle flakes scattered all over the floor. I took the usual samples, labelling and sealing them, and then returned to Lyndhurst police station where the four suspects had been taken in the intervening period. They denied all knowledge of the premises.

I therefore took possession of their clothing, giving them a blanket in return, combed their hair onto a sheet of white paper, all of which was again labelled and sealed, and drove direct to Aldermaston for everything to be checked as a matter of urgency. The scientists were delighted with the paint samples, saying they had never dealt with 17 different layers, all different colours and thicknesses, before – it was a record for them.

Suffice it to say, identical flakes were found on the clothing of two of the men, one of them with some flakes in his hair, and when informed of this they put their hands up and admitted their involvement. A satisfactory conclusion for me.

Another happy conclusion came my way in October when I was told to report to the clothing store at Winchester to collect my uniform clothing. I was to be promoted to uniformed sergeant and posted to Portswood station on 1 November 1968.

On 7 November the local *Daily Echo* duly reported my promotion, an event that was customarily reported at this period, but this seems to no longer apply.

COMMENDED OFFICER PROMOTED

HAMPSHIRE Police announce the promotion of Det. Con. James William Maxton Brown—Southampton-born and with the police in the city since 1952—to sergeant.

A man with six Commendations during his 16 years' service, he is stationed at Portswood.

Married, with two children, he joined the Southampton City Force in August, 1952. He has served, before and since amalgamation, in Portswood, Shirley and Southampton Central divisions. His home is in Bitterne.

Sgt. Brown's work has included service with the CID when, as a detective constable, he operated from both Shirley and Central divisions, for six years.

He was also a scenes-of-crime officer in the Shirley area, working for the South-West Support Headquarters at Winchester.

His career has included a spell as a police motor cyclist and two years as assistant Coroner's officer at the Civic Centre.

He joined the police when 20, after two years' National Service as a sergeant in the Royal Army Education Corps.

(Southern Daily Echo)

20. UNIFORMED SERGEANT – 1968

I had waited six months after passing the promotion board and it was made clear that if I had elected to 'unfreeze' and be available for promotion anywhere in Hampshire, my promotion would have come much sooner. But I was quite happy to wait and remain in my beloved Southampton.

My first duty was a 9.00am to 5.00pm shift, getting acclimatised to Portswood police station, meeting the other officers and generally settling in. I had one duty to perform, another first time for me, to accept a charge for a shoplifter arrested by PC Ian Fox. Straightforward, but I found it strange to be responsible for having to decide if there was sufficient evidence to proceed with the charge.

My first real duty was in charge of the 6.00am shift the following morning and to allocate the beat officers. I arrived early and when I went into the parade room I found the 'parade' to be vastly different from those I had attended as a PC. No longer did officers stand up presenting their truncheons and handcuffs, notebooks in hand to write down their beat etc. They now sat around a table, informally, to chat with their section sergeant - me.

However, I had to display my rank from the outset as when I entered the room I saw Bob Smith, my section friend from Shirley beat days, leaning back in his chair, feet on the table and reading a newspaper. He looked up as I walked in, and said, casually "Carry on Jim" and continued to read the paper. I barked at him "Put that paper away", and he removed it, grinning as he did so. I carried on with allocating the men their duties, concluding with "My office, PC Smith". When we were alone I said "Don't you ever take the piss again Bob. I am Sarg or Skipper when on duty, don't you forget it. If you do that again I'll have your guts for garters". He apologised and all was forgiven, but Bob made a point of always addressing me correctly thereafter.

For a considerable period my pocket book merely showed entries of my arriving and departing Portswood police station, my time taken up with checking constables' reports, and going out to 'book' them on their point. The first entry of significance was on 17 December when I was summoned to the Civic Centre to see Supt George Mansell (my former section sergeant who had made me a witness when he reported Mr Beirne for displaying artificial excrement.)

He explained that there was yet another 'first' waiting for me, if I was willing. An embryo crime intelligence system was going to be set up in January, 1969, with PC Ron Sayers at F Central division, compiling information on the movement and association of criminals. Known as a 'Collator', his function was to obtain information about crimes, criminals and suspects, maintain efficient records and ensure this information was passed onto others in a methodical way. George Mansel told me that this Local Intelligence Office was going to be increased in scope later that year, when a sergeant would be in charge. Was I interested? I most certainly was, so although I continued to be a section sergeant at Portswood I maintained contact with Ron Sayers, visiting him regularly, discussing what ideas he had and suggesting improvements. He took this well and we formed a good working relationship from the outset.

As my full-time move was some unknown time in the future I carried on as a patrol sergeant, with my first problem coming to light on a tour of night duty. It was the normal custom for the duty sergeant on the night shift to patrol Portswood with the emergency driver and PC in the divisional car. (On nights I was the sole supervising officer, virtually the Chief Constable of Portswood – although an Inspector from F Central would sometimes make a visit).

We had a call to an RTA (road traffic accident) at Portswood Junction and when we arrived I immediately saw that the driver of the offending vehicle showed signs of being under the influence. I had never even seen a breathalyser, let alone used one, so I said to the PC "Breathalyse him, will you", getting the unexpected reply "I've never done it Skipper, I don't know how". I then turned to my driver and asked him to carry it out, but was horror stricken when I received the same reply.

I thus had no option but to carry it out myself, reading the instructions as I did so, watched carefully by my two colleagues. For some strange reason the result proved negative, for which I was grateful.

In November I attended a nasty fatal accident, in dense fog, on the Winchester Road dual carriageway. A coupe sports car had driven directly underneath a parked articulated lorry and trailer, decapitating the unfortunate driver. What absolutely amazed me was that the fog was so thick that you could not see the opposite side of the road, but we could hear vehicles driven past at speeds greater than 50mph, although their stopping distance could not have been more than a few feet. It was absolutely unbelievable, also bearing in mind that at the scene of the fatality were two police cars, a fire engine and an ambulance, all with their warning lights flashing, lighting up both sides of the road and penetrating the dense fog.

I later became a brutal and unfeeling sergeant when I made a policewoman cry. It had been snowing and the roads were icy, and when I went through my in-tray I saw that two summons had to be served in Honeysuckle Road, Bassett. I looked out of my office, saw a young policewoman standing there, and asked her what work she had on. She had none at the moment, so I asked her to serve the summons for me. She told me she had never served a summons before, so I told her now was a good time to learn and explained the procedure.

To my surprise I then saw her go the front enquiry desk, controlled by PC Bert Vanstone, go behind the counter, take hold of the radio microphone and call the Portswood car back to the station. I asked her what on earth she was doing, getting the reply "To serve the summons Sarg". I immediately cancelled the car from returning and told her that if I had wished the car to serve the summons I would have called it back myself. I had asked her to do it, on foot. She then said "But the roads and pavements are icy", to which I replied, "Then you had better walk carefully". I added that if she returned saying the occupants were out, I would call the car back to take me there to check, and if they were in she would be on a misconduct form. Whereupon she burst out crying, but as I had several beat constables out on patrol, walking throughout their shift, I did not feel the slightest bit sorry for her, and she eventually returned with the summons duly served. I don't think she ever forgave me.

That February I was called out from home to assist with controlling the area following a large-scale fire in Bevois Valley Road. Barriers were erected across Bevois Valley Road, at the junction with Lawn Road, whilst the fire brigade dealt with the fire. Whilst I was standing near the barrier, which was lit with warning lamps, I saw, to my dismay, a motor cyclist hurtling down Portswood Road, towards Bevois Valley Road, oblivious of the lit barrier across the road. He hit the barrier with some force, catapulted from his machine over the top of the barrier and landed in a heap. I went across and found he was, miraculously, uninjured, other than a slight bruise on his arm. He told me he came this way every morning and the road had never been blocked before.

Another early turn saw me on duty in Wide Lane, controlling pickets who were trying to stop Ford workers entering the factory during a strike. I then had my first confrontation with a trade union official, who thought he had the right to stop men entering the gates. I calmly pointed out that if his men obstructed the footpath or road they would be arrested. He did not believe I had the power to interfere in an industrial dispute, but I made it very clear indeed that his pickets could shout all they liked, wave placards or in any way try to dissuade others from entering the factory, but if they caused an obstruction he would be the first to be arrested. We had a face to face confrontation, with me looking very determined indeed and luckily he was the first to back down. I was most relieved.

A few weeks later I used my truncheon in anger for the first time. Because there had been a press outcry over the use of handcuffs when a large contingent of stowaways were taken from the Docks, some high-ranking genius decided that handcuffs should no longer be carried by officers but only be available in police cars. This instruction only lasted a week or so, but it had a dramatic effect on me.

The same week as the handcuffs instruction I was in the team car at 11.40pm, with the driver and a PC, when we saw two men urinating in the centre of Kent Road. I got out, went up to them, saying "That's a disgusting thing to do", but got the drunken reply from one of them "It's a police state, shut your mouth, you f........ Gestapo bastard". That was enough for me to arrest him for drunk and disorderly, but his friend caught hold of my arm, telling me "leave him alone". I told him not to interfere and go away, but he then caught hold of the arm of one of the PCs, who had joined me, and lashed out at me, kicking my left leg and punching me in the chest.

The three of us then struggled with the two men, who became most violent and we had great difficulty in restraining both of them simultaneously. The second man was arrested for obstruction, but when we managed to get them as far as the police van a fight developed, with the three of us being punched and kicked by both men.

As we were not carrying our handcuffs, they were in the van, and we could not get away to get them, I told the man who was hitting me "Stop this nonsense or we shall have to use our sticks". This only seemed to provoke them, so I had no option but to draw my stick and aiming at my prisoner's shoulder, missed and struck him on the head by accident.

Assistance then arrived and the men were taken to the Civic Centre where Dr Bridger, the police surgeon, was summoned to treat my prisoner, who was bleeding profusely from a head wound. Dr Bridger also saw and confirmed the bruising we three officers had sustained. One man was taken to the RSH Hospital and given 17 stitches in his head wound, and both men were charged with assault on police and being drunk and disorderly. They appeared at court three days later and each, after their previous convictions were given, sentenced to nine months imprisonment.

A week later I was on early turn, driving the Portswood car in Wide Lane, when I heard a radio message that a Triumph 2000 saloon had been stolen from Hill Lane in the previous three minutes. 'Lucky Jim' came to the fore again as I decided to park on the forecourt of the Fleming Arms, facing the junction with Wessex Lane. I have no idea why I decided to do that, but I radioed my position and was then joined by PC Eric Fielder in his dog van.

We had only been in position for ten minutes when, lo and behold, what should turn up facing us, waiting at the traffic lights showing red, but the Triumph saloon. I immediately drove straight across Mansbridge Road, blocking the car in, and was able to arrest the driver with no trouble at all. He was taken to Portswood police station where he readily admitted not only taking the car from Hill Lane, but several other identical offences, leaving the vehicles where they could be found. I later charged him with TADA (Taking and Driving Away Without Consent) and driving uninsured, and he was subsequently fined and disqualified.

One late evening, whilst on patrol in the divisional Commer van, with driver and PC, we were driving along Portswood Road and saw that a long line of approaching vehicles ahead kept stopping, some swerving, and starting again. As we got closer I saw that a young idiot, part of a large group of youngsters, thought it funny to unexpectedly jump out in the road, into the path of oncoming cars, forcing them to suddenly brake, and then run back to the pavement. His friends obviously thought it a huge joke, but I was annoyed. This was before the days of seat belts and the constant sudden unexpected braking could throw a passenger, possibly an elderly one, onto the windscreen or dashboard, with the potential to cause serious injury. Vehicles could also have collided.

I told my driver to pull up behind the young man, who was now at the rear of the bunch, and told the PC to open the rear doors of the van. I then jumped out, grabbed the man from his rear by the scruff of the neck and seat of his pants, just as he was about to again jump into the road, and dragged him back to the police van, throwing him into the back. We shut the doors and drove off back to Portswood police station, all without saying a word. As we passed the group of youngsters I saw them look round for their friend, who had just disappeared.

When we arrived at the station I told him "When you are sober you will be charged with being drunk and disorderly", to which he replied "I've only had one drink". He was searched and placed in a cell and, as I anticipated, a few minutes later his group of friends, realising what had taken place, called to ask what was going to happen.

They were told that their friend had carried out a very dangerous manoeuvre and would be charged later that night and bailed to appear at court the next morning. They reluctantly accepted this ruling, realising he had been foolish. It was duly carried out and the young 18 year-old pleaded guilty and paid a fine of £3. I think he learnt his lesson, albeit I bent the rules slightly.

My final experience as a patrol sergeant involved my poor 14 year-old daughter. She had asked if she and a friend could go to the Top Rank Ballroom in Portswood. I was on night duty, so agreed, with the proviso that to ensure their safety I would collect them in the police car and bring them part way home. Accordingly, at around 10.30pm I duly collected the two girls from the Ballroom, in the Portswood team car, with driver and PC, and took them as far as the Bullar Road bus stop. I could not take them all the way home as that was too far off my area; I had gone well over the border as it was, and I could be in trouble if an emergency call came through.

When we dropped them at the bus stop, from where they could safely return home, there were several people waiting at the stop and a little devil came into my head. As we pulled away those waiting saw the sergeant in the police car open the window, point at the two girls and call out "Any more trouble from you two and you are going straight back in the Remand Home". We then pulled away, leaving them very discomforted indeed and it was a long time before my daughter forgave me.

I had by now been a patrol sergeant for only six months before the next change of direction came my way – to take charge of the Southampton Local Intelligence Office, the L.I.O.

21. CRIME INTELLIGENCE – 1969

After 1 January 1969, when Ron Sayers started the F Central Local Intelligence Office, I made many visits to the new office, on the ground floor west wing of the Central police station. I spent a large number of full 8-hour days with Ron, discussing the systems he had started, amending them, devising new ones with him and ordering stationery and equipment. We maintained contact, carried out regular consultations and worked together very well indeed.

Ron was an excellent worker, enthusiastic and intelligent, and we worked as a team from the outset. I joined him, officially, on 18 May, when two PCs, including my friend from my schooldays, PC Gordon Grimstead , were also attached to the new unit.

This date coincided with the introduction of Unit Beat Policing, a new concept in policing, designed to 'overcome a shortage of police officers by combining resources and the use of new distinctly marked beat mini-cars' (Pandas). The LIO was an integral part of this innovation, to ensure, as the Chief Constable, Douglas Osmond, said in his official Routine Order, 'an increased and improved flow of information'.

F Central division now included Portswood, Chilworth and Eastleigh, and the entire area was arranged into nine 'mobile beats', each patrolled by a constable in a single-manned mini-car on shifts throughout the 24 hours. Officers on the mobile beats were in groups of five, to ensure 24 hour coverage. The min-cars were not fitted with radios as the drivers carried their personal radios, ensuring they were accessible at all times.

'Area constables', on foot, were also incorporated into the system, with additional foot patrols on main roads and likely trouble spots. Each Area PC was to become the 'Village Policeman', his prime functions being to retain a close link with the public, a source of crime intelligence and to cultivate informants.

My office was staffed on a shift system, worked by the three PCs covering 6.00am to 2.00am, with the indices and other records available via the Communications Room staff outside those times. I worked a basic 9.00am to 5.00pm shift, Monday to Friday; something that my wife was delighted about, although I invariably arrived well before that time and more often than not remained for some time at the end of the shift, depending on the workload. This was considerable in the early days as there was so much to set up.

I travelled around Southampton and made personal contact with other agencies, such as British Transport police, HM Customs, Immigration, and Special Branch, agreeing to make my information available to them in return for a supply from them. Sadly, in the case of HM Customs this never materialised; they happily used the information I supplied them daily, but not once did we get even a scrap of information back from them.

One example, updating details of vehicles owned by criminals and suspects, was always a useful piece of information. Although HMC made arrests, assisted by information my staff supplied, they never considered giving us details of the vehicles used or owned by their prisoners. Such is life, I suppose.

The LIO maintained various indices, with a Master Index that contained the names of individuals coming to notice locally, whether convicted or merely suspected. Full names, aliases and nicknames were recorded, typed and cross referenced on cards.

In connection with these index cards, my sense of humour came home to roost a few years later, in October 1972, when I was the Chief Security Officer on the Southampton Container Terminal. I was amazed to read an article in the local Daily Echo saying the local Church Army Captain, Gordon Kitney, had made an official complaint that the police held a criminal record card about him in their files, giving his nickname as 'Soupy'. The nickname was clearly a reference to his late night handing out cups of soup to vagrants. The card said he was 'an associate of prostitutes, drug addicts and lower class police officers' and that he 'frequented downtown public houses and derelict properties'.

Capt. Kitney stated the card had been removed from the official police files by a social worker and he was concerned that this access was available. Capt. Kitney added that his name had also been circulated on an internal police bulletin.

He had made a statement to the police complaining that he failed to see why any citizen should be circulated and watched by the police, unless there were very good grounds.

Captain hits out at Soton police

"Echo" Staff Reporter

FRICTION between Captain Gordon Kitney, head of the Church Army in Southampton, and the city's police force has come to a head with an allegation that the police made up a "joke" criminal record card on him.

On the card, says the captain, he is nicknamed "Soupy" — presumably a reference to his late-night tours of Southampton, handing out cups of soup to vagrants.

His associates are listed as "all prostitutes, drug addicts and lower class police officers," says Capt. Kitney.

Today, police at the Central Station are inquiring into the affair, and will say no more. They confirm that yesterday Capt. Kitney went to see them and made a statement.

According to Capt. Kitney the card—an official police document—has been removed from the files by a social worker, and the fact that this could have been done also worries the Church Army chief.

"I could see it was a joke, but I would like to feel that criminal records are indeed confidential."

Capt. Kitney also claims that his name was circulated on an internal police bulletin. Yesterday he went to the station to make a statement and a complaint.

He later told the "Echo" that during the course of the interview at the station it had been suggested that he himself obtained the card, and typed the "joke" details on it. He denied this strenuously.

"The police do quite often keep information of citizens, whether they have a criminal record or not," said Capt. Kitney. I just fail to see why any citizen should be circulated and watched by the police unless there are grounds for suspicion."

(Southern Daily Echo)

I was angry about what I knew to be a completely false and unfair allegation. I had typed out this card in 1969 and given it to Robbie, Capt. Kitney's assistant, to give to the Captain. Gordon Kitney was well known to us, and liked because of his care for 'down and outs'. The 'lower class police officers' referred to the area beat constables on Capt. Kitney's district. Robbie later told me that the Captain had been amused at the card and had placed it in his scrap book.

I immediately contacted the Echo, explaining the circumstances and pointing out that the joke card had never been in the filing system and that Capt. Kitney had placed it in his scrap book. Capt. Kitney was interviewed by a reporter and admitted the card had been placed in his scrap book and that he knew it was a joke, so further articles appeared in the Echo.

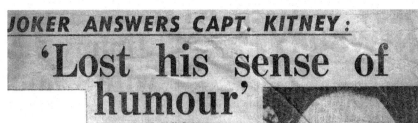

JOKER ANSWERS CAPT. KITNEY:
'Lost his sense of humour'

"Echo" Staff Reporter

A FORMER Southampton police sergeant claimed today that he typed the joke criminal record card, centre of controversy between Captain Gordon Kitney of the Church Army and the police, and that the card was produced about four years ago.

"This card was never in the official police index and it is scandalous to suggest that anyone other than the police have access to criminal record files," he said.

Ex-Sgt. Jim Brown, now a security officer with a firm at Southampton Docks, was officer in charge of the Local Intelligence Office, Southampton Central police station, until he left Hampshire Police in February, 1976.

ASTONISHED

"I was astonished and very angry when I read the report in yesterday's "Echo." Captain Kitney must have completely lost his sense of humour, taking an unfair opportunity to hit out at serving police officers who must remain silent because of the disciplinary inquiry now going on," he said.

"I typed the joke CRO card. An assistant of Captain Kitney's, whom I knew as Robbie, was there at the time. He thought it was very funny and I am virtually certain we gave the card to him to show to Captain Kitney. I was told later that the Captain had stuck it in his own scrapbook."

GOOD TERMS

Mr. Brown said that in his police days Captain Kitney, who was on good terms with the local beat policeman, was known humorously and without malice as "Soupey"—the joke alias or nickname referred to on the card — and that the Captain had sometimes used this name himself when leaving occasional messages for the police. The "lower class police officers" also referred to on the card meant the area beat police constable who knew Captain Kitney very well.

Captain Kitney, who—as reported in yesterday's "Echo"—made an official complaint to the police on Monday, wouldn't say today whether his former colleague known as "Robbie" was the person who showed him the card.

"I have made a statement and I have said I cannot say who the social worker was. I first knew about the card's existence early this year, possibly in January or February, Captain Kitney said.

"I knew it was a joke on me and I do have a copy of it stuck in my scrapbook.

"My major concern was that someone should have access to police files. I do not think that anyone should have access to such files unless they have signed the Official Secrets Act."

Captain Kitney denied that at any time he had referred to himself as "Soupey" in

Captain Gordon Kitney, of the Church Army holding the record card.—Photo: Roger Quilter.

Church Army chief retracts allegations against police

CAPTAIN GORDON KITNEY, head of the Church Army in Southampton, has withdrawn his complaint against the police that they made up a "joke" criminal record card under his name.

But he has withdrawn the complaint, he says, only because of police pressure.

Capt. Kitney claimed that "people we are trying to help are being put under extreme pressure by the police. You just can't get to the bottom of the truth so it is better to withdraw it."

He added: "I personally feel that the time has come in this country when there has got to be a independent body looking into complaints against the police."

A senior police officer at Southampton Civic Centre police station commented today that it was "totally wrong" to suggest that the police would ever bring pressure to bear on the person in order that a complaint should be withdrawn.

"In this case, despite anything that Capt. Kitney has said now, the matter is still under investigation," said Chief Insp. John Dean.

"Any complaint against the police is investigated thoroughly until the Chief Constable is satisfied. If the complaint involves an allegation of a criminal offence being committed by a policeman then it is always referred to the Director of Public Prosecutions for his decision."

One article, with a photo of Capt. Kitney and the card in question, giving my explanation of the true circumstances, and another, a few days later, stating he had withdrawn his allegations. *(Southern Daily Echo)*

Sadly, even then Capt. Kitney felt compelled to say that he had only withdrawn his complaint because of police pressure, something the police strongly denied. The allegation was, of course, nonsense. I remain puzzled to this day why the Church Army Captain made such a complaint, especially when the serving officers were in no position to refute his claim, something I was delighted to be able to do publicly.

I maintained a vehicle index, which Ron and I had decided would be referenced on cards in four ways, by colour and type, make, alphabetically and numerically, from the appropriate part of the vehicle registration number. This index was invaluable when only a part of a vehicle number was obtained by a witness. Vehicles would not only be those used by known criminals or suspects, but included those seen in unusual or suspicious circumstances. In the latter case we would obtain details of the registered owners to include in our files, having first checked on whether they had a record.

We also maintained an MO Index, i.e. a modus operandi card index system, setting out the methods that different individuals used when committing offences. Examples of this would be such things as housebreakers defecating in attacked premises; pasting paper on the pane of glass before breaking it, to reduce the sound; climbing through insecure transom windows, climbing drainpipes and similar peculiarities known to relate to certain individuals.

A Beat/Street index was also maintained, kept in a street geographical order, using coloured cards to denote the addresses of convicted or suspected individuals and the types of buildings in the area attacked, cross referenced to the other indices. This enabled us to create a Crime Pattern Chart, showing a break-down of all crimes on each beat, displayed in a conspicuous position to enable trends to be easily recognised.

Radio equipment, on a new UHF network, with Pye Pocketphone radios allocated to beat officers, was installed in the LIO, keeping us in touch with events as they took place.

As Crime Intelligence Sergeant, I maintained a liaison with the Force Crime Intelligence Bureau at Winchester Headquarters. An important function, one that was my personal responsibility, was compiling a Daily Bulletin, giving brief details of all matters within the Division I considered worthy of attention. I was able to compile this early each morning, my first duty, by looking through all the messages on the consecutively numbered Daily Record Sheets that had been prepared by the duty LIO staff during the previous 24 hours. They would highlight matters they thought worthy of inclusion.

This would be typed on a Gestetner duplicating 'skin', with typing errors painted over with a special red solution that hardened immediately, enabling me to retype over the offending error. Once completed to my satisfaction, I would run off several dozen copies on the Gestetner (often a messy business, with ink staining my hands for the rest of the day) and distribute them to the various offices, with bundles made available for collection by HMC, Docks Police, Shirley and Bitterne Divisions etc.

The files were small initially, but as the feed of information into the office gradually built up, and officers, especially detectives, realised its value, the volume of information increased, building up to a constant and regular flow that kept the LIO staff busy throughout their shift. It was very satisfying, as far as the efficiency of the office was concerned, but as the months passed I gradually realised that I was no longer an active police officer, dealing directly with the public, victims and offenders, but merely an office worker handling nothing but paper.

It was also becoming clear that although I was one of the fortunate ones who had been promoted after the amalgamation, I had no real prospect of a further promotion unless I agreed to 'unfreeze' and be prepared to serve anywhere in the county. This I was not prepared to do. I therefore gave a good deal of thought about my position, culminating in a decision I made at the start of the New Year, 1970.

22. GOODBYE – 1970

I knocked on the door of Chief Superintendent Eric Coleman's office, entered when invited and gave him that morning's Daily Bulletin as well as a short report. He thanked me, and I said, "It's my half sheet Sir. I'm giving a month's notice". He looked at me astonished, "What do you mean, Jim? Don't be bloody stupid, you can't really want to leave. I don't believe you." I then managed to convince him that I was serious, and he patiently listened as I explained my reasons.

I was now 38 and, at that time, the magic age beyond which employers didn't want to take on a prospective new employee, was 40. I had enjoyed my police service, during which I had received six commendations, but after amalgamation it felt as though I had left a family firm for a remote large conglomerate. In the Southampton Force we all knew one another, but we were now supervised by many strangers who did not know our individual strengths and weaknesses or the nature of policing Southampton.

I was not happy with the new Force. Senior former county officers often failed to appreciate that a city force worked in a different way, the pace was faster and the stress levels higher. In Southampton quick decisions often had to be made, but in the county there was usually far more time and the pace was much slower. Procedures were also becoming more and more bureaucratic, with government directives interfering more and more with the way we worked.

The Force that I had served in for many years had changed in character, not for the better, I believed. Decisions were taken that I did not agree with, such as Southampton being split into three separate parts, with Shirley enlarged to include Totton; Central to include Chilworth and Eastleigh and Bitterne to take in Bursledon and Netley. No doubt, from the view of a remote office desk, there were sound psychological reasons for this, to break up Southampton and get away from a 'them and us' attitude, but it created real operational problems.

Separate radio networks were allocated to the three parts of Southampton, meaning a Bitterne officer could be in serious trouble on one side of Northam Bridge, calling for help, but there could be a considerable delay before Central officers, sitting in their car on the other side of the bridge, got to hear of it.

Another example of how things had changed was that when a new Street Offences Act came into law Hampshire Constabulary brought out a new 'Prostitutes Caution Register'. Women had to be cautioned more than once before they could be arrested for importuning. It could not be a loose leaf type of Register, as detectives using prostitutes as informants could be tempted to remove pages. Accordingly an expensive beautifully bound Register was issued to all stations. Comically, Registers were issued to Totton, Hythe, Romsey and similar county stations, who were unlikely to see a prostitute more than once in a decade.

Southampton Central was also issued with a Register, and I was in the main enquiry office a few weeks later when PS Joe Cass phoned Winchester Headquarters. He eventually got through to the department responsible for the issue of the Registers, and asked for a further Register. The clerk at the other end became most concerned, pointing out that these Registers cost a lot of money and there would be trouble if it had been lost. Joe, with a broad grin, said, "No, we've filled the bugger up."

But among the reasons for my decision to leave was that although I had never been overly ambitious, the fact was that further promotions were very unlikely to come my way if I continued to keep the protection of Regulation 20 and remain in Southampton, where I was born and had lived all my life. The continuing education of my two daughters was a very high priority for me and any move out of the area would seriously disrupt it.

I had sought, found and been accepted for a senior management position, with a higher salary, including a company car with unlimited free petrol. I would not be in danger of shift working, as I would be if I remained, but would have a permanent day job with every week-end off. I realised that was what I currently had, but among the many factors I considered was that my current position in the LIO meant I no longer had contact with the general public or offenders. I was purely an office worker, behind a desk, and had become bored with my present situation.

Eric discussed the matter with me at length, after all he was one of the few remaining old Southampton officers, and finally agreed with my decision. Accordingly, my retirement took place on 28 February 1970, and for the following months I must confess I had pangs of regret whenever I passed a Southampton police station. I found it very strange to have to wait in front of the counter, if calling to make an enquiry, and not able to just walk past it with a nod.

Current serving officers may be interested to know that my last pay advice note for February 1970 showed that my sergeant's basic monthly pay was £119. 11s 8d, with boot and rent allowance of £23.8s 7d, bringing my gross pay to £143. 0s 3d, but deductions of tax, pension and graduated pension contributions and National Insurance, brought my final net pay down to £109. 18s 10d. The final irony was that I was due well over £600 refund of my pension contributions, but this was taxed by over £200, bringing my net refund, after 18 years service, to £411. 18s 5d.

I trust the reader will now have a good grasp of what policing in Southampton was really like in the 1950/60s and will forgive the many instances of what is now considered to be 'politically incorrect', although our intentions were always to act in the best interests of the citizens of Southampton. I also trust that serving officers will appreciate the vast differences between my old fashioned methods and modern policing.

J.W.M. Brown, July 2013.

APPENDIX A

FORCE STRUCTURE AND VARIOUS PROCEDURES

In common with the general population, a six-day 48 hr week was the norm in 1952, meaning that the one rest day a week had to be allocated within each section of 12 or more officers. A rest day during the tour of night duty was the worst of all, particularly if it had to be taken on a Monday, following the first night on Sunday. It meant considerable disruption to the digestive system. But this was all accepted, albeit not cheerfully, but treated as part of 'The Job'.

The system allowed two men off on weekdays, only one on a Saturday but up to four on a Sunday, the quietest day of the week. Booking normal rest days was in accordance with a list, published on the parade room notice board weekly, with officers booking in order of priority, moving from the bottom of the list to the top in sequence. This allowed Saturday off when top of the list and the adjacent Sunday off when second on the list. This full weekend leave happened once in roughly every three months.

The shift system for beat officers was, in sequence, 6.00am to 2.00pm; 10.00pm to 6.00am; 5.00pm to 1.00am; 8.30am to 4.30pm and 2.00pm to 10.00pm. It can thus be seen that there was an overlap of shifts between 8.30am and 1.00am, with 2/5 of the force strength on duty for that, the busiest period. This system meant that there were five sections, each of 12 to 15 officers, at each of the four police stations, namely Civic Centre (also the Police Headquarters), Shirley, Bitterne and Portswood (with fewer officers due to the area's smaller size).

Each section (numbers depending on annual and sick leave), had to parade a quarter of an hour before their shift commenced, otherwise they were late and subject to discipline. They were supervised by two sergeants and an inspector, who worked a basic three-shift pattern so as to cover the five shifts worked by the men. I say 'men' as policewomen, who received less than male pay, did not work night shifts or patrol beats. There were only twelve policewomen, two based at each station, more at Police Headquarters, and they mainly worked day shifts. Their duties concentrated on matters dealing with women and children, victims of sexual offences, dealing with and searching women prisoners etc.

WPS 1 Doris Coles was the sole supervising policewoman sergeant who joined in 1942 and retired in 1965. She was a lovely gentle woman, always relaxed and unruffled, but steely and determined to get her way when dealing with awkward individuals or wayward policewomen.

WPS 1 Doris Coles (*Hampshire Constabulary History Society*)

Home-going shifts were not released from their beats until the incoming shifts had been allocated their individual beat, their respective duties etc. and were marching out from the station. The officers waiting to answer a flashing light signal from the police pillars on their beat were then told they could proceed home. This often meant having to wait several minutes, sometimes five to ten minutes, beyond their normal time, but again that was accepted.

Paid overtime just did not exist. Uniformed officers working beyond their normal tour of duty, because of dealing with an incident, received one hour time off for every three quarters of an hour worked. This would build up and could be taken at the officer's request or as directed by the station's clerk sergeant. If not taken within three months it would be eligible for payment, under police regulations, but this situation just never arose. Before the three month period was reached officers would be directed to take time off, as allocated by the clerk sergeant, whether they wished to or not. I have no knowledge of an officer ever actually being paid. Detectives received a weekly allowance of 17 shillings, based on £44 a year (we were all paid weekly at this period, in cash) to cover both overtime and plain clothes allowance. This meant that no matter how many hours they worked, and this could average well over 60 hours in what was otherwise a 48 hour week, no overtime payment was made.

Police Headquarters, also "A" Central Division, on the west face of the Civic Centre.

The large block on the right of the photo, surrounding the tower, housed the Law Courts and Police Station. The large imposing front entrance led directly to the three law courts on the left, right and rear of the clock tower.

The CID office and Detective Superintendent's office was on the corner of the rear left ground floor, with the Divisional Superintendent's office directly above it. The front left ground floor block housed the Criminal Record Office and canteen, with various offices right along that face. On the front left upper floor was the Coroner's Officer, General Office and Chief Constable's office. The Information Room and main Enquiry Office were to the extreme right on the ground floor.

Portswood police station in 1952 (*Hampshire Constabulary History Society*)

Shirley (B Division) boundary ran from the length of Hill Lane in the east to Tanners Brook in the west and Bitterne (C Division) was the area to the east of the River Itchen. Central (A Division) was the area between Hill Lane and the River Itchen, including Portswood as a sub-division. Each Division incorporated 'Beats', 11 in Shirley (increased to 14 when the borough boundary was extended as far west as the River Test in 1954, to include Millbrook and Redbridge) and a similar number in town. Bitterne was also extended to include Harefield and Thornhill. Some Beats would be coupled between 1am and 8.30am to become cycle beats. Coxford and Lordswood beats were already cycle beats because of their large area.

Traffic was a separate division, with a garage and offices based in Hulse Road with the Training School. In 1952 this consisted of five Wolseley cars and 10 Triumph motor cycles. They worked two shifts, 8.00am to 4.00pm and 4.00pm to midnight, and maintained a constant patrol within the town limits, only venturing into the adjoining county area on specific enquiries or in pursuit of a vehicle. In such cases they kept radio contact with the county HQ Winchester control room via a link with their radio system. The Hulse Road premises also housed the force training school, where refresher courses were held on new legislation and local issues. I attended one such course in March 1953, the Instructor being, of course, my old friend Inspector 'Judy' Garland.

There was also a vehicle based at every station with an 'emergency driver' available to deal with 999 calls within his division. This vehicle, originally a Hillman Estate, was changed some years later to a Commer van. If the emergency driver was involved in an incident one of the traffic officers would attend any further call. Emergency drivers did not work the five shift system but a three shift system, 6.00am to 2.00pm, 10.00pm to 6.00am and 2.00pm to 10.00pm, the same as the supervising officers. Each station also had a 24/7 enquiry office, manned by a police officer, usually one of the older experienced officers.

Previous page: Some of the traffic department being inspected at the Hulse Road garage. *(Hampshire Constabulary History Society)*

All 999 calls for the police went direct to the Civic Centre control room, otherwise direct to the ambulance or fire station, both of whom would immediately contact the police control room. We attended every single fire or ambulance emergency call, no matter its nature, as an apparent minor matter could rapidly change to a major one, so we were always on hand to assist. This automatic attendance at every fire or ambulance incident no longer takes place.

Sadly, I have recently spoken to both fire officers and ambulance drivers who tell me that not only is there now no automatic response, but the police have sometimes failed to attend when requested to deal with unsocial behaviour or other problems at the scene. Because emergency vehicles were based at all stations, as well as the traffic patrolling cars and motor cyclists, it was rare for the Southampton police not to attend the scene within minutes in the 50's and 60's.

The Southampton control room, based in the Civic Centre, was manned by older experienced officers and could be linked to the country network at the touch of a switch. The fire brigade were also on the same radio frequency and this was useful during incidents. The only radio contact, of course, was with vehicles, as in the 1950's individual portable handsets had yet to be invented. This system, with the control room staff having detailed knowledge of the town through their beat experience, ensured good deployment of vehicles to any situation.

A special duty was seeing children across the road at school times, a particular burden for the 8.30am-4.30pm officers. It took place four times a day, covering children starting and leaving as well as lunch time exits and entries, and this duty tied us down considerably on our patrol. It was considered of paramount importance and the thought of being late for this cover, with an injured or dead child as a consequence, was too terrible to contemplate. You also had to take especial care that traffic stopped on your signal before allowing children to cross, so concentration was important. There were no school crossing attendants or traffic wardens at this period; it was part of the police responsibility of protecting the public, and escorting children across the road was a very high priority indeed. If unable to attend because of another incident, the station had to be informed immediately so that somebody else could attend, a traffic officer if need be.

Our uniform, with light blue shirts and black tie, included an old fashioned closed neck tunic, only to be worn on night duty. This shows Supt. Bert Adams, as a pre-war PC with his closed neck tunic, together with a photo of my cap and neck badges. The latter was worn on the shoulder epaulets of the day-wear open neck tunics, with collar and tie.

The uniform right hand trouser pocket had an additional deep narrow pocket to hold the truncheon, so that only the leather strap showed hanging out of the pocket. Likewise, only a small section of the handcuffs showed out of the left hand trouser pocket.

The whistle and chain was also not only a decorative part of the uniform, but a necessary part of equipment as it was the only means of summoning assistance. However, the only time I ever tried to use my whistle, when chasing a suspect who was faster than me, proved impossible as I had run out of breath.

Flat caps had to be worn at all times in police vehicles, and the issued heavy cape proved to be a godsend in bad weather, keeping both hands and pocket book dry no matter the conditions. (I later discovered that when rolled up and carried it was also invaluable in subduing a violent prisoner without injuring him.)

Helmet, pair of waterproof leggings, rubber boots and cape meant that patrols in the worst of weather presented no problem whatsoever. Also, the winter overcoat was extremely thick and heavy, giving useful bulk when persuading somebody to move. One idiosyncrasy was that winter overcoats or tunics could only be worn as and when the Chief Constable decreed it. Similarly, in the summer the Chief decided when shirt sleeve order came into use and it was his personal decision on whether or not the heat was bearable in full uniform.

Gannex raincoats later replaced the overcoats, but again could not be left off until the Chief decided it was now summer. Because changes came about on the first Sunday after the Standing Order was issued, it could be several days while officers continued to wear a heavy duty overcoat or Gannex in searing heat. The whole point was that all officers had to be dressed the same; it was not permitted for some to be wearing tunics, others an overcoat or Gannex and yet others in shirt sleeve order.

Everything I did had to be recorded in my pocket book, at the time or as soon as possible after an event or occurrence. Each tour of duty started with writing down the times of the shift, the number of the beat(s), ringing in time and meal break time. Books were numbered consecutively when issued and held in a thick leather case with a strong elastic band to keep it on the correct page.

The case also held a printed card which set out, in detail, the 'Judge's Rules' regarding statements made by suspected persons. (Appendix C) It was very important that the caution "You are not obliged to say anything unless you wish to do so but what you say may be put into writing and given in evidence" was said to a suspect when there was evidence affording reasonable grounds for suspecting that person had committed an offence.

The Rules went into great detail as to the procedures relating to questioning and charging a person, or taking statements from them, and a failure to follow these rules to the letter could result in evidence becoming inadmissible and a prosecution could collapse as a result. I was baffled when I was first instructed on these Rules. To my simple mind it meant that a guilty person could be stopped from incriminating himself, but what was wrong with him doing just that? After all, we only wanted to get at the truth. It also could mean that an innocent person might act on the caution and keep quiet, resulting in being charged, kept in custody and not disclosing a perfect alibi until appearing in court.

Only a guilty person gained by not answering further questions, but I assumed (and still do) that the rules were framed by lawyers to assist them in defending their clients, not to further justice. (The caution has now been changed to "You do not have to say anything but it may harm your defence if you do not mention when questioned something which you later rely on in court. Anything you do say may be given in evidence." A far more sensible caution.

Daily Orders were issued two or three times a week and displayed on station noticeboards, keeping us abreast of various duties, promotions, transfers, changes in the law etc. One item, in February 1953, would appear strange to serving officers today. It stated "Fatal accidents – Police photographers are to attend only if it is going to serve some useful purpose, on the authority of an Inspector".

Another item informed us that testing of air raid sirens in the Borough would be carried out at 11.00am on 7 March. The sirens were based at Honeysuckle Road, Woolston Fire Brigade, Butts Road, Palm Road, Carlisle Road, B.A.T. in Regents Park Road, Old Docks and New Docks. This testing continued to take place for many years.

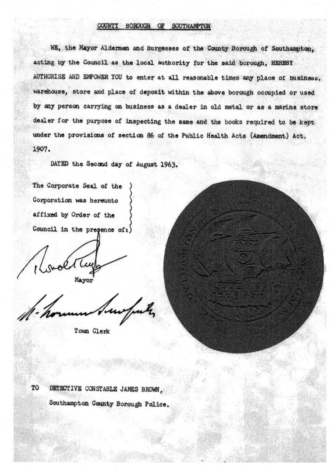

One useful asset for Southampton detectives was the personal issue of a magnificent warrant that gave officers the power to enter, "at all reasonable times", any place of business within the Borough used for dealing in metal or as a marine store, and to inspect the premises and the books **(previous page)**.

It had a massive red seal and, heaven forbid, was imposing enough to be shown at ANY building where urgent last minute entry was needed. (Not that I ever carried out such an unlawful act.)

1 April 1954 saw the Millbrook Estate and Redbridge, including parts of Nursling, Rownhams, Thornhill and Harefield incorporated into the Borough of Southampton. The western extension now went from the River Test instead of the former Tanners Brook, to include Millbrook and Redbridge, and Bitterne 'C' Division increased in the east to include Harefield and Thornhill. Police pillars had still yet to be erected in the new area so on our allocated ringing-in times we had to remain at a nominated telephone kiosk for ten minutes so that the station could phone us if needed.

The new police pillars were to be installed at Oakley Road/Cumbrian Way (P23), Redbridge Road/Gove Road (P24), Windermere Ave/Mansel Road (P25), Romsey Road/Brownhill Road (P26) and a new police box erected at Millbrook Roundabout, but this did not come about until July 1955. The western extension then went from the River Test, to include Millbrook and Redbridge, instead of the former Tanners Brook. The enlarged Shirley Division establishment was then increased to one Superintendent, three Inspectors, ten Sergeants, 66 Constables, two Policewomen, one Cadet, one Shorthand Typist and two Telephone Operators.

A Daily Order on 1 May 1956 set out the distribution of personnel within the Force:

'A' Central Div., Portswood A-sub and Traffic 158 and six policewomen.

'B' Shirley, 85 and two policewomen

'C' Bitterne and Woolston, 78 and two policewomen

Headquarters, 22 and CID 28 and two policewomen.

The total strength was 371 plus 12 policewomen, eight male civilians and 31 female. The senior officers then were:

Chief Constable Charles G. Box, OBE; Deputy Chief Constable Supt. A.T. Cullen, MBE; 'A' Div. – Supt. G. Baker; A-sub - C/Insp. R. Tribe, BEM; Traffic – Insp. F. Muddiman; 'B' Div. – Supt. W. Moore, BEM; 'C' Div. – Supt. S. Pearce; C.I.D. – D/Supt. H. O'Connor

May, 1959, saw the Rent Allowance rise to a maximum of £2. 12s 6d a week for Constables, £2.15s 0d for Sergeants and £2. 17s 6d for Inspectors.

That September saw the introduction of an amazing means of communication, modern technology at its best – it was called 'Telex'. One machine was installed in the Information Room, capable of receiving and sending messages at the rate of 60 words (400 characters) a minute. Some other Forces had already had this service installed and it was regarded as the leading and most efficient way of Forces communication with each other. Only Information Room staff were trained in its use.

6 December 1959 saw the end of the Five-Relief System, reverting to a Three-Relief system, i.e. 6.00am-2.00pm, 10.00pm-6.00am and 2.00pm-10.00pm, but at that time my duties were not affected; I still worked the usual CID 'Split' shifts.

1 April 1967 brought about the amalgamation of the Southampton and Portsmouth City Forces with Hampshire Constabulary, with Police Headquarters in Winchester. Chief Constable Alf Cullen resigned and was replaced by a Chief Superintendent in charge of what was now Southampton Division, later called an OCU (Operational Command Unit). The Southampton City strength was then 525, including 15 police-women.

Unit Beat Policing came in to being on 1 May 1969. Under this new system tradi-tional Beat Officers were replaced by community based 'Area Officers' who patrolled their personal designated area on foot. The object was to get to know the local resi-dents and liaise with local groups, such as schools. Patrols were also carried out in small cars, known as 'Panda' cars (because of their distinctive markings) with drivers able to contact the Area Officer and their Station via two-way radio.

APPENDIX B

NOTES FOR THE GUIDANCE OF POLICE

This small blue covered booklet, dated 1 January 1949, was a summary of local information and contained a wealth of detail.

Southampton County Borough Police

(CONFIDENTIAL)

NOTES
for the
GUIDANCE
of
POLICE

by

H. S. KEMBLE

It started with a brief description of the Borough, stated to be "The Gateway of the Empire", with its area of 9,600 acres and population of 176,000

(12,802 acres and population of 236,700 in 2011).

Policing of the Docks, it said, was carried out by a Division of the Railway Executive Police, with the Harbour Board Police responsible for the Royal Pier, Town Quay, Isle of Wight boats, Harbour Board offices and the warehouses opposite the Town Quay. It added "all criminal matters are referred to the Borough Police by these two private forces."

The British Transport Police, who later took over the Harbour Board responsibilities, managed the day to day policing of the docks at this period, only involving the Borough when serious matters arose. They had full police powers and considerable expertise when it came to cargo documentation and knowledge of dock working, but they no longer exist and the current private security, with no powers, depends entirely upon the Hampshire Constabulary to deal with all dock issues.

The Southampton force establishment was set out as a Superintendent in charge of headquarters and each of the three divisions, with a Detective Chief Inspector in charge of the CID. There were 17 Inspectors, 46 sergeants, 275 male constables and 12 policewomen. Mention was made of the Police College, which had opened in June 1948.

Paragraphs in the booklet ranged, alphabetically, from absentees & deserters, animals injured on the highway and annual leave (one week taken in the winter and one in the summer), to witnesses at court and women police. Details were also given of the procedures to be followed during the Annual Inspection of the force by one of "His Majesty's Inspectors of Constabulary".

Previous page: Inspection at the Stadium, Banister Road at 11am on 21 April 1953. *(The St John's Ambulance Brigade silver badge can be seen on the officers' right upper arm)* **The inspecting officers are, left to right, Supt. Gordon Baker; HMI W.C. Johnson, CMG, CBE; Chief Constable Charles Box and Superintendent Alfred Cullen.**

(I was none too pleased to take part, being on 5.00pm–1.00am duty for both the rehearsal the preceding day as well as the actual parade and this made for two very long days.)

Further paragraphs dealt with all manner of aspects of carrying out duties, many of which will amuse serving officers, such things as:

"Children found begging (including exhibiting 'guys' on Guy Fawkes Day), will be taken to their homes and handed over to parents, with a report submitted to the divisional superintendent."

"Any person using any street or public place for bookmaking or betting to be arrested under the Street Betting Act, 1906."

"Bicycles found to be taken to the station and descriptive forms completed, to be checked against special cycle theft reports with possible identical descriptions." All machines were taken to St Mary's Police Station each week for regular inspections by those who had lost their bicycle.

The Coroner's Officer was a full time duty, carried out by a Detective Sergeant.

Drugs – the only mention of drugs was a nominated detective constable's duty to visit chemists and examine the dangerous drugs registers and stocks.

"No person shall, in any street or public place, throw or leave orange peel, banana skin or other like substance on any footway, *(Bye-law, penalty £2)*" The amount of the fine was more than it appears today, bearing in mind that a probationer constable's pay was then £9. 13s a week.

Dog licences, renewable every January at a cost of 7/6d, had to be in force and in possession of the owner, or occupier of a building, if the animal was over 6 months old.

"Driving vehicles under the influence of drink or drugs – if the examining doctor objects to the presence of a constable during the examination, the constable should withdraw but exercise care to prevent any escape by the accused."

(It should be noted there were no medical tests available. The police surgeon was responsible for confirming that the accused was not suffering from a medical condition affecting his balance or speech. In practice, he confirmed that the accused was under the influence.) The question of being unfit whilst in possession of a motor vehicle was also determined by the police officer's opinion, based on simple tests and observation.

"Sergeants and constables must carry, when on duty, a field dressing in the back trouser pocket."

"Footwear – boots must be worn at all times by sergeants and constables on patrol." *(Police Regulations)*

A list of all the principal forms in use was set out. Those most in use were simple forms for traffic accident report (Form 17); occurrence report (Form 19); and offence report (Form 22). *(Modern forms are far lengthier and more complicated, to comply with Ministerial Directives.)*

"Funerals – police on duty will salute the hearse as the procession passes."

Hackney carriages, i.e. taxis, were dealt with by a PC as a full time duty, dealing with their licensing and complaints against drivers.

"Handcuffs will only be required in exceptional circumstances, to prevent escape or control an unusually violent prisoner."

"Identification of an offender should be confirmed by the production of their identity card."

"Members of the force when parading for duty will travel to and from their homes in uniform, unless permission to wear other dress has been received from a senior officer in particular circumstances."

"Members of the force doing duty in plain clothes should recognise the need for reasonably sober dress, and a hat should be worn except in special cases when headwear would render the individual conspicuous."

One section in the booklet was devoted to describing the location of the Borough's police pillars and boxes, and an explanation of the wireless system that was installed in 1942.

The Police Social and Athletic Club at 17 Hulse Road, opposite the force training school, is mentioned. Founded in 1921, officers had the princely sum of six pence a week (2½ p) deducted from their pay if they wished to remain a member.

Rent Allowance – Regulation 65 of the Police (Consolidation) Regulations, 1948 meant that every officer was entitled to free accommodation or a rent allowance in lieu. The scale of weekly allowances increased with rank, ranging from a maximum of £1. 10s for a married PC (15s if single), to £2 for a Chief Superintendent (£1 if single). The actual rent would be paid if it was less than the maximum scale. One amazing

aspect of this allowance was that it was regarded as tax-free by the police authority but not by the Inland Revenue. The result was that a lump sum "Compensatory
Grant" was paid at the end of each tax year, repaying the tax paid by the officer, but
this was also taxed, together with the next allowance, the following year. This continued year after year.

(It was not unknown for some officers to neglect informing their spouse of the
Compensatory Grant and if it arose in conversation state it was merely the tax they
had to pay on the allowance.)

River patrol – the police launch "Versatile" was manned by a crew of three from the
traffic department and patrolled the Solent area, excluding the docks.

Scenes of crime – there were no specialists in this field. Officers were instructed to
ensure nothing was touched until the arrival of a senior officer or a detective.

Special Constabulary – the establishment for the Borough comprised 200 officers,
including a Special Superintendent, a Chief Inspector, four Inspectors and 21 Sergeants. They were controlled by the Clerk Sergeant in each division.

Spitting in public places, such as carriages, halls, waiting rooms, shelters or places
of entertainment was subject to a penalty of £5 under a Bye-law.

Truncheon "is issued to be used only against superior odds to protect the constable, or to prevent the escape of a prisoner."

Street cries – "No person shall, when selling newspapers or other articles, call or
shout to the annoyance of the inhabitants in the neighbourhood" *(£5 penalty under
a Bye-law.)*

Unoccupied houses (persons on holiday) – "Dwellings reported to the police must
receive careful attention by beat constables. On the first visit you must be satisfied
that doors and windows are secure and on visiting thereafter you must be alert to
detect unlawful entry."

The Watch Committee was the police authority for the area, appointed by the Borough Council from its members. They appointed constables on the recommendation
of the chief officer. One half of the annual cost of maintaining the force was borne
by the National Exchequer, the remainder contributed by the local rate. As the Chief
Constable saw them on a regular basis, to discuss police matters, he was always made
fully aware of local complaints and problems. Although they could not dictate any
course of action to him, he nevertheless always acted on such matters as a matter of
policy.

Women police – carried out duty between 6.00am and 10.00pm, but were available at night to care for female prisoners. Their duties were set out in some detail, all relating to dealing with women and young children.

APPENDIX C

THE JUDGES' RULES

Memorandum approved by Her Majesty's Judges of the Queen's Bench Division regarding Statements made by Persons suspected of Crime or by Prisoners in Police Custody

1. When a police officer is trying to discover whether, or by whom, an offence has been committed he is entitled to question any person, whether suspected or not, from whom he thinks that useful information may be obtained. This is so whether or not the person in question has been taken into custody so long as he has not been charged with the offence or informed that he may be prosecuted for it.

2. As soon as a police officer has evidence which would afford reasonable grounds for suspecting that a person has committed an offence, he shall caution that person or cause him to be cautioned before putting to him any questions, or further questions, relating to that offence.
The caution shall be in the following terms:—
   "You are not obliged to say anything unless you wish to do so but what you say may be put into writing and given in evidence."
When after being cautioned a person is being questioned, or elects to make a statement, a record shall be kept of the time and place at which any such questioning or statement began and ended and of the persons present.

3. (a) Where a person is charged with or informed that he may be prosecuted for an offence he shall be cautioned in the following terms:—
   "Do you wish to say anything? You are not obliged to say anything unless you wish to do so but whatever you say will be taken down in writing and may be given in evidence."
   (b) It is only in exceptional cases that questions relating to the offence should be put to the accused person after he has been charged or informed that he may be prosecuted. Such questions may be put where they are necessary for the purpose of preventing or minimising harm or loss to some other person or to the public or for clearing up an ambiguity in a previous answer or statement.
Before any such questions are put the accused should be cautioned in these terms:—
   "I wish to put some questions to you about the offence with which you have been charged (or about the offence for which you may be prosecuted). You are not obliged to answer any of these questions but if you do the questions and answers will be taken down in writing and may be given in evidence."
Any questions put and answers given relating to the offence must be contemporaneously recorded in full and the record signed by that person or if he refuses by the interrogating officer.
   (c) When such a person is being questioned, or elects to make a statement, a record shall be kept of the time and place at which any questioning or statement began and ended and of the persons present.

4. All written statements made after caution shall be taken in the following manner:—
   (a) If a person says that he wants to make a statement he shall be told that it is intended to make a written record of what he says.

He shall always be asked whether he wishes to write down himself what he wants to say; if he says that he cannot write or that he would like someone to write it for him, a police officer may offer to write the statement for him. If he accepts the offer the police officer shall, before starting, ask the person making the statement to sign, or make his mark to, the following:—
   "I, ..., wish to make a statement. I want someone to write down what I say. I have been told that I need not say anything unless I wish to do so and that whatever I say may be given in evidence."
   (b) Any person writing his own statement shall be allowed to do so without any prompting as distinct from indicating to him what matters are material.
   (c) The person making the statement, if he is going to write it himself, shall be asked to write out and sign before writing what he wants to say, the following:—
   "I make this statement of my own free will. I have been told that I need not say anything unless I wish to do so and that whatever I say may be given in evidence."
   (d) Whenever a police officer writes the statement, he shall take down the exact words spoken by the person making the statement, without putting any questions other than such as may be needed to make the statement coherent, intelligible and relevant to the material matters: he shall not prompt him.
   (e) When the writing of a statement by a police officer is finished the person making it shall be asked to read it and to make any corrections, alterations or additions he wishes. When he has finished reading it he shall be asked to write and sign or make his mark on the following Certificate at the end of the statement:—
   "I have read the above statement and I have been told that I can correct, alter or add anything I wish. This statement is true. I have made it of my own free will."
   (f) If the person who has made a statement refuses to read it or to write the above mentioned Certificate at the end of it or to sign it, the senior police officer present shall record on the statement itself and in the presence of the person making it, what has happened. If the person making the statement cannot read, or refuses to read it, the officer who has taken it down shall read it over to him and ask him whether he would like to correct, alter or add anything and to put his signature or make his mark at the end. The police officer shall then certify on the statement itself what he has done.

5. If at any time after a person has been charged with, or has been informed that he may be prosecuted for an offence a police officer wishes to bring to the notice of that person any written statement made by another person who in respect of the same offence has also been charged or informed that he may be prosecuted, he shall hand to that person a true copy of such written statement, but nothing shall be said or done to invite any reply or comment. If that person says that he would like to make a statement in reply, or starts to say something, he shall at once be cautioned or further cautioned as prescribed by Rule 3(a).

6. Persons other than police officers charged with the duty of investigating offences or charging offenders shall, so far as may be practicable, comply with these Rules.

Printed by Printforce, United Kingdom